W. D. Ross

THE RIGHT AND THE GOOD

Edited by
Philip Stratton-Lake

CLARENDON PRESS · OXFORD

OXFORD

UNIVERSITY PRESS

Great Clarendon Street, Oxford OX2 6DP

Oxford University Press is a department of the University of Oxford.
It furthers the University's objective of excellence in research, scholarship,
and education by publishing worldwide in

Oxford New York

Auckland Cape Town Dar es Salaam Hong Kong Karachi Kuala Lumpur
Madrid Melbourne Mexico City Nairobi New Delhi Shanghai Taipei Toronto

With offices in

Argentina Austria Brazil Chile Czech Republic France Greece
Guatemala Hungary Italy Japan Poland Portugal Singapore
South Korea Switzerland Thailand Turkey Ukraine Vietnam

Oxford is a registered trade mark of Oxford University Press
in the UK and in certain other countries

Published in the United States
by Oxford University Press Inc., New York

British Library Cataloguing in Publication Data

Data available

Library of Congress Cataloging in Publication Data

Ross, W. D. (William David), 1877–
The right and the good/W. D. Ross; edited by Philip Stratton-Lake.–[New ed.].
p. cm.
Includes bibliographical references and index.
1. Good and evil. 2. Right and wrong. I. Stratton-Lake, Philip. II. Title.
BJ1401.R6 2002   170—dc21   2002066234

ISBN 978-0-19-925265-7 (pbk)

Typeset by Hope Services (Abingdon) Ltd
Printed in Great Britain
on acid-free paper by
the MPG Books Group

PREFACE

W. D. Ross

IT is with much diffidence that I send into the world this essay on two of the most important conceptions that occupy the attention of moral philosophers. I am conscious of the great difficulty of most of the main problems of ethics, and of the fact that almost all the assumptions that it seems most natural to make raise problems that for their proper treatment would demand long and careful discussion. I fancy that in some places, in my anxiety to take account of the complications and opposing considerations that demand to be taken account of, I may have made the main outlines of my view difficult to follow; and that in others, in my wish to avoid undue complexity, I may have made general statements without qualifications which will suggest themselves as necessary. I have tried to strike a mean between undue simplicity and undue complexity; but I cannot flatter myself that I have always, or even usually, been successful. Some of the conclusions I have reached seem to me almost certainly true, and others seem to me very doubtful; and I have tried to indicate which I think the more and which the less doubtful.

My main obligation is to Professor H. A. Prichard. I believe I owe the main lines of the view expressed in my first two chapters to his article 'Does Moral Philosophy rest on a Mistake?' (*Mind*, 1912, 21–37). In addition to this, I have repeatedly discussed many of the main ethical problems with him, and have learnt something from every discussion; I have also had the advantage of reading a good deal that he has written but not published. And finally, he has read in manuscript most of what I have written, and has helped me greatly by exhaustive comments and criticisms. These have been very profitable to me both where (as in the treatment of rightness) he is (I believe) in general agreement with my point of view, and where (as in the treatment of the question what things are good) he to a large extent disagrees.

I wish also to say how much I owe to Professor G. E. Moore's writings. A glance at the index will show how much I have referred to him; and I will add that where I venture to disagree, no less than where I agree, I have always profited immensely from his discussions of ethical problems.

October 1930.

CONTENTS

INTRODUCTION

Philip Stratton-Lake

Ross's *The Right and the Good* (1930) marked the pinnacle of ethical intuitionism, a doctrine that had been the dominant moral theory in Britain for much of the preceding two hundred years. But within twenty years of its publication intuitionism had come to be rejected out of hand by most moral philosophers, so that by the 1960s it became difficult to see what its appeal had been.[1] This negative opinion prevailed for much of the second half of the twentieth century, and meant that very few philosophers were inclined to read the central texts of intuitionism with any care or sympathy. This in turn led to a caricature of intuitionism which encouraged the view that intuitionism could easily and quickly be dismissed before moving on to 'more serious' moral theories.

Ross's intuitionist moral theory suffered as much as others from this neglect. Some critics maintained that his intuitionism tells us nothing that we did not already know, that he is content merely to list our common-sense opinions.[2] Others objected that his intuitionism is metaphysically and epistemologically extravagant in so far as it assumes the existence of 'otherworldly' non-natural properties that can be directly perceived by a mysterious special moral faculty.[3] But all of this misrepresents Ross's views, and once the caricature is put aside, and we look at Ross's actual views and arguments, we discover a serious, honest, and persuasive moral philosopher, whose views deserve far more serious consideration than they often receive.

---

[1] Thus, for example, in 1967 G. J. Warnock wrote that 'Intuitionism seems, in retrospect, so strange a phenomenon—a body of writing so acute and at the same time so totally unilluminating—that one may wonder how to explain it, what its genesis was' (*Contemporary Moral Philosophy* (MacMillan: London, 1967), 16).

[2] See e.g. Mary Warnock, *Ethics since 1900* (Oxford University Press: Oxford, 1968), 50, G. J. Warnock, *Contemporary Moral Philosophy*, 12–13, and Alasdair MacIntyre, *A Short History of Ethics: A History of Moral Philosophy from the Homeric Age to the Twentieth Century*, 2nd edn., (Routledge: London, 1998), 254.

[3] William K. Frankena, *Ethics* (Prentice-Hall: Englewood Cliffs, NJ, 1963), 86–7.

The Central Theses

What, then are these views? In *The Right and the Good* Ross argues for a distinctive view in the metaphysics of morals, in normative ethics, and in moral epistemology. Ross is a moral realist. He believed that rightness and goodness are objective features of the world in just the way that shape, size, and mass are. '. . . there is', he writes, 'a system of moral truth, as objective as all truth must be' (p. 15),[4] and later on claims: 'The moral order . . . is just as much part of the fundamental nature of the universe (and, we may add, of any possible universe in which there are moral agents at all) as is the spatial or numerical structure expressed in the axioms of geometry or arithmetic' (pp. 29–30).[5]

We do not make actions right or good by our moral attitudes, conventions, culture, or whatever, any more than we make some thing square in these ways. Rather our moral attitudes are responses to 'perceived'[6] goodness and rightness. And when our attitudes are appropriate, it is because something is the way we think it is— that is, it really is good, bad, right, or wrong. What makes our moral belief that *X* is good true (when it is true) is the property, or objective characteristic, *X* has of being good, according to Ross. In this respect value judgements are like colour judgements.[7] If my judgement that the wall is red is correct, this will be because the wall has a certain colour property, the property of being red. Similarly, if my judgement that something is good is correct, this will be because this thing has a certain value property, the property of being good.

Ross's realism has the consequence that if there are no value properties in the world—no objective values—then all of our value

---

[4] Page numbers in parentheses in the text refer to *The Right and the Good*.

[5] Here Ross commits himself not only to objective moral truth, but to necessary moral truths.

[6] I put the word 'perceived' in inverted commas as Ross did not think that we literally perceive rightness and goodness. We judge that something is right or good not on the basis of a perception of these properties, but on the basis of a perception of other properties (*The Foundations of Ethics* (Clarendon Press: Oxford, 1939), 168).

[7] Though it should be noted that there are many ways in which moral judgements differ from colour judgements. For example, it is plausible to think that colour judgements are true if a certain subjunctive condition is true, namely, if we would have the relevant sensation under certain specified circumstances. It is not the case, however, that value judgements would be true if it is true that we would respond in a certain positive way under certain conditions. Ross notes certain other differences between colour and value (pp. 88 and 121–2).

judgements will be mistaken. For if it is the existence of moral properties that *make* our moral judgements true, then if there are no such properties then none of our moral judgements would be true. To think that all of our moral judgements are false is to embrace an error theory about value. According to the error theory, moral disagreements are like disagreements about what colour something is in an objectively colourless world. You might think that the ball is red, whereas I might think it is orange. But we would both be mistaken. For we both think it has a colour which, in a colourless universe, it does not. The same would be true of disagreements about the value of something in an objectively valueless world. You might think that something is good, whereas I might think it is bad. But we would both be mistaken. For we both think it has a value which, in a valueless universe, it does not.

Although Ross's moral realism commits him to the view that in an objectively valueless universe all of our evaluative judgements would be mistaken (p. 82), he maintained that there is no reason to think that the universe is valueless (p. 82). His view is, then, that some of our moral judgements are true, and what makes them true is the presence of the relevant objective value.

Not only was Ross a realist; he was a *non-naturalist* realist. This means that he thought that moral properties cannot be understood in wholly non-moral terms.[8] Moral terms are evaluative or deontic terms, such as 'good', 'valuable', 'ought', 'duty', 'fitting', 'appropriate', or 'merited'. Non-moral terms are psychological, sociological, evolutionary, or scientific terms, such as 'desire', 'approval', 'society', 'survival', etc. For Ross, to understand moral properties in wholly non-moral terms is to provide a reductive, naturalistic definition of these properties.

If you define 'right' as meaning what is approved by the community, you are putting forward a naturalistic definition. If you define 'good' as meaning 'such that it *ought* to be desired', you are putting forward a non-naturalistic definition. Consequence theories also may be either naturalistic or non-naturalistic. If you define 'right' as 'productive of the greatest pleasure', you are putting forward a naturalistic definition. If

---

[8] *The Foundations of Ethics*, 6. We shall see later that this understanding of the non-naturalness of non-natural properties is inadequate.

you define it as 'productive of the greatest amount of *good*', you are putting forward a non-naturalistic definition.[9]

If moral properties can be defined in terms of natural properties, then moral issues will be decidable by means of empirical observation. If moral properties cannot be defined in this way, then moral issues are not empirically decidable. Ross does not deny that certain empirical matters will be relevant to deciding whether we ought or ought not to act in certain ways. His point is just that even when all of the empirical facts are in, there is still a further, *moral* judgement to be made—namely, that these empirical facts make a certain act *right*, or *good*.

As well as insisting that rightness and goodness are non-natural properties, he held that they are simple properties. The view that rightness and goodness are simple properties is the view that they are not combinations of two or more properties or relations, such as the relation of being appropriate (moral) and the property of being approved (non-moral), or the causal relation (non-moral) and the property of being best (moral).[10] Ross held that if a property is simple it cannot be defined. Consequently, he held that the simplicity of rightness and goodness implies that these properties are indefinable.

In his normative theory, Ross defends a form of methodological intuitionism. Methodological intuitionists maintain that there is a plurality of first principles that may conflict, and that no explicit priority rules for resolving such conflicts can be provided.[11] This means that principles of duty cannot ultimately be grounded in a single foundational principle as consequentialists and Kantians believe. This pluralism applies not only to the right, but to the good also. There is, Ross maintains, no master value, such as pleasure,

---

[9] Ibid., 6–7.

[10] For Ross, a property is not complex simply in virtue of being a determinate form of a determinable property. He did not, for example, think that redness is a complex property because it has the (determinable) property of being a colour and the (determinate) property of being red (p. 92 n.). In this he follows J. Cook-Wilson, *Statement and Inference, ii* (Clarendon Press: Oxford, 1926), 502–4.

[11] B. Williams, 'What does Intuitionism Imply?' in Williams, *Making Sense of Humanity and Other Philosophical Papers 1982–1993* (Cambridge University Press: Cambridge, 1995), 182. Not all pluralists are methodological intuitionists, for a rationalized pluralism might have priority rules. Methodological intuitionists form, therefore, a subclass of pluralist theories. In what follows, however, I shall use the term 'methodological intuitionism' and 'pluralism' interchangeably.

well-being, or happiness, in terms of which the value of all other goods can ultimately be understood. There are, rather, a number of things that are good on their own account (Ross lists virtue, pleasure, knowledge, and justice[12]) and whose value does not, therefore, need to be derived from the value of anything else.

Ross was an epistemological as well as a methodological intuitionist. Epistemological intuitionists maintain that we can know directly (intuitively) that certain things are good or right on their own account. We can know these things directly because the propositions which state that these things are good or right are self-evident. To say that these propositions are self-evident is to say that they can be known on the basis of an understanding of them, and so can be known *a priori*. Ross did not maintain that all moral propositions are self-evident. Only the most fundamental moral propositions can be known in this way, according to Ross. Particular judgements based on these foundations about what we should do in specific situations are not self-evident, or even knowable. For Ross, we can only have a probable opinion about such things.

We can, therefore, identify four key views which are at the centre of Ross's intuitionist moral theory. The first is moral realism, the second is the view that moral properties are simple, non-natural properties, the third is his commitment to an irreducible pluralism about the right and the good, and finally the view that fundamental moral propositions are self-evident. The first two express his view in the metaphysics of morals, the third expresses his normative theory, and the fourth his epistemology. In what follows I consider each of these aspects of Ross's view in more detail. In Section I I discuss Ross's metaphysics of morals; in Section II I focus on his normative theory—his pluralism about the right and the good; and in Section III I assess his moral epistemology.

---

[12] By justice Ross means the allocation of happiness, or pleasure, in proportion to merit (virtue). He does not always mention this value when he lists the basic goods, and so sometimes says that there are three things that are intrinsically good. It is clear, however, that he thought that justice is a distinct intrinsic good which differs in structure from the other three in that it is complex, while they are simple.

I

Moral Truth and Moral Realism

Why should we think that there are moral as well as non-moral properties in the world? Why think that values are sewn into the fabric of the world, as it were? Ross claims that moral realism is built into our everyday ethical discourse and thought. For example, although we can only discover the value of certain things by attending to them, we think of them as having this value before we attended to them, and as possessing this value even if we did not attend to them (p. 81). We think that the positive feelings we have towards those things we judge good are *responses to* value rather than as conferring value on their objects (p. 89), and we think of moral judgements as expressing moral beliefs which aim to track objective evaluative facts (p. 85).

More generally, Ross thinks that simply in virtue of being an adjective there is an assumption that 'good' refers to a property. 'When some entity is commonly referred to by an adjective, there is a certain presumption that it is a quality, just as when it is commonly referred to by a prepositional phrase, there is a presumption that it is a relation or a relational property.'[13] When we think that some adjective applies to something, we naturally think of that thing as having a certain feature, of being a certain way; and to think of it as being a certain way is to think of it as having a certain property. This presumption may, on reflection, be overturned.[14] It may turn out that the adjective 'good' refers to a relation, or relational property, rather than an intrinsic property of the things of which it is predicated. It may even turn out that in judging that something is good we are saying nothing at all about that thing, but are either simply expressing our positive attitudes towards it, or are saying that such attitudes would be appropriate. But Ross rejects these alternatives and insists that there is no good reason to think that the presumption that 'good' and 'right' do not refer to properties of the things of which they are predicated (p. 114).[15] The realist construal of moral-

---

[13] *The Foundations of Ethics*, 278. See also *The Right and the Good*, 81.

[14] Ross was an irrealist about colour even though 'red' is an adjective (p. 86).

[15] See *The Foundations of Ethics*, 32 ff., for Ross's rejection of Carnap's theory, pp. 34 ff. for his critique of Ayer's emotivism, and pp. 279 ff. for his response to Brentano's claim that 'good' is a *Scheinsqualität*.

ity is, therefore, the best way of capturing the moral phenomenolo-
gy and what might be called the platitudes of ordinary moral
thought.

Recently, however, philosophers have denied this. They accept
that the platitudes of ordinary moral thought give us good reason to
think of moral judgements as truth apt—that is, as being either true
or false—but deny that truth in ethics commits us to any sort of realism. They do this by claiming that moral judgements are true (or
false) only in a minimal sense.[16] According to this minimal sense
one says no more in saying ' "Rape is wrong" is true' than if one had
said 'Rape is wrong'. To add 'is true' to a quoted sentence is just to
note the appropriateness of disquoting. It does not imply that reality *corresponds* to the way the sentence represents it as being. Minimal
truth in ethics does not, therefore, imply that the world is a certain
way, as realists like Ross think, but implies simply that one has moral
commitments.[17]

But as Jackson, Oppy, and Smith have pointed out,[18] the minimalist conception of truth is inadequate because it fails to pick out
what it is about a certain discourse that makes it truth apt. Not
everyone agrees that moral judgements have a truth value.
Emotivists think that moral judgements express non-cognitive attitudes rather than beliefs, and these attitudes cannot be true or false.
So why should we think that moral discourse is truth apt, and that
emotivism is mistaken? Moral discourse is truth apt, minimalists
maintain, if certain syntactical and normative conditions are met.
The syntactical conditions are that sentences be significantly
embeddable in suitable constructions, e.g. negation, conditional,
propositional attitude, and truth ascriptions. The normative
conditions are that there are certain well-established standards in a
community governing the use of such sentences. Since these syntactical and normative conditions are easily met, minimalists have no
trouble allowing that moral sentences (as well as sentences within

[16] See e.g. S. Blackburn, *Ruling Passions: A Theory of Practical Reason* (Clarendon Press: Oxford, 1998).

[17] M. Smith, 'Moral Realism', in H. LaFollette (ed.) *Ethical Theory* (Blackwell: Oxford, 2000), 18.

[18] F. Jackson, G. Oppy, and M. Smith, 'Minimalism and Truth Aptness', *Mind*, 103 (1994), 287–302. See also Smith, 'Moral Realism', 15–37, for an excellent account of minimalism about truth and the problem with it.

other problematic discourses) are truth apt. But since these conditions only qualify a discourse for truth in the minimalist sense, truth aptness does not imply any problematic realism.

The problem with the minimalist criterion of truth aptness, however, is that it is arbitrarily selective about which platitudes it allows to determine how we are to understand truth aptness. One of the platitudes of a truth apt sentence is that it be used to give the content of a belief of someone who asserts the sentence.[19] This condition is neither syntactical nor normative, but is, nonetheless, central. If, however, it is included amongst the platitudes determining truth aptness, then truth aptness will no longer be a minimal matter. For beliefs are states that are designed to fit the facts, are sometimes action-guiding, and tend to evolve in a rational manner.[20] Whether the utterance of certain sentences expresses such a state is a substantial rather than a minimal matter. It is not, therefore, clear that we can admit that moral discourse is truth apt without realist assumptions, as minimalists maintain.[21]

Simplicity and Non-Naturalism

But even if moral discourse is truth apt in a fairly robust sense—that is, in the sense that moral sentences are true if and only if the world is the way they represent it as being—Ross's moral realism might be mistaken. We might have good reason to think that there are no such things as moral properties. Moral properties might be metaphysically weird, or have no place in a modern scientific view of the world. If this were the case, then the conditions for the truth of our moral judgements would never obtain, and an error theory would be correct. The question we have to address now, therefore, is whether we have good reason to think that there are no such things as moral properties.

We would have no problems accepting that moral properties exist if these properties are natural properties, for no one thinks that natural properties are peculiar or incompatible with the scientific *Weltanschauung*. It is for this reason that most contemporary moral

---

[19] Jackson *et al.*, 'Minimalism and Truth Aptness', 294.   [20] Ibid. 296.
[21] Minimalists could insist that such utterances express beliefs *minimally construed*. But if this is to be pursued, then minimalists owe us an account of what makes a state one of belief rather than something else (ibid. 296–7).

realists are naturalists. Ross, however, like all intuitionists, thought that moral properties must be *non-natural* properties, and (like many other intuitionists) that rightness and goodness are *simple* non-natural properties.

Two questions arise at this point. (1) Why did Ross think that rightness and goodness are simple non-natural properties? (2) Do such properties exist? If Ross can provide us with no good reason for thinking that rightness and goodness are simple, non-natural properties, then the view that such properties exist would be uncontroversial, for no one denies the existence of natural properties. If, however, Ross can provide us with good reason to think that truth in ethics depends on the existence of simple, non-natural properties, then the view that there are such properties will be controversial, as many philosophers deny the existence of non-natural properties. If they are right, and if moral truth depends on the existence of non-natural properties, then an error theory will be true.

Most discussions of the intuitionist view of moral properties do not clearly distinguish between the claim that goodness and rightness are simple, and the claim that they are non-natural properties. These are, however, very different and independent claims. A naturalist might agree with Ross that rightness and goodness are simple properties, but insist that they are simple *natural* properties, or a non-naturalist might insist that rightness and goodness are complex properties, but agree with Ross that they are non-natural.[22] It is, I believe, important to note this distinction, for if we do not, then it will not be clear whether a particular problem is generated by the simplicity of rightness and goodness, or from their non-naturalness. I shall, therefore, deal with these separately.

Why does Ross think that goodness and rightness are simple properties? He rests his view on two closely interconnected arguments. The first may be called the 'transparency argument'. According to the transparency argument, if 'good' could be defined, the term would have to stand for a certain complex property, for the definition would consist in specifying what this complex

---

[22] A. C. Ewing argued that goodness is a complex non-natural property (*The Definition of Good* (Routledge & Kegan Paul: London, 1947), ch. 5), and in *Principia Ethica* (rev. edn. (Cambridge University Press: Cambridge, 1993), 196) Moore argued that rightness is complex, but non-natural.

is. If 'good' stood for a complex and could thus be defined, then we could only use the term 'good' intelligently and intelligibly to the extent that we had this definition in mind. But we use this term intelligently and intelligibly without having any definition in mind. Therefore, 'good' and the property this term stands for must be simple (p. 92).

The second argument Ross proposes is Moore's open question argument. According to this argument every attempt to define 'good' must fail, for it is always possible to enquire whether something that answers to the supposed definition is good. We can show, for example, that being good is not the same as being desired by somebody, for even if we know that war is desired by someone, we may still doubt whether it is good (p. 92). If the definition were correct, however, we could have no such doubt. One could not, for example, intelligibly doubt that John is a bachelor if one knew that John is a male and is unmarried. Since such doubts are always possible in relation to any definition of 'good', all such definitions must be false. Consequently, 'good' must stand for a simple property.

Although these are different arguments, Ross regards the second as adding nothing to the first.[23] He recognizes, however, that the transparency argument cannot be accepted as it stands, for, he notes, we do not always have a certain complex property in mind when we use a term that denotes a certain complex.

... there seem to be cases in which we seek for the definition of a term and finally accept one as correct. The fact that we accept some definition as correct shows that the term did somehow stand for a complex of elements; yet the fact that we are for some time in doubt whether the term is analysable, and if so, what the correct analysis is, shows that this complex of elements was not distinctly present to our mind before, or during, the search for a definition. It appears as if we cannot avoid recognizing that there is such a thing as using a term which implicitly refers to a certain complex, while yet the complex is not explicitly present to our minds . . . (pp. 92–3)

This acknowledgement seems to be fatal to Ross's argument for the simplicity of moral properties. If a term may be definable even

---

[23] He says they both express the same thought, namely, that if good stood for a complex we would have this complex in mind when we use the term. Yet we have no such complex in mind when we use the term 'good'.

though we do not have this definition in mind when we use the term, then the term 'good' could be definable (complex) despite the fact that we do not have this definition in mind when we use the term, and so may intelligibly question whether something that satisfies the definition is good. But Ross insists that this opacity only shows that we cannot know straight off, as it were, that all definitions of 'good' must fail. What we must do is attend to any definition that seems at all plausible, and ask ourselves whether this is what we meant by 'good' all along (p. 93). If the answer to this question is 'no', then we should reject the proposed definition. And if we reject all of the most plausible definitions of 'good' in this way 'we may feel fairly confident that "good" is indefinable' and stands for a simple property (p. 93). Ross's point is that even if good is an opaque complex notion, once the definition is presented to us we should be able to respond by saying, 'that is what I meant all along, though I was unable to formulate it'. Applying this method to both rightness and goodness, Ross concludes that they are both simple properties.

Ross thought that goodness and rightness are not only simple, but non-natural properties. If 'good' and 'right' cannot be defined, then they cannot be defined in wholly natural (non-moral) terms. But even if goodness and rightness cannot be defined (are simple properties), they may still be natural properties.[24] Ross did not clearly separate the question of whether moral properties are simple from the question of whether they are natural. As a result of this he offers no argument against the view that moral properties might be simple natural properties. In one respect his failure to distinguish these issues is unproblematic, for it is difficult to imagine any *simple* natural property that might plausibly be identified with goodness (or rightness). And even if some simple natural property could be found that could plausibly be identified with goodness (or rightness), Ross could use the same argument against this identification that he did to establish the simplicity of goodness. He could claim we should consider whether we have always had this simple natural property in mind when we think of something as good (or right). Although we cannot know for certain beforehand that all such

[24] Ross held that complex properties presuppose simple ones (p. 93). Since he does not seem to think that the natural realm is reducible to some other realm, he is committed to there being simple natural properties.

identifications must fail, the absence of any plausible candidate property means that it is highly unlikely that goodness is identical with some simple natural property. If, therefore, naturalists are right, then goodness and rightness are identical with some *complex* natural property. Consequently, if Ross is right to reject all definitions of rightness and goodness, then he is right that the moral cannot be reduced to the non-moral (natural).

I do not, however, think that Ross is right that all definitions of rightness and goodness are inadequate. Ross thinks that the open question argument illustrates the fact that we do not have some definition in mind when we think of something as good. But I think this argument shows something different. I think it shows the essential normativity of evaluative judgements.[25] To say that evaluative judgements are normative is to say that they express conclusions about what would be *reasons* for acting or responding in certain (positive) ways. Natural facts may provide the ground for such practical conclusions, but judging that these natural facts obtain does not by itself involve explicitly drawing these conclusions. It is for this reason, therefore, that questions such as 'This is N, but is it good?' (where 'N' stands for some natural property) have an open feel. They have an open feel because when we decide that something is good we conclude that we have reason to adopt some pro-attitude towards it. But in judging simply that it has some natural property, we have not yet concluded that we have reason to adopt such an attitude towards it.[26]

This is not to say that natural properties cannot give us reason to respond in certain positive ways. On the contrary, the fact that something will give another person, or me, pleasure gives me a reason to get it, either for the other person or for myself. The point is that the judgement that I have reason to respond in a certain way is always a further judgement over and above the judgement that the natural property obtains. It is one thing to judge that something will be pleasant, and quite another to judge that its pleasantness gives me a reason to pursue it.

---

[25] I here follow T. M. Scanlon's account of the open question argument and the conclusion he draws from this in *What We Owe to Each Other* (Harvard University Press: Cambridge, Mass., 1998), 96 ff.

[26] Ibid. 96.

But the judgement that we have reason to respond in a certain positive way to something does not seem to be a judgement over and above the judgement that this thing is good. On the contrary, it seems that in judging that something is good we are judging that we have reason to respond in certain positive ways.[27] If this is right, then it strongly suggests that thinking of something as good is thinking of it as having features that give us reason to respond in certain ways (to adopt some pro-attitude or to do some action). The open question argument should not, therefore, lead us to conclude that goodness is indefinable, but to the conclusion that a certain definition is correct—namely one in terms of reasons, pro-attitudes, and actions. But although the open question argument does not support the view that goodness is a simple property, it does, I believe, support the view that it is a non-natural property. For what this argument makes clear is that goodness is a normative property whereas natural properties are not. If they were, then we would be able to judge that we have reason to adopt some pro-attitude towards something simply in judging *that* it has some natural property. Since the judgement that we have such reason is always additional to the judgement that something has a certain natural property, natural properties are not normative.

Someone might insist that the property of being a reason is a natural property. But I think no naturalistic account of reasons can be accepted. The most plausible ones try to define reasons in terms of what we would desire under certain conditions. But either some explicitly normative term will appear in the list of conditions—in which case the analysis will not be reductive—or the analysis is reductive, in which case it will be vulnerable to a version of the open question argument. For we can always doubt that something gives us a reason even though we know that the reductive definition is satisfied.

What we get from the open question argument, then, is not that goodness is indefinable, but that it is indefinable in naturalistic, or non-normative, terms.[28] The open question argument actually

[27] Ibid. 97 ff.
[28] This was in fact what Moore was most concerned to show with the open question argument (*Principia Ethica*, 19).

favours a certain non-naturalistic definition of goodness—it makes clear that for X to be good is for X to have features that give us reason to adopt some pro-attitude towards it.

Since the open question argument can be applied to rightness as well as to goodness, it would seem that we can draw similar conclusions about rightness—that is, we can conclude that rightness cannot be understood in wholly natural terms, and that it should be understood in terms of reasons. But since, as Ross rightly notes, rightness (where rightness is understood as equivalent to ought-to-be-doneness) is distinct from goodness, the property an act has of being right cannot be the property it has of having features that give us reason to adopt some positive attitude to it. It is, rather, the property an act may have of having features that give us overall reason to do it. It is for this reason that questions of the form 'Action A is N, but is it right?' (where 'N' stands for some natural property) have an open feel. They have an open feel because in asking whether an action is right (whether we should do it) we are asking whether we have overall reason to do it, and although N may *give* us overall reason to do A, we do not conclude that we have such reason simply in judging that the action is N. There is, however, no question of whether we have overall reason to do A once we have concluded that A is the right act. This is, I believe, best explained by identifying rightness with the property A has of having features that give us overall reason to do it.

So I think that Ross was wrong to conclude that rightness and goodness are simple properties, and that 'right' and 'good' are indefinable. But Ross does not need to insist on the indefinability of these notions to maintain that rightness and goodness are non-natural properties. For although pro-attitudes and actions are natural properties, the property of being a reason is, I believe, a non-natural property. The property of being a reason is a normative property, and one that cannot be understood in wholly non-normative (naturalistic) terms. This point is obscured by Ross's characterization of non-natural properties as those which cannot be understood in wholly non-moral terms. For the term 'reasons' is neither an explicitly moral nor a natural term. So once we note that reasons are non-natural properties, we have to characterize the natural–non-natural distinction in some other way. I do not know of a wholly adequate characterization of this distinction,[29] but Moore captures the flavour of this distinction when he says that natural properties are those that are the business of the empirical sciences (including psychology) to study, and non-natural properties are those that cannot be studied empirically. This characterization of the distinction allows us to capture the view that the property of being a reason is a non-natural property. For although science can tell us, for example, that certain animals feel pain, it cannot tell us that this empirical fact gives us *reason* not to do certain things, say, boil them alive. In pointing out that certain animals can feel pain, most scientists will have little doubt that this empirical fact gives us reason not to boil them alive. But their belief that we have such reason will not be the result of scientific investigation. All such investigation reveals is the non-normative (empirical) fact that a certain animal can feel pain. It does not reveal the normative fact that this empirical fact gives us reason to act in certain ways.

So far, I have argued, Ross has provided us with reason to think that moral properties are non-natural properties, but no good reason to suppose that they are simple. But as we noted earlier, many philosophers feel that if the truth of moral judgements commits us to the existence of non-moral properties, then we must abandon our belief that some moral judgements are true and accept an error theory. For non-natural properties are unacceptably weird and mysterious. Now the question of whether such properties are as metaphysically suspect as naturalists insist raises deep and complex issues that cannot be gone into here. We can, however, make a number of brief points on this topic.

First, we may put aside two objections that are based on confusion. Sometimes the weirdness of non-natural moral properties is expressed by saying that they are *otherworldly* properties. But Ross did not think that moral properties exist in some other world. He doesn't think that certain things in this world are good because in

---

[29] Thomas Baldwin suggests that we understand non-natural properties as properties that lack causal powers (introduction to *Principia Ethica*, p. xxii). Although I think that this, like Moore's definition, is helpful in characterizing the natural–non-natural distinction, I do not think it can be accepted as a definition. For some philosophers think that dispositional properties, such as fragility or solubility lack causal efficacy. If they are right, then all dispositional properties would be non-natural properties, according to Baldwin's definition. But fragility and solubility are clearly natural properties, whether or not they have causal powers.

some other world goodness exists. Moral properties are ways in which natural things *in this world* are. Since the way in which something is cannot be separated from the thing that is in that way, if moral properties are non-natural properties of natural (thisworldly) things, then moral properties must be thisworldly also.

A second common objection to Ross's view about moral properties is that they are mysterious because nothing can be said about them.[30] This objection is confused in a number of ways. First, it has nothing to do with the supposed non-naturalness of moral properties. If it is true that moral properties are mysterious because nothing can be said about them, then it is true not because these properties are non-natural but because they are indefinable. Second, it is not clear that a property is mysterious simply in virtue of being indefinable. For Ross, a property is indefinable if and only if it is simple, but there is nothing mysterious about simple properties as such. I take it that no naturalist will claim that the basic elements of the material world are mysterious just because they are simple. Finally, Ross did not think that nothing could be said about simple, indefinable properties. All their simplicity rules out is a definition. It does not prevent there being many informative, non-definitional things that can be said about such properties.[31] So in so far as this criticism has any force at all, it does not count against the view that there are non-natural properties, but against the view that there are *simple* moral properties, and it does not have much force against this view. In any case, I have claimed that Ross's arguments only support the view that moral properties are non-natural properties, and actually support the view that they are certain complex properties. If I am right, then the claim that such properties are mysterious because they are simple is irrelevant (as well as confused).

A third common objection is epistemological. It is that non-natural moral properties could only be known by means of a special moral faculty. But such a moral faculty is as mysterious as the properties it is supposedly able to detect. There is a real problem here for non-naturalists like Ross, but it is not at all clear that he can-

---

[30] Warnock, *Contemporary Moral Philosophy*, 13.
[31] In *The Foundations of Ethics* Ross claims that moral fittingness is indefinable, but points out what it has in common with utilitarian and aesthetic fittingness, and how it differs from these (pp. 51 ff.).

not provide a decent response. First, once we recognize that non-natural properties are, for Ross, thisworldly, our knowledge of them will seem less mysterious, for it will be knowledge of this, rather than of some other, world. Secondly, as we shall see later, Ross did not think that we know that certain things are intrinsically good or *prima facie* right literally by perceiving the property of goodness or *prima facie* rightness certain things have, let alone by perceiving them by means of a special faculty. We know these things by reflection on certain moral propositions, and such reflection requires nothing more than the ability to know anything by *a priori* reflection—that is, the ability to understand and think.[32]

Other objections to non-natural properties are, however, harder to deal with. But if we abandon the view that rightness and goodness are *simple* non-natural properties and understand them in terms of reasons, it is much harder for worries about non-natural properties to lead one to adopt an error theory about value. If moral properties are simple, then pervasive error in our evaluative judgements will be relatively local. For we can doubt the existence of simple moral properties without doubting anything other than those properties and the complex moral properties that are formed out of them. If, however, value is to be understood in terms of reasons, then (assuming one has no problem with actions and psychological attitudes) one's scepticism about value would have to stem from scepticism about reasons. But if an error theory about value rests on an error theory about reasons, then the error theorist would be committed both to the view that we have good reason to deny the existence of reasons, and that this implies that all of our reasons judgements are false. But such a view seems to undermine itself, for it is to say that we have reason to be sceptical about reasons, and implies that it is false that we have reason to be sceptical about reasons.

One might try to avoid this conclusion by limiting one's scepticism to *practical* reasons—that is, reasons to do some act or adopt some pro-attitude. This form of localized scepticism would leave epistemic reasons (reasons to believe) untouched, and so would not land the error theorist with a self-undermining view. But I do not see how scepticism about reasons could be limited in this way. The

[32] See L. Bonjour, *In Defence of Pure Reason: A Rationalist Account of A Priori Justification* (Cambridge University Press: Cambridge, 1998), 107–9.

difference between practical and epistemic reasons is not that they stand in different warranting relations to certain things (one relation queer and the other innocuous), but that they warrant different things. Practical reasons warrant pro-attitudes and actions, whereas epistemic reasons warrant beliefs. If, therefore, one has doubts about the normative (warranting) relation itself, these doubts could not be localized in such a way as to avoid scepticism about epistemic as well as practical reasons.

If the above argument is along the right lines, then the naturalist must abandon either the view that moral discourse is truth apt—the option taken by emotivists—or deny that its truth aptness implies the existence of non-natural properties—the option taken by naturalist realists. But I believe that we have good reason to think of moral discourse as truth apt, and Ross offers a persuasive argument that moral properties (the truth-makers of moral judgements) cannot be identified with any natural property. My view is thus that we should abandon naturalism.

II

Critique of Consequentialism

Intuitionists are often accused of being obsessed with defining 'right' and 'good'. But Ross clearly thought (wrongly, I have argued) that nothing interesting could be said on this subject, for he thought that goodness and rightness are simple and thus indefinable. Ross's concern with the definition of rightness and goodness was purely negative. He clearly thought that all definitions of goodness and rightness are mistaken, and that this mistake had implications for our thinking about normative ethics. For if one thought, as Moore did in *Principia Ethica*, that to think of an act as right is to think of it as maximizing good outcomes, then consequentialism *must* be correct, despite the fact that we often do not seem to look to future consequences when considering what we should do. But as Ross points out, and Moore eventually came to see,[33] if consequen-

---

[33] There is evidence that Moore recognized this point in his *Ethics* (Oxford University Press: London, 1966). For a discussion of this, see Ross, pp. 8–11. This recognition is explicit, however, in his 'A Reply to my Critics', in P. A. Schilpp (ed.), *The Philosophy of G. E. Moore* (Northwestern University Press: Evanston, Ill., 1942), 558.

tialism is true, then it would not be *analytically* true, but would be a substantive (synthetic) truth. In so far as consequentialism is at all plausible, it does not tell us what it is for an act to be right, but offers an account of the ultimate reason why all right acts are right—that is, the ultimate *ground* of rightness. If consequentialists cannot force their doctrine through by insisting that it is analytically true, then the case for consequentialism must be made by considering different types of right action and considering what makes these actions right (p. 36). Ross argues that once consequentialists are forced to defend their view in this piecemeal fashion, they become vulnerable to a series of objections. These objections may not be thought to be individually decisive, but together they do form a compelling case against consequentialism.

First, Ross thinks consequentialism oversimplifies the morally relevant relations in which we stand to others. Consequentialism, Ross maintains, implies that 'the only morally significant relation in which my neighbours stand to me is that of being possible beneficiaries by my action' (p. 19). But, he objects, although the benefactor–beneficiary relation is morally important, it is not the only morally relevant relation. The relations of promiser to promisee, of creditor to debtor, of wife to husband, of child to parent, of friend to friend, of fellow countryman to fellow countryman are also morally relevant to determining what we should do (p. 19).

Ross, however, overstates his case here. Consequentialism does not imply that the only morally significant relation in which we stand to others is that of beneficiary to benefactor. Consequentialists can allow that all of the relations Ross mentions are morally significant also. Consequentialists do not claim that these relations are morally insignificant, but that their significance is derivative, and contingent on the fact that keeping one's promises, paying one's debts, etc. happens to produce the best outcome. But a consideration that is morally relevant under certain conditions *is* morally relevant when those conditions obtain. Ross's objection must, therefore, be that these other relations are morally significant *in their own right*, and thus do not need to acquire this significance because luck would have it that respecting these relations maximizes good.

But why should we agree with Ross that these considerations are morally relevant in their own right and reject the consequentialist account of their relevance? Ross offers a number of arguments to suggest that being productive of the best outcome is not the only basic moral consideration. The first is that the fact that we have made a promise can decide what we should do where breaking our promise will produce as much good as keeping it.

If, so far as I can see, I could bring equal amounts of good into being by fulfilling my promise and by helping some one to whom I had made no promise, I should not hesitate to regard the former as my duty. Yet on the view that what is right is right because it is productive of the most good I should not so regard it. (p. 18)

If all moral considerations acquire their moral significance from consequence-based considerations, then if the value of the consequences of keeping a promise is the same as the value of the consequences of breaking it, we should have no moral reason to keep our promise rather than break it. But we have no doubt that in such a situation we should keep our promise rather than break it. This can only be explained by the fact that promise-keeping has a moral importance that does not stem from the value of outcomes.[34]

  Ross's second argument is that consequentialism ignores what he calls the 'highly personal character' of duty (p. 22).

If the only duty is to produce the maximum of good, the question of who is to have the good—whether it is myself, or my benefactor, or a person to whom I have made a promise to confer that good on him, or a mere fellow man to whom I stand in no such special relation—should make no difference to my having a duty to produce that good. But we are all in fact sure that it makes a vast difference. (p. 22)

The thought here seems to be that we are more certain that these relations make a difference to whom we should confer the good than we are of the truth of consequentialism. If this is correct, then if consequentialism implies that these relations make no such difference, then we should reject consequentialism rather than our conviction that these relations make a difference.[35]

---

[34] Brad Hooker addresses this sort of difficulty as it applies to rule consequentialism in his *Ideal Code, Real World* (Oxford University Press: Oxford, 2000), 114–16.
[35] This argument from degrees of confidence is pervasive in Ross, and bears a close affinity to Moore's argument against scepticism about the external world in his 'Some Judgements of Perception', in *Philosophical Studies* (Routledge & Kegan Paul: London, 1922).

Ross also notes that we do not think that the tiniest increase in overall value would necessarily justify us in breaking a promise. If, for example, my keeping my promise to *A* would produce 1,000 units of good for him, but by doing some other act I could produce 1,001 units of good for *B*, I would not think that I should break my promise to *A* (p. 34).[36] 'To produce the 1,001 units of good for *B* rather than fulfil our promise to *A* would be to take, not perhaps our duty as philanthropists too seriously, but certainly our duty as makers of promises too lightly' (p. 35).

Ross goes on to offer two variants of the same thought experiment. The first involves producing 1,001 units of good for *A* by doing something other than what I promised, which would produce 1,000 units of good for *A*. The other is where I have made no promise, but have the option of producing 1,000 units of good for *A*, who is a very good man, or 1,001 units of good for *B*, a very bad man. In the first case we should, Ross claims, do what we promised *A*, while in the second we should produce the benefits for *A*. But in both cases what we should do is produce the lesser good.

Ross argues further that, 'if it were self-evident that the right coincides with the optimific, it should be self-evident that what is *prima facie* right is *prima facie* optimific. But whereas we are certain that keeping a promise is *prima facie* right, we are not certain that it is *prima facie* optimific' (p. 36). What each of these arguments aims to do is to show that on reflection we do not think that considerations of fidelity are morally relevant just because they are instrumental to bringing about the best state of affairs. These considerations have intrinsic deontic relevance which, as such, does not need to be inherited from anything else. The duty to keep our promise may be overridden if breaking it would bring about a considerably better state of affairs. But the fact that considerations of fidelity can be defeated by consequence-based considerations does not imply that when we should keep our promises this is also explained by consequence-based considerations.

---

[36] Ross later considers a response to this objection, that failing to keep one's promise will have effects that will always tip the evaluative balance in such cases in favour of keeping one's promise to *A* (p. 38), but rightly rejects this.

Other Attempts to Derive the Right from the Good

Consequentialists maintain that rightness is grounded in goodness—that the ultimate reason why some act is right is because it is, in a certain sense, good. Consequentialism is not, however, the only theory that attempts to ground the right in the good. Certain theories attempt to ground the rightness of right acts, not in the value of their outcomes, their instrumental goodness, but in their intrinsic moral value. On this view, we ought to do certain acts because those acts are morally good on their own account. Egoists also attempt to ground the right in the good. For them we ought to do certain actions because doing these acts will, in the long run, promote our own good. Ross quickly disposes of both of these attempts to derive the right from the good. The egoistic theory is rejected on the ground that 'a great part of duty consists in an observance of the rights and a furtherance of the interests of others, whatever the cost to ourselves may be' (p. 16). Furthermore, even if it were true that doing morally right acts always benefits the agent in the long run, this would be irrelevant to the moral rightness of those actions. 'As soon as a man does an action *because* he thinks he will promote his own interests thereby, he is acting not from a sense of its rightness but from self-interest' (p. 16).

Given that Ross thinks that the rightness of an action is completely independent of the motive from which it is done (pp. 4 ff.), it is not clear how this point about acting from different motives is relevant. But I take Ross's point to be this. When we think of ourselves as doing the morally right act, we regard ourselves as responsive to considerations such as fidelity, intrinsic value, gratitude, etc. We do not, however, think of self-interest as a *moral* consideration—that is, as one that could generate a *moral* obligation. So when we think of ourselves as responding solely to considerations of self-interest, we do not think that we are doing what we morally ought to do. The 'ought' that considerations of self-interest generate is not a *moral* ought. It is for this reason that considerations of self-interest are irrelevant to the moral rightness of an act. What is relevant are the considerations that can *make* an act morally right, but considerations of self-interest will not appear on a list of such considerations. Consequently, considerations of self-interest are irrelevant to the rightness of morally right acts even if all morally right acts tend to promote the agent's interest.

Ross spends a little more time on the attempt to derive the right from the morally good. He does this in the chapter on the meaning of 'right', and so does not explicitly consider this view as a theory of the *ground* of rightness. But by arguing that what is morally good is never morally required he tries to show that 'morally good' need not be coextensive with 'morally right'. If this attempt is successful, it would show not only that 'right' cannot mean 'morally good', but also that moral goodness cannot be the sole ground of morally right acts.

Ross's arguments against the view that we are never required to do morally good actions rest on the assumption that the only morally good actions are those that are done from morally good motives (p. 4). Granted this assumption, if he can show that we are never required to act from a morally good motive, then he will have shown that we are never morally required to do a morally good act.

In *The Right and the Good* Ross proposes two arguments for the view that we are never morally required to act from morally good motives.[37] His first argument is that such a requirement would transgress the 'ought implies can' principle. His second argument is that the requirement to act from the morally best motive (the motive of duty) leads to an infinite regress.

We cannot be required to act from a good motive, because we can only be required to do what we can, at a moment's notice, choose to do. But we cannot choose to have a motive if we do not have it, and even if we possess the relevant motive, we cannot choose to be motivated by it rather than by some other motive. The object of choice, *what* we choose, is some action, and although we choose to do this action from some motive, the motive from which we choose it is never part of what is chosen.[38] Since we cannot choose to be motivated in a certain way, we cannot be required to be motivated in a certain way.

This argument is far from persuasive. It rests on a dubious understanding of the 'ought implies can' principle which has very counter-intuitive consequences. If this understanding of the

[37] Further arguments against this view can be found in *The Foundations of Ethics*, ch. 6.
[38] Ibid. 120–1 and 138.

principle were correct, then we would be freed from obligations from which we do not think we are free. For example, suppose I have promised John that I would pay back the money I owe him at midday, and that John is counting on my doing so (he really needs the money then). Suppose further that I have the money, and set off to meet him and pay him back. En route, however, I pass a casino and, in a moment of weakness (and bad luck), lose all of the money at the blackjack table. If Ross's understanding of the 'ought implies can' principle is correct, then as soon as I have lost the money I am freed of the obligation to repay John. For although I could have chosen to pay him back at noon before I lost the money, I can no longer choose to do this, for it is not in my power to conjure up the money at will. But this seems wrong. It seems that I still ought to pay back the money to John at midday even though I can no longer choose to do so.

Ross might respond by saying that I no longer have *this* obligation, but have acquired a different one—namely, to apologize to John and to find some other way of paying him back as quickly as possible. This is partly right. I do acquire those extra obligations as a result of my action. But it is wrong to assume that these other obligations *replace* the first one. I cannot so easily free myself of this obligation. On the contrary, what I did was wrong *because* it meant that I would no longer be able to fulfil my obligation to John (to pay him at midday). We can only make sense of this if we assume that I have made myself unable to fulfil an obligation that survives my inability to fulfil it.

Ross's second argument against the view that we are required to do morally good actions claims that this view leads to an infinite regress. If we are required to act from a good motive, then we will, at least sometimes, be required to act from the best motive. The motive of duty is, Ross argues, the best motive (pp. 164–5). To act from the best motive is, therefore, to act from a sense of duty. On this view we will not have done what we should simply in doing some act, say an act of helping another person. We will have done our duty only if we help someone from a sense of duty, for this is what is required of us. But if helping someone from a sense of duty is our duty, then, according to the theory under consideration, all of this (helping from a sense of duty) must itself be done from a sense of duty. This gives rise to a new duty (helping from a sense of duty, from a sense of duty), which in turn must be done from a sense of duty. This process will have to be repeated again, and again, leading to a vicious infinite regress (pp. 5–6).

Ross regards this as a *reductio ad absurdum* of the view that we are required to act from duty. This does not show that we cannot be required to act from other good motives. But Ross rightly points out that it would be paradoxical to assert that we are required to act from good motives but can never be required to act from the best (p. 6).

Since the most plausible monistic deontic theories are those that attempt to ground the right in the good, if such theories are false it is a safe bet that all monistic deontic theories are false. If all monistic theories are false, then if we are bound by any duties at all, pluralism must be true.

Prima Facie *Duties*

This brings us to Ross's positive theory—his doctrine of *prima facie* duties. This doctrine rests on a distinction between '*prima facie* duty' and 'duty proper', or what Ross sometimes calls our 'actual duty' (pp. 19–20). It is tempting to understand this distinction as one between what merely *seems* to be our duty and what *really is* our duty, but Ross is clear that it should not be understood in this way. In fact the term '*prima facie* duty' is doubly misleading, for Ross intended it to pick out a feature of actions that is neither a type of duty nor *prima facie* (in the sense of being merely apparent).

The phrase '*prima facie* duty' must be apologized for, since (1) it suggests that what we are speaking of is a certain kind of duty, whereas it is in fact not a duty, but something related in a special way to duty. Strictly speaking, we want not a phrase in which duty is qualified by an adjective, but a separate noun. (2) '*Prima' facie* suggests that one is speaking only of an appearance which a moral situation presents at first sight, and which may turn out to be illusory; whereas what I am speaking of is an objective fact involved in the nature of the situation, or more strictly in an element of its nature, though not, as duty proper does, arising from its *whole* nature. (p. 20)

For an act to be *prima facie* right is not for us to have some kind of duty to do this act, but is for this action to have some feature that

gives us a moral reason to do it. For some feature of an act to be
prima facie wrong is not for us to have some kind of duty not to do it,
but is for it to have some feature that gives us a moral reason not to
do it. These features are not what we should do (our duty), but are
considerations which we (should) take into account in deciding
what it is we should do.

Ross does not make this clear in his official subjunctive conditional definition of *prima facie* duties,[39] or in his account of them in
terms of a certain tendency, or disposition.[40] But this is, I believe,
what Ross means when he says that a *prima facie* duty 'is not a duty,
but something related in a special way to duty'. This interpretation
is given support by the fact that Ross discusses the doctrine of *prima
facie* duties in a chapter called 'What Makes Right Acts Right?' in
The Right and the Good, and in 'Theories about the Ground of
Rightness' in *The Foundations of Ethics*. So *prima facie* duties should
be understood as features that give us genuine (not merely apparent) moral reason to do certain actions.

Because the term '*prima facie* duty' is so misleading Ross was
keen to find some other term. 'Strictly speaking', he writes, 'we
want not a phrase in which duty is qualified by an adjective, but a
separate noun.' At the time of writing *The Right and the Good*, however, Ross could not think of a better term. He considered the term
'claim', but rejects this for two reasons. First, it captures what he
wants to express from the wrong point of view—from the point of
view of the other person, the person who has a claim against me,
rather than of the agent. Secondly, it does not capture the fact that
we have a *prima facie* duty to ourselves, for only others can have a
claim against us (p. 20). In *The Foundations of Ethics*, however, he
accepts that the term 'responsibility' is a better way of expressing
what he was getting at with the term '*prima facie* duty'. *Prima facie*
duties are, he there states, responsibilities to ourselves and to others,
and what we should do (our duty proper) is determined by the balance of these responsibilities.

[39] 'I suggest '*prima facie* duty' . . . as a brief way of referring to the characteristic . . . which an
act has . . . of being an act which would be a duty proper if it were not at the same time of another
kind which is morally significant' (p. 19).

[40] On p. 28 Ross characterizes the *prima facie* rightness of actions as their tending to be our
duty. See also *The Foundations of Ethics*, 86.

He also accepts C. D. Broad's notion of fittingness, for unlike rightness this allows of degrees. It makes no sense to say that a right act is the one that is *most* right, but it makes perfect sense to say that a right act is the one which is most fitting, or appropriate to the total situation. Ross's account of duty proper in terms of fittingness is very close indeed to the definition in terms of reasons offered above. According to this definition, to say that an act is right is to say that it has features that give us overall reason to do the action, whereas for Ross it is to say that it has features that make it most appropriate to the situation.

His account of rightness in terms of fittingness allows Ross to understand *prima facie* right features of actions as those that are fitting to some aspect of the situation. We can offer an account of *prima facie* duties in terms of reasons also. To say that an act is *prima facie* right is just to say that it has a feature that gives us moral reason to do the act (or, as Ross would put it, a feature that is fitting to some aspect of the situation). So if one is troubled by the term 'fitting' one can replace Ross's account in *The Foundations of Ethics* with an account which replaces fittingness with reasons.

We have seen that Ross rejects the view that all moral considerations can be reduced to, or grounded in, one, as consequentialists claim. Initially he lists seven fundamental *prima facie* duties—that is, seven intrinsically (moral) reason-giving features of actions from which all other moral features derive their reason-giving force. They are (1) considerations of fidelity, (2) of reparation, (3) of gratitude, (4) of justice, (5) of beneficence, (6) of self-improvement, and (7) of non-maleficence (p. 21). Later on, however, he claims that (4) to (6) can all be subsumed under the promotion of intrinsic value (p. 27), for happiness, virtue, and justice are intrinsic goods. This reduces the list of fundamental *prima facie* duties to five: fidelity, reparation, gratitude, promotion of the good, and non-maleficence (avoidance of the bad).

One might think that considerations of honesty should appear on the list of basic moral considerations, but Ross thinks the reason-giving nature of honesty is not basic but derivative. The fact that our act is one of lying gives us moral reason not to do it only because (and if) in lying we break an implicit promise to tell the truth, or harm someone (pp. 54–5). In most cases one or both of these basic considerations will be relevant, but not always. For example, in a game of Contraband[41] one is expected to deceive, so there is no implicit promise to tell the truth, no trust to be betrayed. If no one is harmed by these lies, then lying falls under neither the *prima facie* duty of fidelity nor that of non-maleficence. In such cases the fact that our act is one of lying gives us no moral reason at all not to do it. This shows that the reason-giving force of dishonesty is derivative, rather than basic. The moral reason we have not to lie stems not from the very nature of lying, but from considerations of fidelity and non-maleficence. It is for this reason that when these basic considerations do not apply, we have no moral reason not to lie.[42]

What this shows is that Ross is not simply *listing* whatever moral obligations we think we have, something he is often accused of doing. He is, rather, attempting to systematize as much as possible the moral convictions we have. He does this by asking which moral considerations are basic and which derivative, with the aim of finding the considerations that underpin all the rest, but that are not themselves underpinned by some other moral consideration. This is basically the same enterprise consequentialists and Kantians are engaged in. The only difference is that they think that all moral considerations can ultimately be grounded in one, whereas Ross thinks that they can be reduced to no fewer than five. This may not satisfy everyone, but it is no more unsatisfactory than the fact that there is an irreducible plurality of geometric axioms. The fact that there is a plurality of axioms in geometry does not render it unsystematic. Similarly, Ross's intuitionism is not unsystematic simply because he thinks that there is an irreducible plurality of fundamental moral principles.

Ross not only thinks that there is vertical structure (from basic to derivative principles) but also some horizontal structure. For although he thinks that any basic moral consideration can outweigh any other, he does not think they carry equal normative weight. He clearly thinks that certain basic considerations are weightier than others. For example, he maintains that considerations of non-maleficence, fidelity, and reparation are weightier than those of

41 I borrow this example from Jonathan Dancy's *Moral Reasons* (Blackwell: Oxford, 1993), 60-1.
42 Another example of a derivative *prima facie* duty is that of political obligation (pp. 27-8).

beneficence (pp. 22, 30). It is, however, hard to specify what this stringency amounts to in the abstract.[43] It is not that considerations of non-maleficence, fidelity, and reparation always outweigh those of beneficence. All that Ross can say is that considerations of, say, fidelity can be overridden only by a *significant* gain in well-being for others. But what is to count as significant will vary from case to case.

It is sometimes said that Ross cannot adequately account for moral conflict.[44] According to this view Ross's theory means that what looks like a real conflict of duties turns out, after all, to be a merely apparent conflict. For, it is said, in deciding which *prima facie* duty generates our actual duty we are deciding which of the conflicting duties is real and which *merely* apparent. On this view, there turns out to be no real conflict at all, just an apparent one.

It should, however, be clear by now that this criticism rests on a misunderstanding of the notion of a *prima facie* duty. Deciding what our actual duty is is not, according to Ross, deciding which *prima facie* duty is real and which merely apparent. It is, rather, deciding which morally relevant consideration gives us the weightier reason. Deciding that the fact that we have made a promise gives us a stronger reason to keep it than the fact that breaking it would produce more good gives us reason to break it is not deciding that the latter fact gives us no moral reason at all. It is just deciding that we have more reason to keep our promise than to break it. Ross shows that he recognized this in claiming that when we decide that some *prima facie* duty is overridden, we feel not guilt, but certainly compunction for the fact that we could not respond to the defeated duty (p. 28).

In 1959 A. C. Ewing described Ross's doctrine of *prima facie* duties as one of the most important discoveries in moral philosophy in the twentieth century.[45] This description may be over the top, but Ross's doctrine is certainly an important step in our understanding of morality. One of the advantages of Ross's theory is that it can accommodate the fact that we sometimes ought to break a promise in order to prevent a bad outcome without conceding everything to

[43] For Ross's discussion of the stringency of the *prima facie* duty to keep one's promises, see *The Foundations of Ethics*, 100–1.

[44] See e.g. J. Searle, '*Prima Facie* Obligations', in J. Raz (ed.), *Practical Reasoning* (Oxford University Press: Oxford, 1978), 81–90.

[45] *Second Thoughts in Moral Philosophy* (Routledge & Kegan Paul: London, 1959), 126.

the consequentialist (p. 18). Furthermore, before Ross, deontologists could only attempt to accommodate the pluralism that is deeply embedded in our moral thinking by insisting that there is a plurality of basic duties (duties proper, that is). The problem with this, however, is that it turned every moral conflict into a tragic moral dilemma whereby we are morally obligated to do two very different actions in the same situation, but can only do one. In such circumstances, whatever we do is wrong in the sense that we will fail to do what we should no matter what we do. With his doctrine of *prima facie* duties Ross frees pluralists from this difficulty. For this doctrine allows us to think of moral conflict not as a conflict of duties, but as a conflict of moral reasons, which is, I believe, how things are.

Pluralism about the Good

Discussions of Ross's pluralism tend to focus on his doctrine of *prima facie* duties. But although Ross's views about the good are almost never discussed, more than two-thirds of *The Right and the Good* is devoted to this subject. Much of this is negative, attacking those who deny that goodness is a simple, non-natural property. But in Chapter V he outlines his positive theory about intrinsic goods—that is, about things that are good on their own account. Following Moore, Ross divides such goods into those that have some parts that have no value, and those that are either simple intrinsic goods, or complex wholes all the parts of which are intrinsically good (p. 69). He calls the latter 'ultimate goods'. Ultimately good things, unlike other intrinsic goods, are good throughout—that is, contain nothing that is not intrinsically good.

Although Ross followed Moore in distinguishing intrinsic from ultimate goods, he differed from Moore in that he thought that for the most part we can work out the intrinsic value of complex wholes (which are not good throughout) from our knowledge of their ultimately good parts.[46] Consequently, he focuses on ultimate goods, on the assumption that we can almost always work out which more complex things are intrinsically good from our knowledge of which

---

[46] '. . . I regard the things that are intrinsically but not ultimately good as owing, generally speaking, their value to those elements in them that *are* ultimately good; as being good, in fact, "in virtue of a part of themselves", the other parts of them being irrelevant to their goodness' (p. 73).

things are ultimately good. So he thinks that the evaluative has the same foundationalist structure as the deontic. There is an irreducible plurality of ultimate goods from which (almost) all other intrinsic goods can be constructed, and in virtue of which they are intrinsically good (p. 141).

Ross argues that there are three simple ultimate goods, and one complex (which cannot be reduced to the value of its elements) (p. 27).[47] The simple goods are virtue, pleasure, and knowledge. The complex good is the distribution of happiness in proportion to merit (virtue). The first thing he claims is ultimately good is virtue. He includes under virtue both virtuous dispositions and actions that express these dispositions. The actions that express these dispositions are actions done from certain motives, such as the desire to do one's duty, the desire to bring into being something good, or the desire to give pleasure to others (p. 134). Hedonists would deny that virtue is intrinsically good. They are monists about the good, and hence insist that pleasure is the only intrinsic good. Ross argues that we can see the falsity of hedonism if we consider a certain thought experiment. If we consider two worlds that contain the same amount of pleasure, though one is full of vicious and the other full of virtuous people, we would not think that they are equally good. Rather we would think that the one that has both virtue and pleasure would be the better world. This thought experiment shows the implausibility of monistic hedonism (p. 134).

Ross uses the reverse thought experiment in support of the view that pleasure is intrinsically good. If we imagine two worlds equal in virtue, though in the first there is widespread and intense pleasure, while in the second there is widespread and intense pain, we would have no doubt that the first is the better (p. 135). This shows that we do not think that virtue is the only thing that is good on its own account, for the two worlds are equal in respect of virtue, though are not equal in respect of value.

Ross brings forward two other considerations in favour of the view that pleasure is intrinsically good. The first is that we can only explain our approval of kindness on the assumption that pleasure is intrinsically good. If we did not think that pleasure is good, we

[47] This view seems to commit Ross to Moore's doctrine of organic wholes, though in Ch. III he is rather sceptical about this doctrine.

would not think that the desire to give pleasure to others is a virtue. Secondly, we think that virtue should be rewarded by happiness. We would not, however, think this unless we thought that happiness (here apparently equated with pleasure and the absence of pain) is intrinsically good (p. 135).

The third (ultimate) intrinsic good is justice. By justice Ross means the proportionment of happiness (again equated with pleasure) to virtue, and misery to the vicious (p. 138).[48] Unlike the first two goods, this is a complex good involving both pleasure and virtue in a certain relation. It cannot, however, be reduced to the value of virtue and pleasure separately. We can see this if we consider two worlds with equal amounts of virtue, vice, pleasure, and pain, but which in one the virtuous are happy and the vicious miserable, while in the other the virtuous are miserable and the vicious happy. Although both worlds contain the same amount of virtue and pleasure, they are not equally good. The former world is better than the latter. To accommodate this we must, Ross thinks, allow justice as a distinct and irreducible ultimate good. This is, he acknowledges, one of the few clear instances of an organic whole. For both vice and misery are intrinsically bad, but a whole involving the combination of these elements is better than one in which the vicious are happy (p. 72).

Finally Ross maintains that knowledge, and to a lesser degree, true belief are intrinsically good (pp. 138–9). Once again, a comparative thought experiment is used to make this clear.

> . . . we . . . may . . . help ourselves to realize the fact by supposing two states of the universe equal in respect of virtue and of pleasure and of the allocation of pleasure to the virtuous, but such that the persons in the one had a far greater understanding of the nature and laws of the universe than those in the other. Can any one doubt that the first would be a better state of the universe? (p. 139)

Ross admits that knowledge of certain trivial facts, like the number of storeys in a building, without knowledge of their relation to other facts, may seem worthless. But he maintains that although such

---

[48] Ross acknowledges that this is only one thing that we might mean by 'justice', but it is this that he thinks is ultimately good (p. 26).

knowledge has much less value than knowledge that involves insight and understanding, it still has some intrinsic value (p. 139).

It is, however, not at all clear to me that knowledge, say, of the number of grains of sand on a certain beach, has any value whatsoever. Ross claims that even of such trivial facts right opinion is better than wrong, and knowledge is better than right opinion. This may be so, but does not show that such knowledge is good in itself. One might think that one thing is better than another without thinking that either is good. Ross is, however, on much stronger ground with the view that knowledge and true belief that involve insight and understanding are good on their own account, independently of any benefit they might bring. (At least one would hope this is true if one thinks that most philosophical enquiry has any value!)

It may be objected that such knowledge has value only in so far as it is a source of satisfaction to its possessor. But Ross rightly responds to this that one might be equally satisfied with a false belief that one thinks is true. But although we might be as satisfied with a false belief as with genuine knowledge, we do not doubt that the latter state is better than the former (p. 140).

In *The Right and the Good*, then, Ross maintains that there are four ultimate goods: virtue, pleasure, justice, and knowledge. In *The Foundations of Ethics*, however, he rejected his earlier view that pleasure is intrinsically good, owing to certain difficulties this view entails.[49] Ross lists a number of difficulties, the most significant of which is that if pleasure were intrinsically good, then we would have a *prima facie* duty to produce pleasure not only for others, but also for ourselves.[50] For if we have a *prima facie* duty to promote the good, and our own pleasure is good, then we have a *prima facie* duty to promote our own pleasure. It is not, however, the case that we have a moral duty to promote our own pleasure. It may be foolish not to promote our own happiness when we have the opportunity to do so, but it is not something that is morally wrong, something about which we have reason to feel guilty. But although Ross abandoned his earlier view that pleasure is

---

[49] *The Foundations of Ethics*, 271 ff.   [50] Ibid. 271–2.

intrinsically good, he never abandoned his pluralism about the good (and the right).[51]

III

Self-Evidence

We saw earlier that Ross was keen to show that moral properties could not be understood wholly in terms of non-moral properties. This meant that he believed in the autonomy of ethics. To think that ethics is an autonomous realm is to believe that ethics is a distinct subject matter that cannot be subsumed under any other science. We have also seen that Ross embraced a foundationalist epistemology. He held that we can know certain derivative moral truths only because we know more basic truths. These more basic truths can in turn be known only on the basis of our knowledge of even more fundamental truths. But this cannot go on for ever, for we cannot know an infinite number of truths. Following Aristotle,[52] therefore, Ross held that if we know anything derivatively, there must be something that we know non-derivatively—something that can be known directly. We do seem to have derivative moral knowledge. We know, for example, that lying is often *prima facie* wrong, and that we have a *prima facie* duty to obey the laws of our country. According to Ross, we know that lying is *prima facie* wrong on the basis of our knowledge that we have made an implicit promise to tell the truth, or because lying will harm someone, and we know that promise-breaking and harming others are *prima facie* wrong. But how do we know that promise-breaking and harming others are *prima facie* wrong? It does not seem that we derive this knowledge from some other, more fundamental, *moral* proposition. If ethics forms an autonomous realm we cannot derive this knowledge from our knowledge of some non-moral premiss. We cannot derive our knowledge that we should keep our promises from knowledge that our society disapproves of promise-breaking, or that the institution

---

[51] Although in *The Foundations of Ethics* Ross abandoned the view that pleasure is intrinsically good, he still held that it is good in some sense (*Foundations*, 275 ff.). But given that he did not abandon the view that we have a *prima facie* duty to promote the good, it is unclear how he can believe that pleasure is good in any sense and avoid the conclusion that we have a *prima facie* duty to promote our own pleasure.

[52] *Posterior Analytics*, bk. 1, chs. 2 and 3.

of promise-keeping has great utility. Since we cannot derive this knowledge from our knowledge of other propositions (moral or non-moral), then if we know that promise-breaking and harming others is *prima facie* wrong we must know this directly.

This is true not only of the deontic, but of the evaluative also. We know that certain things are instrumentally good, but this knowledge is derivative. It is based on our knowledge that certain things are non-instrumentally good, and that something else is a means to obtaining this good. But our knowledge that certain things are intrinsically good does not seem to be derived from other evaluative knowledge, and given the autonomy of ethics, this knowledge cannot be derived from non-evaluative premises, such as our knowledge that we desire or approve of that thing. Given that this knowledge cannot be derived from moral or non-moral premises, if we know that certain things are intrinsically good, this must be known directly—that is, non-inferentially. If, therefore, we have any moral knowledge at all—be it deontic or evaluative—we must know certain fundamental moral propositions directly, on the basis of an understanding of them. This means that the most fundamental moral propositions are self-evident.

But although Ross held that the principles of *prima facie* duty are self-evident, he did not think that we know the *stringency* of these duties. We only have a probable opinion about the degree of their *prima facie* obligatoriness (p. 31).[53] Furthermore, Ross was sceptical about our ability to know what our actual duty is in particular situations. 'Our judgements about our actual duty in concrete situations have none of the certainty that attaches to our recognition of the general principles of [*prima facie*] duty' (p. 30). This is for three reasons. First, we can never be sure that there is some *prima facie* consideration that we have failed to notice. Second, 'any particular act will in all probability in the course of time contribute to the bringing about of good or of evil for many human beings, and thus have a *prima facie* rightness or wrongness of which we know nothing'.[54] And finally, even if we know which *prima facie* considerations are relevant to the particular case, we cannot know which is the

[53] See also *The Foundations of Ethics*, 188.
[54] Ross seems to think of this second point simply as an illustration of the first (p. 31). It is, however, a distinct epistemological difficulty.

more stringent. So although Ross's view on moral epistemology may seem overly optimistic in so far as he thinks that basic moral propositions are self-evident, his overall view is in fact rather pessimistic.

Nonetheless, many moral philosophers think that Ross's epistemological intuitionism is utterly unacceptable, and reject it out of hand. It is, however, worth asking what it is that is supposed to be so untenable about this view. The most common response is that it presupposes a mysterious sixth sense, a moral sense, by means of which we apprehend the presence of moral properties—intrinsic goodness and *prima facie* rightness. This objection is, however, based upon a myth. If one looks at Ross's moral writings one will find no reference to such a mysterious faculty. Is he *committed* to belief in such a faculty? The simple answer is 'No'. Ross thinks that fundamental moral propositions are self-evident. This means that we are able to know these propositions solely on the basis of an understanding of them—that is, that they are knowable *a priori*.[55] If this is right, then Ross is not committed to the view that we have a faculty of apprehending moral properties, but only an ability to know certain propositions *a priori*. Moral knowledge is no more mysterious than any other *a priori* knowledge.

One may be suspicious of *a priori* knowledge in general on the ground that it presupposes a mysterious faculty for apprehending eternal truths. But I see no reason why we should think that *a priori* knowledge requires such a mysterious faculty. All it requires is the ability to understand and think. We should, therefore, quickly put to one side the most common objection to epistemological intuitionism, and see if there are any objections with more substance to them.

It is sometimes argued that if the basic principles of duty were self-evident, there would be no moral disagreement. There is moral disagreement. Therefore, the basic principles of duty are not self-evident. Ross considered this argument and rejected the conclusion.

---

[55] It should be noted that, according to Ross, we come to know self-evident universal principles by first knowing particular instances that fall under these principles. So, for example, we come to know that promise-breaking is *prima facie* wrong by first knowing that some particular act of promise-breaking is *prima facie* wrong. But knowledge of these particulars is, for Ross, simply a way of ascending to knowledge of the universal, knowledge which, once attained, can be known directly (pp. 32–3).

'. . . the diversity of opinion on moral questions is found to rest not on disagreement about fundamental moral principles, but partly on differences in the circumstances of different societies, and partly on different views which people hold, not on moral questions but on questions of fact'.[56] The sort of difference in circumstances Ross had in mind is illustrated by the presence or absence of a system for the enforcement of public laws. Private vengeance may be right in an unsettled state of society that lacks the proper provision for the punishment of murderers, but wrong in a more settled society that has such provisions. This moral difference is explained not by a difference in opinion about the fundamental principles of morality, but by the fact that in an unsettled state of society private vengeance may be 'the only way of securing respect for life, while in a more settled state of society this is better left to the arm of the law'.[57]

Different moral views may also be explained by differences about the non-moral facts.

. . . the difference between those who think vaccination right and those who think it wrong turns largely on a difference of opinion on the question of fact whether vaccination does or does not prevent smallpox, while both parties accept the principle that parents should try to save their children from disease. And the difference of opinion between fox-hunters and those who condemn fox-hunting turns largely on a difference of view as to the comparative intensity of the pain of the fox and the enjoyment of his hunters.[58]

One might not think that these examples accurately represent the non-moral differences that underpin these moral disagreements. Nonetheless, the point should be clear that many moral differences rest on different views about the non-moral (but morally relevant) facts, rather than on differences about the fundamental principles that Ross maintains are self-evident.

Ross acknowledges, however, that not all moral differences can be accommodated in this way. He writes:

While all men are probably at bottom agreed in thinking we ought [*prima facie*] to produce as much good as we can, and agreed also as to the goodness of certain things—virtue, intelligence, thought and happiness—there is a real difference of opinion as to the comparative worth of

[56] *The Foundations of Ethics*, 18.   [57] Ibid.   [58] Ibid.

different goods; and this is a difference not on an ordinary matter of fact but on a moral question.[59]

This fact should, Ross thinks, weaken our confidence in our own opinion. But we have already noted that he did not think that the comparative stringency of our basic *prima facie* duties is self-evident, even though their *prima facie* rightness is. One would assume, therefore, that he does not think that the comparative value of certain goods is self-evident, even though it is self-evident that certain things are intrinsically valuable. If this is right, then difference about comparative value is not damaging to his view about self-evident moral propositions.

Ross could have made the more general point that self-evident propositions need not be obvious. Complex as well as simple mathematical proofs are self-evident in that we can know them *a priori* by reflection on their meaning. But in so far as they are complex they may not be at all obvious. Self-evidence, therefore, does not entail obviousness. Once this is noted we can reject the first premiss of the argument against self-evident moral principles—the claim that if the basic principles of morality are self-evident there would be no moral disagreement. This would only be true if self-evident moral principles must be obvious to everyone, as there is no general and protracted disagreement about obvious truths. But Ross is clear that self-evident moral principles are not obvious, at least, not obvious to everyone. He writes:

the nature of the self-evident is not to be evident to every mind however undeveloped, but to be apprehended directly by minds which have reached a certain degree of maturity, and for minds to reach the necessary degree of maturity the development that takes place from generation to generation is as much needed as that which takes place from infancy to adult life. (p. 12)

And later on he states that a *prima facie* duty is self-evident,

not in the sense that it is evident from the beginning of our lives, or as soon as we attend to the proposition for the first time, but in the sense that when we have reached sufficient mental maturity and have given sufficient attention to the proposition it is evident without any need of proof, or of evidence beyond itself. (p. 29)

To many ears talk of 'mental maturity' and 'developed minds' may sound arrogant, chauvinistic, or at best unacceptably complacent. But Ross was neither arrogant nor complacent. Although he thinks that there is moral progress, he does not think that we should accept uncritically whatever moral system we inherit as the most developed and mature thinking on the issue. A sincere questioning in ethics reflects, he believes, 'a desire to get down to bedrock in morality; and this is all to the good'. He goes on to write:

Moral codes that will not survive such questioning do not deserve to survive it, and those that do deserve to survive it will do so. *Magna est veritas et praevalet.* Acquiescence in moral codes merely because they are accepted by the society in which one lives spells death to progress in moral insight.[60]

These passages were not written by someone who thought that his own thinking, or the moral thinking in his own culture, was so developed and mature that it is beyond question.

Does the fact that one can have a good understanding of these propositions yet deny that they are true show that they cannot be self-evident? I do not see how it could. For a proposition to be self-evident is for it to be know*able* on the basis of an understanding of it. It does not follow from this that if *P* is self-evident and one understands *P*, then one will believe that *P*. All it means is that one's understanding of *P* provides a sufficient warrant for believing that *P*, not that one must *recognize* one's understanding as a sufficient warrant.

Some object to the idea that certain moral propositions are self-evident on the ground that this leads to dogmatism. Thus, for example, Korsgaard claims that all that intuitionists can do in the face of disbelief is insist that what they are saying is true,[61] and Nowell-Smith writes: 'If I do not recognize the truth of your statements of objective moral fact, you can do nothing to convince me by argument but are, like the subjectivist, thrown back on force or

---

[60] Ibid. 21.
[61] C. Korsgaard, *The Sources of Normativity* (Cambridge University Press: Cambridge, 1996), 38.

xlviii   INTRODUCTION

acquiescence'.[62] We should be on the guard against dogmatism, and be aware that many of our moral beliefs may be the product merely of upbringing, self-interest, or ideology. But a commitment to self-evident moral propositions does not make intuitionists like Ross especially vulnerable to dogmatism. For Ross does not dogmatically assert the self-evidence of any moral proposition that seems true to him, but claims this status only for those apparently basic moral convictions that survive careful reflection.[63] Such reflection is aimed at getting a clear understanding of the proposition in question in order to ascertain whether we really do think it expresses a morally basic truth. It also aims at providing arguments for its truth and self-evidence. If the proposition survives such reflection, then Ross can do more than merely assert the truth of the moral proposition that someone else denies. He can take them through the form of reflection that convinced him of the truth and self-evidence of this proposition.

It may be thought that this is incoherent, that someone who thinks that P is self-evident cannot offer an argument for P.[64] But there is nothing about the fact that a proposition can be known solely on the basis of an understanding of it that rules out the possibility that it can be known in some other way as well, i.e. that it is epistemologically overdetermined.[65] It may not be that every self-evident proposition is epistemologically overdetermined, but the thought that some are is in no way absurd.

In *The Right and the Good* Ross seemed to deny this. Here he states that self-evident moral propositions 'cannot be proved, but . . . just as certainly need no proof' (p. 30). But elsewhere in *The Right and the Good* he makes only the more restricted claim that such propositions do not *need* any proof,[66] and despite the fact that he sometimes makes the further claim that they *cannot* receive any proof (justification) I do not think this further claim expresses his

---

[62] *Ethics* (Penguin: London, 1956), 46.
[63] See my 'Pleasure and Reflection in Ross's Ethical Intuitionism', in Stratton-Lake (ed.), *Ethical Intuitionism: Re-Evaluations* (Clarendon Press: Oxford, 2002).
[64] Mary Warnock seems to think this (*Ethics since 1900*, 53).
[65] See David O. Brink, 'Common Sense and First Principles in Sidgwick's Methods', *Social Philosophy and Policy*, 11 (1994), 179–201, for an alternative view.
[66] See e.g. p. 29.

considered view.[67] Three years before the publication of *The Right and the Good* Ross explicitly states that 'the fact that something can be inferred does not prove that it cannot be seen intuitively'.[68] If he thinks that some proposition can be inferred from (justified by) other propositions and be self-evident, he clearly thinks that its being self-evident does not rule out the possibility of a proof. So the occasions in *The Right and the Good* where he denies this are, I think, instances where Ross was not as careful in what he said as he should have been.

I have argued that the view that basic moral propositions are self-evident is not as easily dismissed as it is so often thought to be. It may, nonetheless, be that in the end Ross's moral epistemology cannot be sustained. But because almost everyone is content with standard objections to epistemological intuitionism—objections which are less than compelling—no one has, to my knowledge, offered decent arguments for the rejection of this view. If Ross's epistemology commits us only to the view that basic moral propositions can be known *a priori*, I for one, am happy to stick with it until such arguments are put forward.

CONCLUSION

Most that is written on Ross focuses on his doctrine of *prima facie* duties, with passing reference to his metaphysics and epistemology. This is probably because this doctrine is regarded as separable from his other views and hence need not be contaminated by their (perceived) untenability. I have tried to provide a more rounded picture of Ross's ethical intuitionism which situates his doctrine of *prima facie* duties within a more general pluralism as well as a distinctive metaphysics and epistemology. I have, however, left out a discussion of Ross's views on a number of topics which, though interesting, are not central to his intuitionism. I have said nothing about his view about rights and their relation to obligations,[69] his view on

---

[67] In this I differ from Robert Audi's view in 'Intuitionism, Pluralism, and the Foundations of Ethics', in W. Sinnott-Armstrong and M. Timmons (eds.), *Moral Knowledge?* (Oxford University Press: New York, 1996).

[68] 'The Basis of Objective Judgements in Ethics', *International Journal of Ethics*, 37 (1927), 121.

[69] App. I of Ch. II of *The Right and the Good*.

punishment,[70] or his stance on the debate between subjective and objective accounts of duty (p. 43) (which changed dramatically in *The Foundations of Ethics*[71]). In general I have argued that many of the standard criticisms of his views are at best less than compelling, and are often based upon an accepted understanding that is little more than a caricature. Ross was not content merely to list our common-sense moral opinions, and his metaphysics does not commit him to a belief in otherworldly properties, or to the view that we need a mysterious special faculty for perceiving these properties. I think Ross should have abandoned his view that goodness and rightness are simple properties, and suspect that he may have been willing to do this if he clearly distinguished the question of the simplicity of these properties from the question of whether they are natural properties. But in the main I think his views are plausible and of lasting significance.

[70] App. II of Ch. II of *The Right and the Good*.
[71] Ch. 7. For an excellent discussion of the arguments in Prichard that led Ross to change his mind, see Jonathan Dancy's 'Prichard, Duty, and Ignorance of Fact', in Stratton-Lake (ed.), *Ethical Intuitionism*.

A NOTE ON THE TEXT

Asterisked cues in the text are to the Editor's Notes at the end of the text.

BIBLIOGRAPHY

WORKS BY ROSS

Books on Moral Philosophy

The Right and the Good (Oxford University Press: Oxford, 1930; Hackett: Indianapolis, 1988).
The Foundations of Ethics (Clarendon Press: Oxford, 1939).

Other Books

Aristotle (Methuen: London, 1923; Routledge: London, 1996).
Aristotle: Metaphysics (ed.), 2 vols., (Clarendon Press: Oxford, 1924).
Aristotle: Physics (ed.) (Clarendon Press: Oxford, 1936).
Plato's Theory of Ideas (Clarendon Press: Oxford, 1951).
Kant's Ethical Theory: A Commentary on the 'Grundlegung zur Metaphysik der Sitten' (Clarendon Press: Oxford, 1954).
Aristotle: Parva Naturalia, (ed) (Clarendon Press: Oxford, 1955).
Aristotle: Prior and Posterior Analytics (ed.) (Clarendon Press: Oxford, 1957).
Aristotle: De Anima (ed.) (Clarendon Press: Oxford, 1961).

Articles on Moral Philosophy

'The Basis of Objective Judgements in Ethics', *International Journal of Ethics*, 37 (1927), 113–27.
'The Nature of Morally Good Action', *Proceedings of the Aristotelian Society*, 29 (1928–9), 251–74.
'The Ethics of Punishment', *Journal of Philosophical Studies*, 4 (1929), 205–11.

Other Writings

The Philosophical Aspect of the Theory of Relativity: A Symposium, by A. S. Eddington, W. D. Ross, C. D. Broad, and F. A. Lindemann, *Mind*, NS 29/116 (1920), 415–45.
'The Authenticity of Aristotle's Categories', in 'Comments and Criticisms', *Journal of Philosophy*, 36 (1939), 427–33.
'The Discovery of the Syllogism', *Philosophical Review*, 48 (1939), 251–72.
'Some Thoughts on Aristotle's Logic', *Proceedings of the Aristotelian Society*, 40 (1939–40), pp. i–xviii.

'The Date of Plato's *Cratylus*', *Revue Internationale de Philosophie*, 9 (1955), 187–96.

WORKS ON W. D. ROSS

AL-HIBRI, A., 'Conditionality and Ross's Deontic Distinction', *Southwestern Journal of Philosophy*, 11 (1980), 79–88.

AQVIST, L., '*Prima Facie* Obligations in Deontic Logic: A Chisholmian Analysis Based on Normative Preference Structures', in C. Fehige (ed.), *Preferences* (de Gruyter: Hawthorne, Nev., 1998).

ATWELL, J., 'Ross and *Prima Facie* Duties', *Ethics*, 88 (1978), 240–9.

BAUMRIN, B. H., '*Prima Facie* Duties', *Journal of Philosophy*, 62 (1965), 736–8.

BECK, L. W., 'Sir David Ross on Duty and Purpose in Kant', *Philosophy and Phenomenological Research*, 16 (1955), 98–107.

BERAN, H., 'Ought, Obligation and Duty', *Australasian Journal of Philosophy*, 50 (1972), 207–21.

BRENNAN, S. K., 'Ross, Promises and the Intrinsic Value of Acts', *Lyceum*, 1 (1989), 43–56.

BROWNE, S. S. S., 'Right Acts and Moral Actions', *Journal of Philosophy*, 42 (1945), 505–15.

CHISHOLM, R. M., 'Epistemic Reasoning', *Dialectica*, 36 (1982), 169–77.

DANCY, J., 'Ethical Particularism and Morally Relevant Properties', *Mind*, 92 (1983), 530–47.

—— 'An Ethic of *Prima Facie* Duties', in P. Singer (ed.), *A Companion to Ethics* (Blackwell: Oxford, 1991).

—— 'Wiggins and Ross', *Utilitas*, 10 (1998), 281–5.

DARWALL, S., 'Under Moore's Spell', *Utilitas*, 10 (1998), 286–91.

EDWARDS, R. B., 'A Criticism of Ross's Hypothetical "I Can" ', *Mind*, 69 (1960), 80–3.

FOX, A. C., 'The Right and the Good Once More', *Australasian Journal of Philosophy*, 28 (1950), 1–28.

FRAZIER, R., 'Moral Relevance and *Ceteris Paribus* Principles', *Ratio*, 8 (1995), 113–27.

GALVIN, R. F., '*Prima Facie* Duty: An Analysis', *Southwest Philosophical Studies*, 100/2 (1990), 41–52.

GARCIA, J., 'On *High-Mindedness*', *Proceedings of the American Catholic Philosophical Association*, 63 (1990), 98–107.

—— 'The Right and the Good', *Philosophia*, 21 (1992), 235–6.

GAY, R., 'Ethical Pluralism: A Reply to Jonathan Dancy', *Mind*, 94 (1985), 250–62.

GIRILL, T. R., 'On the Defeasibility of Duties', *Journal of Value Inquiry*, 12 (1978), 197–209.

HOOKER, B., 'Ross-Style Pluralism versus Rule-Consequentialism', *Mind*, 105 (1996), 531–52.

—— 'Reply to Stratton-Lake', *Mind*, 106 (1997), 759–60.

JACK, H. H., 'More on *Prima Facie* Duties', *Journal of Philosophy*, 63 (1966), 521–3.

—— 'Note on Doubts about *Prima Facie* Duties', *Philosophy*, 46 (1971), 160–1.

—— 'Utilitarianism and Ross's Theory of *Prima Facie* Duties', *Dialogue*, 10 (1971), 437–57.

JONES, P., 'Doubts about *Prima Facie* Duties', *Philosophy*, 45 (1970), 39–54.

LEWIS, H, 'Moral Freedom in Recent Ethics', in W. Sellars and J. Hospers (eds.), *Readings in Ethical Theory* (Appleton-Century-Crofts: New York, 1952).

MACBEATH, A., 'Duty', *Philosophy*, 23 (1948), 99–115.

MCCLOSKEY, H. J., 'Ross and the Concept of a *Prima Facie* Duty', *Australasian Journal of Philosophy*, 41 (1963), 336–45.

MCCONNELL, T., 'Ross on Duty and Ignorance', *History of Philosophy Quarterly*, 5 (1988), 79–95.

MCNAUGHTON, D., 'An Unconnected Heap of Duties?', *Philosophical Quarterly*, 46 (1996), 433–47.

MORREAU, M., '*Prima Facie* and Seeming Duties', *Studia Logica*, 57 (1996), 47–71.

NEBLETT, W. R., 'W. D. Ross and the Nature of Moral Obligation', *Journal of Value Inquiry*, 7 (1973), 40–51.

NYSTEDT, H., 'The Problem of Duty and Knowledge', *Philosophy*, 26 (1951), 333–46.

PIETROSKI, P., '*Prima Facie* Obligations: Ceteris Paribus Laws in Moral Theory', *Ethics*, 103 (1993), 489–515.

ROSEN, B., 'In Defense of W. D. Ross', *Ethics*, 78 (1968), 237–41.

SAYWARD, C., 'W. D. Ross on Acting from Motives', *Journal of Value Inquiry*, 22 (1988), 299–306.

SEARLE, J. R., '*Prima Facie* Obligations', in J. Raz (ed.), *Practical Reasoning* (Oxford University Press: Oxford, 1978).

SHAW, L. M., 'Can we Choose our Motives?', *Australasian Journal of Philosophy*, 22 (1944), 93–105.

SHOPE, R. K., '*Prima Facie* Duty', *Journal of Philosophy*, 62 (1965), 279–86.

SNARE, F., 'The Definition of *Prima Facie* Duties', *Philosophical Quarterly*, 24 (1974), 235–44.

STRASSER, M., 'Guilt, Regret and *Prima Facie* Duties', *Southern Journal of Philosophy*, 25 (1987), 133–46.

—— 'Ross on the Sense of Duty', *Philosophical Papers*, 16 (1987), 195–207.

STRATTON-LAKE, P., 'Can Hooker's Rule-Consequentialist Principle Justify Ross's *Prima Facie* Duties?', *Mind*, 106 (1997), 751–8.

WHEELER, A. M., '*Prima Facie* and Actual Duty', *Analysis*, 37 (1977), 142–4.

WIGGINS, D., '*The Right and the Good* and W. D. Ross's Criticism of Consequentialism', *Utilitas*, 10 (1998), 261–80; and in A. O'Hear (ed.), *Philosophy, the Good, the True and the Beautiful, Philosophy*, 47, suppl. (2000), 175–95.

WOLF, J. C., 'Ein Pluralismus von *Prima Facie* Pflichten als Alternative zu monistischen Theorien der Ethik', *Zeitschrift für philosophische Forschung*, 50 (1996), 601–10.

WORKS ON ETHICAL INTUITIONISM

ATKINSON, G. M., 'A Defense of Intuitions: Their Role in Moral Knowledge', *Proceedings of the American Catholic Philosophical Association*, 64 (1990), 107–17.

AUDI, R., 'Ethical Reflectionism', *Monist*, 76 (1993), 295–315.

—— 'Intuitionism, Pluralism, and the Foundations of Ethics', in W. Sinnott-Armstrong and M. Timmons (eds.), *Moral Knowledge?* (Oxford University Press: New York, 1996).

—— 'Moderate Intuitionism and the Epistemology of Moral Judgment', *Ethical Theory and Moral Practice*, 1 (1998), 15–44.

—— 'Self-Evidence', *Philosophical Perspectives*, 13 (1999), 205–28.

—— 'A Kantian Intuitionism', *Mind*, 110 (2001), 601–35.

BALGUY, J., *The Foundation of Moral Goodness* (1728), facs. edn. (Garland: New York, 1978), and in L. A. Selby-Bigge (ed.), *The British Moralists: Being Selections from the Writers Principally of the Eighteenth Century*, ii (Dover: New York, 1965).

BINKLEY, L. J., *Contemporary Ethical Theories* (Philosophical Library: New York, 1961).

BRINK, D. O., 'Common Sense and First Principles in Sidgwick's *Methods*', *Social Philosophy and Policy*, 11 (1994), 179–201.

BROAD, C. D., *Five Types of Ethical Theory* (Kegan Paul: London, 1930).

BRODY, B. A., 'Intuitions and Objective Moral Knowledge', *Monist*, 62 (1979), 446–56.

BURTON, R. G., 'Neointuitionism: The Neglected Moral Realism', *Southern Journal of Philosophy*, 25 (1987), 147–52.

BUTLER, J., *Fifteen Sermons Preached at the Rolls Chapel* (1726), in *The Works of Bishop Butler*, ed. J. H. Bernard, i (Macmillan: London, 1900); and in L. A. Selby-Bigge (ed.), *The British Moralists: Being Selections from the Writers Principally of the Eighteenth Century*, i (Dover: New York, 1965).

CARRITT, E. F., *The Theory of Morals* (Oxford University Press: London, 1930).

—— *Ethical and Political Thinking* (Clarendon Press: Oxford, 1947).

CLARKE, S., *A Discourse Concerning the Unalterable Obligations of Natural Religion* (1706), in *The Works of Samuel Clarke*, ii (J. & P. Knapton: London, 1738), facs. edn. (Garland: New York, 1978); and in L. A.Selby-Bigge (ed.), *The British Moralists: Being Selections from the Writers Principally of the Eighteenth Century*, ii (Dover: New York, 1965).

COHEN, C., 'Natural and Non-Natural Qualities', *Journal of Philosophy*, 55 (1958), 412–29.

CUDWORTH, *A Treatise Concerning Eternal and Immutable Morality* (1731), in *The Collected Works of Ralph Cudworth*, ii (Olms: Hildesheim, 1979), and in L. A. Selby-Bigge (ed.), *The British Moralists: Being Selections from the Writers Principally of the Eighteenth Century*, ii (Dover: New York, 1965).

DALY, C. B., 'Inter-War British Ethics, 2: Critics of Intuitionism', *Philosophical Studies* (Ireland), 15 (1965), 96–111.

DANCY, J., 'Intuitionism in Meta-Epistemology', *Philosophical Studies*, 42 (1982), 395–408.

—— 'Intuitionism', in P. Singer (ed.), *A Companion to Ethics* (Blackwell: Oxford, 1991).

DARWALL, S., 'Moore to Stevenson', in R. J. Cavalier (eds.), *Ethics in the History of Western Philosophy* (St Martin's Press: New York, 1989).

—— *The British Moralists and the Internal 'Ought': 1640–1740* (Cambridge University Press: Cambridge, 1995).

DURFEE, H. A., 'The A Priori, Intuitionism and Moral Knowledge', *Philosophical Studies* (Ireland), 27 (1980), 55–66.

EWING, A. C., *The Definition of Good* (Routledge & Kegan Paul: London, 1947).

—— *Ethics* (Macmillan: London, 1947).

—— *The Fundamental Questions of Philosophy* (Routledge & Kegan Paul: London, 1951).

EWING, A. C., *Second Thoughts in Moral Philosophy* (Routledge & Kegan Paul: London, 1959).

FRAZIER, R. L., 'Intuitionism in Ethics', in E. Craig (ed.), *Routledge Encyclopedia of Philosophy*, vi (Routledge: London, 1998).

GAUT, B., 'Moral Pluralism', *Philosophical Papers*, 22 (1993), 17–40.

—— 'Rag-Bags, Disputes and Moral Pluralism', *Utilitas*, 11 (1999), 37–48.

GEIGER, G., 'Why there are No Objective Values: A Critique of Ethical Intuitionism from an Evolutionary Point of View', *Biology and Philosophy*, 7 (1992), 315–30.

HEYTING, A., *Intuitionism: An Introduction* (North-Holland: Amsterdam, 1956).

HILL, T. E., *Contemporary Ethical Theories* (Macmillan: New York, 1950).

HUDSON, W. D., *Ethical Intuitionism* (Macmillan: London, 1967).

—— *A Century of Moral Philosophy* (St Martin's Press: New York, 1980).

—— *Modern Moral Philosophy*, 2nd edn. (St Martin's Press: New York, 1983).

JOHNSON, O. A., 'Rightness, Moral Obligation, and Goodness', *Journal of Philosophy*, 50 (1953), 597–607.

—— 'Ethical Intuitionism: A Restatement', *Philosophical Quarterly*, 7 (1957), 193–203.

—— *Rightness and Goodness: A Study in Contemporary Ethical Theory* (Martinus Nijhoff: The Hague, 1959).

JOSEPH, H. W. B, *Some Problems in Ethics* (Clarendon Press: Oxford, 1931).

KARANI, R. N., 'Vindication of Ethical Intuitionism', *Mind*, 71 (1962), 535–8.

KEKES, J., 'Moral Intuition', *American Philosophical Quarterly*, 23 (1986), 83–93.

LEVENBOOK, B. B., and GIRILL, T. R., 'The Parti-Resultantness of Requirement: An Explanation that Failed', *Philosophical Studies*, 37 (1980), 237–49.

LUCAS, J. R., 'Ethical Intuitionism II', *Philosophy*, 46 (1971), 1–10.

MCCLOSKEY, H., 'Intuitionism and Rational Ends: Regan's Account of the Intuitionist's Dilemma', *Journal of Value Inquiry*, 9 (1975), 59–66.

MACINTYRE, A. C., *A Short History of Ethics: A History of Moral Philosophy from the Homeric Age to the Twentieth Century* (Macmillan: New York, 1966); 2nd edn. (London: Routledge, 1998).

MACLAGAN, W. G., 'On being Sure of One's Duty', *Philosophical Quarterly*, 1 (1950), 35–49.

McNAUGHTON, D., 'Intuitionism', in H. LaFollette (ed.), *The Blackwell Guide to Ethical Theory* (Blackwell: Oxford, 2000).

MARGOLIS, J., 'G. E. Moore and Intuitionism', *Ethics*, 87 (1976), 35–48.

MOORE, G. E., *Principia Ethica* (Cambridge University Press: Cambridge, 1903; rev. edn. 1993).

—— *Ethics* (Oxford University Press: London, 1966).

—— 'The Conception of Intrinsic Value', in *Principia Ethica*, rev. edn. (Cambridge University Press: Cambridge, 1993).

MUIRHEAD, J. H., 'The New Deontology', *Ethics*, 50 (1940), 441–9.

NELSON, M., 'Intuitionism and Conservatism', *Metaphilosophy*, 21 (1990), 282–93.

—— 'Intuitionism and Subjectivism', *Metaphilosophy*, 22 (1991), 115–21.

—— 'Morally Serious Critics of Moral Intuitions', *Ratio*, 12 (1999), 54–79.

NOWELL-SMITH, P. H., *Ethics* (Penguin: London, 1956).

ODEGARD, D., 'On Two Arguments against Moral Certainty', *Mind*, 90 (1981), 79–90.

PHILLIPS, R. L., 'Intuitionism Revisited', *Journal of Value Inquiry*, 6 (1972), 185–99.

PRICE, R., *A Review of the Principal Questions in Morals* (1758), ed. D. D. Raphael (Clarendon Press: Oxford, 1974); and in L. A. Selby-Bigge (ed.), *The British Moralists: Being Selections from the Writers Principally of the Eighteenth Century* ii (Dover: New York, 1965).

PRICHARD, H. A., *Moral Obligation*, ed. W. D. Ross (Clarendon Press: Oxford, 1949).

RAPHAEL, D. D., 'Sidgwick on Intuitionism', *Monist*, 58 (1974), 405–19.

—— *Moral Philosophy* (Oxford University Press: Oxford, 1981).

—— 'Les Intuitionnistes d'Oxford', *Archives de Philosophie*, 57 (1994), 281–93.

RASHDALL, H., *A Theory of Good and Evil* (Clarendon Press: Oxford, 1929).

REGAN, T., 'McCloskey on Rational Ends: The Dilemma of Intuitionism', *Journal of Value Inquiry*, 9 (1975), 42–58.

REID, T., *Essays on the Active Powers of Man* (1788), in *The Works of Thomas Reid* (1863), ii, ed. W. Hamilton (Thoemmes: Bristol, 1994); and in D. D. Raphael (ed.), *British Moralists 1650–1800*, ii (Clarendon Press: Oxford, 1974).

SCHNEEWIND, J. B., 'First Principles and Common Sense Morality in Sidgwick's Ethics', *Archiv für Geschichte der Philosophie*, 45 (1963), 137–56.

SCHNEEWIND, J. B., *Sidgwick's Ethics and Victorian Moral Philosophy* (Clarendon Press: Oxford, 1977).

SHAW, W. H., 'Intuitionism and Moral Philosophy', *American Philosophical Quarterly*, 17 (1980), 127–34.

SIDGWICK, H., *The Methods of Ethics*, 7th edn. (Macmillan: London, 1907 and 1967); and in *The Works of Henry Sidgwick*, ed. J. Slater, (Thoemmes: Bristol, 1996).

—— *Outlines of the History of Ethics for English Readers* (Macmillan: London, 1954); and in *The Works of Henry Sidgwick*, ed. J. Slater, iv (Thoemmes: Bristol, 1996).

SIMON, C. J., 'On Defending a Moral Synthetic *A Priori*', *Southern Journal of Philosophy*, 26 (1988), 217–33.

SINNOTT-ARMSTRONG, W. 'Intuitionism', in L. C. Becker (ed.), *The Encyclopedia of Ethics*, I (Garland: New York, 1992).

SMITH, M. B. E., 'Ethical Intuitionism and Naturalism: A Reconciliation', *Canadian Journal of Philosophy*, 9 (1979), 609–29.

STRATTON-LAKE, P., 'Why Externalism is not a Problem for Ethical Intuitionists', *Proceedings of the Aristotelian Society*, 99 (1999), 77–90.

—— *Ethical Intuitionism: Re-Evaluations* (Oxford University Press: Oxford, 2002).

STRAWSON, P. F., 'Ethical Intuitionism', *Philosophy*, 24 (1949), 23–33.

SWANTON, C., 'The Rationality of Ethical Intuitionism', *Australasian Journal of Philosophy*, 65 (1987), 172–81.

URMSON, J. O., ' A Defence of Intuitionism', *Proceedings of the Aristotelian Society*, 75 (1975), 111–19.

WARNOCK, G. J., *Contemporary Moral Philosophy* (St Martin's Press: New York, 1967).

WARNOCK, M., *Ethics since 1900* (Oxford University Press: London, 1960).

WHITTEMORE, R. C., 'Does the Neo-Intuitionist Theory of Obligation Rest on a Mistake?', *Tulane Studies in Philosophy*, 6 (1957), 101–27.

WILLIAMS, B., 'What does Intuitionism Imply?', in J. Dancy (ed.), *Human Agency* (Stanford University Press: Stanford, 1988); and in Williams, *Making Sense of Humanity and Other Philosophical Papers 1982–1993* (Cambridge University Press: Cambridge, 1995).

I

THE MEANING OF 'RIGHT'

THE purpose of this inquiry is to examine the nature, relations, and implications of three conceptions which appear
to be fundamental in ethics—those of 'right', 'good' in general,
and 'morally good'. The inquiry will have much in common
with the inquiries, of which there have been many in recent
years, into the nature of value, and I shall have occasion to
discuss some of the more important theories of value; but my
object is a more limited one. I offer no discussion, except at most
a purely incidental and illustrative one, of certain forms of value,
such as economic value and beauty. My interest will throughout be ethical, and value will be discussed only so far as it seems
to be relevant to this interest.

I propose to begin with the term 'right'. A considerable
ambiguity attaches to any attempt to discuss the meaning of
any term. Professor G. E. Moore has well indicated three main
objects that such an attempt at definition may have. 'When we
say, as Webster says, "The definition of horse is, 'A hoofed
quadruped of the genus Equus'," we may, in fact, mean three
different things. (1) We may mean merely: "When I say 'horse',
you are to understand that I am talking about a hoofed quadruped of the genus Equus." This might be called the arbitrary
verbal definition. . . . (2) We may mean, as Webster ought to
mean: "When most English people say 'horse', they mean a
hoofed quadruped of the genus Equus." This may be called
the verbal definition proper. . . . But (3) we may, when we
define horse, mean something much more important. We may
mean that a certain object, which we all of us know, is composed
in a certain manner: that it has four legs, a head, a heart, a liver,
etc., etc., all of them arranged in definite relations to one
another.' [1]

We must ask ourselves whether, in discussing the meaning
of 'right', we are attempting any one of these kinds of definition,
or something different from them all. I certainly do not wish

[1] *Principia Ethica*, 8.

merely to indicate a sense in which I propose to use the term 'right'. I wish to keep in touch with the general usage of the word. While other things may be called 'right' (as in the phrases 'the right road', 'the right solution'), the word is specially applied to acts, and it is the sense (by general consent a very important one) in which it is so applied that I wish to discuss. But we must be prepared to find that the general usage of the word is not entirely consistent with itself. Most of the words in any language have a certain amount of ambiguity; and there is special danger of ambiguity in the case of a word like 'right', which does not stand for anything we can point out to one another or apprehend by one of the senses. Even with words that do stand for such things there is this danger. Even if two people find that the things the one calls red are just the things the other calls red, it is by no means certain that they mean the same quality. There is only a general presumption that since the structure of their eyes (if neither is colour-blind) is pretty much the same, the same object acting on the eyes of the two men produces pretty much the same kind of sensation. And in the case of a term like 'right', there is nothing parallel to the highly similar organization of different people's eyes, to create a presumption that when they call the same act right, they mean to refer to the same quality of it. In point of fact, there is a serious difference of view as to the *application* of the term 'right'. Suppose, for instance, that a man pays a particular debt simply from fear of the legal consequences of not doing so, some people would say he had done what was right, and others would deny this: they would say that no moral value attaches to such an act, and that since 'right' is meant to imply moral value, the act cannot be right. They might generalize and say that no act is right unless it is done from a sense of duty, or if they shrank from so rigorous a doctrine, they might at least say that no act is right unless done from *some* good motive, such as either sense of duty or benevolence.

This difference of view may be due to either of two causes. Both parties may be using 'right' in the same sense, the sense of 'morally obligatory', and differing as to the further character an act must have in order to have this quality. *Or* the first party may be using 'right' in this sense, and the second in the sense of 'morally good'. It is not clear to me which of these two things is usually happening when this difference of view arises. But it seems probable that both things really happen—that some people fail to notice the distinction between 'right' and 'morally good', and that others, while distinguishing the meaning of these terms, think that only what is morally good is right. A discussion of the first of these positions only is strictly in point here, where we are discussing the *meaning* of 'right'. It seems to me clear that 'right' does not mean the same as 'morally good'; and we can test this by trying to substitute one for the other. If they meant the same thing we should be able to substitute, for instance, 'he is a right man' for 'he is a morally good man'; nor is our inability to do this merely a matter of English idiom, for if we turn to the sort of moral judgement in which we do use the word 'right', such as 'this is the right act', it is clear that by this we mean 'this act is the act *that ought to be done*', 'this act is *morally obligatory*'; and to substitute either of these phrases for 'morally good' in 'he is a morally good man' would obviously be not merely unidiomatic, but absurd. It should be obvious, then, that 'right' and 'morally good' mean different things. But some one might say that while 'morally good' has a wider application than 'right', in that it can be applied to agents as well as to acts, yet when applied to acts they mean the same thing. I should like therefore to convince him that 'right act' cannot mean the same as 'act that ought to be done' and *also* the same as 'morally good act'. If I can convince him of this, I think he will see the propriety of not using 'right act' in the sense of 'morally good act'.

But we ought first to note a minor difference between the meaning of 'right' and the meaning of 'something that ought to be done' or 'that is my duty' or 'that is incumbent on me'. It may sometimes happen that there is a set of two or more acts one or other of which ought to be done by me rather than any act not belonging to this set. In such a case any act of this set is right, but none is my duty; my duty is to do 'one or other' of them. Thus 'right' has a somewhat wider possible application than 'something that ought to be done' or any of its equivalents. But we want an adjective to express the same meaning as 'something that ought to be done', and though we have 'obligatory' at our disposal, that also has its ambiguity, since it sometimes means 'compulsory'. We should have to say 'morally obligatory' to make our meaning quite clear; and to obviate the necessity of using this rather cumbrous expression, I will use 'right' in this sense. I hope that this paragraph will prevent any confusion arising from this slightly inaccurate usage.

Some might deny the correctness of the distinction just drawn. They might say that when there are two or more acts one or other of which, as we say, we ought to do (it not being our duty to do one rather than another), the truth is that these are simply alternative ways of producing a single result, and that our duty is, strictly, not to do 'one or other' of the acts, but to produce the result; this alone is our duty, and this alone is right. This answer does, I think, fairly apply to many cases in which it *is* the production of a certain result that we think obligatory, the means being optional: e.g. to a case in which it is our duty to convey information to some one, but morally immaterial whether we do so orally or in writing. But in principle, at any rate, there may be other cases in which it is our duty to produce one or other of two or more *different* states of affairs, without its being our duty to produce one of them rather than another; in such a case each of these acts will be right, and none will be our duty.

If it can be shown that nothing that ought to be done is ever morally good, it will be clear *a fortiori* that 'morally good' does not *mean* the same as 'that ought to be done'. Now it is, I think, quite clear that the only acts that are morally good are those that proceed from a good motive; this is maintained by those whom I am now trying to convince, and I entirely agree. If, then, we can show that action from a good motive is never morally obligatory, we shall have established that what is morally good is never right, and *a fortiori* that 'right' does not *mean* the same as 'morally good'. That action from a good motive is never morally obligatory follows (1) from the Kantian principle, which is generally admitted, that 'I ought' implies 'I can'.* It is not the case that I can by choice produce a certain motive (whether this be an ordinary desire or the sense of obligation) in myself at a moment's notice, still less that I can at a moment's notice make it effective in stimulating me to act. I can act from a certain motive only if I have the motive; if not, the most I can do is to cultivate it by suitably directing my attention or by acting in certain appropriate ways so that on some future occasion it *will* be present in me, and I shall be able to act from it. My *present* duty, therefore, cannot be to act here and now from it.

(2) A similar conclusion may be reached by a *reductio ad absurdum*. Those who hold that our duty is to act from a certain motive usually (Kant is the great exemplar) hold that the motive from which we ought to act is the sense of duty. Now if the sense of duty is to be my motive for doing a certain act, it must be the sense that it is my duty to do that act. If, therefore, we say 'it is my duty to do act *A* from the sense of duty', this means 'it is my duty to do act *A* from the sense that it is my duty to do act *A*'. And here the whole expression is in contradiction with a part of itself. The whole sentence says 'it is my duty to-do-act-*A*-from-the-sense-that-it-is-my-duty-to-do-act-*A*'. But the latter part of the sentence implies that what I think is that it is my duty to-do-act-*A* simply. And if, as the theory in question requires, we try to amend the latter part of the expression to bring it into accord with the whole expression, we get the result 'it is my duty to do act *A* from the sense that it is my duty to do act *A* from the sense that it is my duty to do act *A*', where again the last part of the expression is in conflict with the theory, and with the sentence as a whole. It is clear that a further similar amendment, and a further, and in the end an infinite series of amendments would be necessary in the attempt to bring the last part of the expression into accordance with the theory, and that even then we should not have succeeded in doing so.

Again, suppose that I say to you 'it is your duty to do act *A* from the sense of duty'; that means 'it is your duty to do act *A* from the sense that it is your duty to do act *A*'. Then *I* think that it is your duty to act from a certain motive, but I suggest that *you* should act under the supposition that it is your duty to do a certain thing, irrespective of motive, i.e. under a supposition which I must think false since it contradicts my own. The only conclusion that can be drawn is that our duty is to do certain things, not to do them from the sense of duty.[1]

The latter of these two arguments ((1) and (2)) cannot be used against those who hold that it is our duty to act from some other motive than the sense of duty; the sense of duty is the only motive that leads to the infinite series in question. But the first of the two arguments seems in itself sufficient against *any* theory which holds that motive of any kind is included in the content of duty. And though the second argument does not refute the view that we ought to act from some other motive, it would be paradoxical to hold that we ought to act from some other motive but never ought to act from a sense of duty, which is the highest motive.[2]

Let us now return to the three senses in which Professor Moore points out that we may understand an attempt to define a certain term.[3] So far, the position we have taken up with regard to 'right' includes something of each of the first two attitudes he distinguishes. In using 'right' as synonymous (but for the minor distinction already pointed out)[4] with 'what is my duty', and as distinct from 'morally good', I believe I am conforming to what most men (if not all men) usually mean when they use the word. But I could not maintain that they always use the word in this way. I am, therefore, to some extent adopting the first of the attitudes he distinguishes, and expressing my own intention to use 'right' in this sense only. And this is justified by the great confusion that has been introduced into ethics by the phrase 'a right action' being used sometimes of the initiation of a certain change in the state of

[1] It should be added, however, that one, and an important one, of our duties is to cultivate in ourselves the sense of duty. But then this is the duty of cultivating in ourselves the sense of duty, and not of cultivating in ourselves, from the sense of duty, the sense of duty.

[2] If any one doubts that it is, I beg him to refer to pp. 164–5, where I give reasons in support of the contention.

[3] Cf. p. 1.

[4] pp. 3–4.

affairs irrespective of motive, and at other times of such initiation from some particular motive, such as sense of duty or
benevolence. I would further suggest that additional clearness
would be gained if we used 'act' of the thing done, the initiation
of change, and 'action' of the doing of it, the initiating of change,
from a certain motive. We should then talk of a right act but
not of a right action, of a morally good action but not of a
morally good act. And it may be added that the doing of
a right act may be a morally bad action, and that the doing
of a wrong act may be a morally good action; for 'right' and
'wrong' refer entirely to the thing done,* 'morally good' and
'morally bad' entirely to the motive from which it is done. *A firm
grasp of this distinction will do much to remove some of the
perplexities of our moral thought. *

The question remains, what attitude we are to take up towards Professor Moore's third sense of 'definition'. Are we to
hold that 'right' can be defined in the sense of being reduced
to elements simpler than itself? At first sight it might appear
that egoism and utilitarianism are attempts to define 'right'—
to define it as 'productive of the greatest possible pleasure to the
agent' or as 'productive of the greatest possible pleasure to
mankind'; and I think these theories have often been so understood by some of those who accept them. But the leaders of
the school are not unanimous in so understanding their theory.
Bentham seems to understand it so. He says [1] that 'when thus
interpreted' (i.e. as meaning 'conformable to the principle of
utility'), 'the words *ought* and *right* . . . and others of that stamp,
have a meaning; when otherwise, they have none'. And elsewhere [2] he says 'admitting (what is not true) that the word *right*
can have a meaning without reference to utility'. Yet, as
Sidgwick points out,[3] 'when Bentham explains (*Principles of
Morals and Legislation*, Chap, I, § 1, note) that his fundamental
principle "states the greatest happiness of all those whose
interest is in question as being the right and proper end of
human action", we cannot understand him really to *mean* by
the word "right" "conducive to the general happiness"; for

---

[1] *Principles of Morals and Legislation*, Ch. I, § 10.   [2] ib. § 14. 10.
[3] *Methods of Ethics*, ed. 7, 26 n.

the proposition that it is conducive to general happiness to take general happiness as an end of action, though not exactly a tautology, can hardly serve as the fundamental principle of a moral system'. Bentham has evidently not made up his mind clearly whether he thinks that 'right' *means* 'productive of the general happiness', *or* that being productive of the general happiness is what makes right acts right; and would very likely have thought the difference unimportant. Mill does not so far as I know discuss the question whether right is definable. He states his creed in the form 'actions are right in proportion as they tend to promote happiness',[1] where the claim that is made is not that this is what 'right' means, but that this is the other characteristic in virtue of which actions that are right are right. And Sidgwick says [2] that the meaning of 'right' or 'ought' 'is too elementary to admit of any formal definition', and expressly repudiates [3] the view that 'right' means 'productive of any particular sort of result'.

The most deliberate claim that 'right' is definable as 'productive of so and so' is made by Prof. G. E. Moore, who claims in *Principia Ethica* that 'right' means 'productive of the greatest possible good'. Now it has often been pointed out against hedonism, and by no one more clearly than by Professor Moore, that the claim that 'good' just means 'pleasant' cannot seriously be maintained; that while it may or may not be true that the only things that are good are pleasant, the statement that the good is just the pleasant is a synthetic, not an analytic proposition; that the words 'good' and 'pleasant' stand for distinct qualities, even if the things that possess the one are precisely the things that possess the other. If this were not so, it would not be intelligible that the proposition 'the good is just the pleasant' should have been maintained on the one hand, and denied on the other, with so much fervour; for we do not fight for or against analytic propositions; we take them for granted. Must not the same claim be made about the statement 'being right means being an act productive of the greatest good producible in the circumstances'? Is it not plain on reflection that

---

[1] *Utilitarianism*, copyright eds., 9.   [2] *Methods of Ethics*, ed. 7, 32.
[3] ib. 25–6.

this is not what we *mean* by right, even if it be a true statement about what *is* right? It seems clear for instance that when an ordinary man says it is right to fulfil promises he is not in the least thinking of the total consequences of such an act, about which he knows and cares little or nothing. 'Ideal utilitarianism'[1] is, it would appear, plausible only when it is understood not as an analysis or definition of the notion of 'right' but as a statement that all acts that are right, and only these, possess the further characteristic of being productive of the best possible consequences, and are right because they possess this other characteristic.

If I am not mistaken, Professor Moore has moved to this position, from the position that 'right' is *analysable* into 'productive of the greatest possible good'. In *Principia Ethica* the latter position is adopted: e.g. 'This use of "right", as denoting what is good as a means, whether or not it is also good as an end, is indeed the use to which I shall confine the word'.[2] 'To assert that a certain line of conduct is, at a given time, absolutely right or obligatory, is obviously to assert that more good or less evil will exist in the world, if it be adopted, than if anything else be done instead.'[3] 'To ask what kind of actions one ought to perform, or what kind of conduct is right, is to ask what kind of effects such action and conduct will produce . . . What I wish first to point out is that "right" does and can mean nothing but "cause of a good result", and is thus always identical with "useful" . . . That the assertion "I am morally bound to perform this action" is identical with the assertion "this action will produce the greatest possible amount of good in the Universe" has already been briefly shewn . . .; but it is important to insist that this fundamental point is demonstrably certain. . . . Our "duty", therefore, can only be defined as that action, which will cause more good to exist in the Universe than any possible alternative. And what is "right" or "morally permissible" only differs from this, as what will *not* cause *less* good than any possible alternative.'[4]

---

[1] I use this as a well-known way of referring to Professor Moore's view. 'Agathistic utilitarianism' would indicate more distinctly the difference between it and hedonistic utilitarianism. [2] p. 18. [3] p. 25.
[4] pp. 146–8. Cf. also pp. 167, 169, 180–1.

In his later book, *Ethics*, Professor Moore seems to have come to adopt the other position, though perhaps not quite unequivocally. On page 8 he names as one of the 'more fundamental questions' of ethics the question 'what, after all, is it that we mean to say of an action when we say that it is right or ought to be done?' Here it is still suggested that 'right' is perhaps analysable or definable. But to this question *Ethics* nowhere distinctly offers an answer, and on page 9 we find, 'Can we discover any single reason, applicable to all right actions equally, which is, in every case, *the* reason why an action is right, when it is right?' This is the question which Professor Moore in fact sets himself to answer. But the *reason* for an action's being right is evidently not the same thing as its *rightness*, and Professor Moore seems already to have passed to the view that productivity of maximum good is not the definition of 'right' but another characteristic which underlies and accounts for the rightness of right acts. Again, he describes hedonistic utilitarianism as asking, 'can we discover any characteristic, over and above the mere fact that they *are* right, which belongs to absolutely *all* voluntary actions which are right, and which at the same time does not belong to any except those which are right?'[1] This is the question which he describes hedonism as essentially answering, and since his own view differs from hedonism not in logical form but just by the substitution of 'good' for 'pleasure', his theory also seems to be essentially an answer to this question, i.e. not to the question what is rightness but to the question what is the universal accompaniment and, as he is careful to add,[2] the necessitating ground of rightness. Again, he describes hedonistic utilitarianism as giving us 'a criterion, or test, or standard by which we could discern with regard to any action whether it is right or wrong'.[3] And similarly, I suppose, he regards his own theory as offering a different criterion of rightness. But obviously a criterion of rightness is not rightness itself. And, most plainly of all, he says, 'It is indeed quite plain, I think, that the meaning of the two words' ('duty' and 'expediency', the latter being equivalent to 'tendency to produce the maximum good') 'is *not* the same;

[1] p. 17.   [2] pp. 44, 54.   [3] p. 43.

for, if it were, then it would be a mere tautology to say that it is
always our duty to do what will have the best possible consequences'.[1] If we contrast this with *Principia Ethica*, page 169,
'if I ask whether an action is *really* my duty or *really* expedient,
the predicate of which I question the applicability to the action
in question is precisely the same', we see how much Professor
Moore has changed his position, and changed it in the direction
in which, as I have been urging, it must be changed if it is to be
made plausible. And if it is clear that 'right' does not mean
'productive of the greatest possible good', it is *a fortiori* clear
that it does not *mean* 'productive of the greatest possible pleasure, for the agent or for mankind', but that productivity of
the greatest possible pleasure for the agent or for mankind is at
most the ground of the rightness of acts, rightness itself being
admitted to be a distinct characteristic, and one which utilitarianism does not claim to define.

But there are theories other than utilitarianism which claim
to define 'right'. It would be tedious to try to refute all such
theories. With regard to many of them [2] it seems to be enough
to ask one's readers whether it is not clear to them on reflection
that the proposed definition of 'right' bears in fact no resem-
blance to what they mean by 'right'. But there is one group of
theories to which some reference should be made, viz. those
that give what may be called a subjective theory of 'right',
that identify the rightness of an act with its tendency to produce
either some feeling or some opinion in the mind of some one
who contemplates it. This type of theory has been dealt with
very thoroughly by Professor Moore,[3] and I should have little
or nothing to add to his convincing refutation. But such theories
are perhaps even more prevalent with regard to 'good' than
to 'right', and in my fourth chapter I discuss them at some
length. I would ask my readers to read the argument there
offered, and to reflect whether the refutation I offer[4] of
subjective accounts of 'good' does not apply with equal force
to subjective accounts of 'right'.

[1] p. 173.
[2] e.g. the evolutionary theory which identifies 'right' with 'conducive to life'.
[3] *Ethics*, Chs. 3, 4.   [4] pp. 80–104.

Any one who is satisfied that neither the subjective theories of the meaning of 'right', nor what is far the most attractive of the attempts to reduce it to simpler objective elements, is correct, will probably be prepared to agree that 'right' is an irreducible notion.

Nor is this result impugned by inquiries into the historical development of our present moral notions from an earlier state of things in which 'what is right' was hardly disentangled from 'what the tribe ordains'. The point is that we can now see clearly that 'right' does not mean 'ordained by any given society'. And it may be doubted whether even primitive men thought that it did. Their thoughts about what in particular was right were to a large extent limited by the customs and sanctions of their race and age. But this is not the same as to say that they thought that 'right' just meant 'what my race and age ordains'. Moral progress has been possible just because there have been men in all ages who have seen the difference and have practised, or at least preached, a morality in some respects higher than that of their race and age. And even the supporters of the lower morality held, we may suspect, that their laws and customs were in accordance with a 'right' other than themselves. 'It is the custom' has been accompanied by 'the custom is right', or 'the custom is ordained by some one who has the right to command'. And if human consciousness is continuous, by descent, with a lower consciousness which had no notion of right at all, that need not make us doubt that the notion is an ultimate and irreducible one, or that the rightness (*prima facie*)[1] of certain types of act is self-evident; for the nature of the self-evident is not to be evident to every mind however undeveloped, but to be apprehended directly by minds which have reached a certain degree of maturity, and for minds to reach the necessary degree of maturity the development that takes place from generation to generation is as much needed as that which takes place from infancy to adult life.

In this connexion it may be well to refer briefly to a theory which has enjoyed much popularity, particularly in France—the theory of the sociological school of Durkheim and Lévy-

---

[1] For this qualification cf. pp. 19–20.

Bruhl, which seeks to replace moral philosophy by the 'science des mœurs', the historical and comparative study of the moral beliefs and practices of mankind. It would be foolish to deny the value of such a study, or the interest of many of the facts it has brought to light with regard to the historical origin of many such beliefs and practices. It has shown with success that many of the most strongly felt repulsions towards certain types of conduct are relics of a bygone system of totems and fetishes, their connexion with which is little suspected by those who feel them. What must be denied is the capacity of any such inquiry to take the place of moral philosophy. The attitude of the sociological school towards the systems of moral belief that they find current in various ages and races is a curiously inconsistent one. On the one hand we are urged to accept an existing code as something analogous to an existing law of nature, something not to be questioned or criticized but to be accepted and conformed to as part of the given scheme of things; and on this side the school is able sincerely to proclaim itself conservative of moral values, and is indeed conservative to the point of advocating the acceptance in full of conventional morality. On the other hand, by showing that any given code is the product partly of bygone superstitions and partly of out-of-date utilities, it is bound to create in the mind of any one who accepts its teaching (as it presupposes in the mind of the teacher) a sceptical attitude towards any and every given code. In fact the analogy which it draws between a moral code and a natural system like the human body (a favourite comparison) is an entirely fallacious one. By analysing the constituents of the human body you do nothing to diminish the reality of the human body as a given fact, and you learn much which will enable you to deal effectively with its diseases. But beliefs have the characteristics which bodies have not, of being true or false, of resting on knowledge or of being the product of wishes, hopes, and fears; and in so far as you can exhibit them as being the product of purely psychological and non-logical causes of this sort, while you leave intact the fact that many people hold such opinions you remove their authority and their claim to be carried out in practice.

It is often said, in criticism of views such as those of the sociological school, that the question of the validity of a moral code is quite independent of the question of its origin. This does not seem to me to be true. An inquiry into the origin of a judgement may have the effect of establishing its validity. Take, for instance, the judgement that the angles of a triangle are equal to two right angles. We find that the historical origin of this judgement lies in certain pre-existing judgements which are its premisses, plus the exercise of a certain activity of inferring. Now if we find that these pre-existing judgements were really instances of knowing, and that the inferring was also really knowing—was the apprehension of a necessary connexion—our inquiry into the origin of the judgement in question will have established its validity. On the other hand, if any one can show that A holds actions of type B to be wrong simply because (for instance) he knows such actions to be forbidden by the society he lives in, he shows that A has no real reason for believing that such actions have the specific quality of wrongness, since between being forbidden by the community and being wrong there is no necessary connexion. He does not, indeed, show the belief to be untrue, but he shows that A has no sufficient reason for holding it true; and in this sense he undermines its validity.

This is, in principle, what the sociological school attempts to do. According to this school, or rather according to its principles if consistently carried out, no one moral code is any truer, any nearer to the apprehension of an objective moral truth, than any other; each is simply the code that is necessitated by the conditions of its time and place, and is that which most completely conduces to the preservation of the society that accepts it. But the human mind will not rest content with such a view. It is not in the least bound to say that there has been constant progress in morality, or in moral belief. But it is competent to see that the moral code of one race or age is in certain respects inferior to that of another. It has in fact an *a priori* insight into certain broad principles of morality, and it can distinguish between a more and a less adequate recognition of these principles. There are not merely so many moral codes which can be described and whose vagaries can be traced to historical causes; there is a system of moral truth, as objective as all truth must be, which, and whose implications, we are interested in discovering; and from the point of view of this, the genuinely ethical problem, the sociological inquiry is simply beside the mark. It does not touch the questions to which we most desire answers.[1]

[1] For a lucid and up to a point appreciative account of the sociological school, and a penetrating criticism of its deficiencies, see ch. 2 of M. D. Parodi's *Le Problème Moral et la Pensée Contemporaine.*

II

WHAT MAKES RIGHT ACTS RIGHT?

THE real point at issue between hedonism and utilitarianism on the one hand and their opponents on the other is not whether 'right' means 'productive of so and so'; for it cannot with any plausibility be maintained that it does. The point at issue is that to which we now pass, viz. whether there is any general character which makes right acts right, and if so, what it is. Among the main historical attempts to state a single characteristic of all right actions which is the foundation of their rightness are those made by egoism and utilitarianism. But I do not propose to discuss these, not because the subject is unimportant, but because it has been dealt with so often and so well already, and because there has come to be so much agreement among moral philosophers that neither of these theories is satisfactory. A much more attractive theory has been put forward by Professor Moore: that what makes actions right is that they are productive of more *good* than could have been produced by any other action open to the agent.[1]

This theory is in fact the culmination of all the attempts to base rightness on productivity of some sort of result. The first form this attempt takes is the attempt to base rightness on conduciveness to the advantage or pleasure of the agent. This theory comes to grief over the fact, which stares us in the face, that a great part of duty consists in an observance of the rights and a furtherance of the interests of others, whatever the cost to ourselves may be. Plato and others may be right in holding that a regard for the rights of others never in the long run involves a loss of happiness for the agent, that 'the just life profits a man'. But this, even if true, is irrelevant to the rightness of the act. As soon as a man does an action *because* he thinks he will promote his own interests thereby, he is acting not from a sense of its rightness but from self-interest.

---

[1] I take the theory which, as I have tried to show, seems to be put forward in *Ethics* rather than the earlier and less plausible theory put forward in *Principia Ethica*. For the difference, cf. my pp. 8–11.

To the egoistic theory hedonistic utilitarianism supplies a much-needed amendment. It points out correctly that the fact that a certain pleasure will be enjoyed by the agent is no reason why he *ought* to bring it into being rather than an equal or greater pleasure to be enjoyed by another, though, human nature being what it is, it makes it not unlikely that he *will* try to bring it into being. But hedonistic utilitarianism in its turn needs a correction. On reflection it seems clear that pleasure is not the only thing in life that we think good in itself, that for instance we think the possession of a good character, or an intelligent understanding of the world, as good or better. A great advance is made by the substitution of 'productive of the greatest good' for 'productive of the greatest pleasure'.

Not only is this theory more attractive than hedonistic utilitarianism, but its logical relation to that theory is such that the latter could not be true unless *it* were true, while it might be true though hedonistic utilitarianism were not. It is in fact one of the logical bases of hedonistic utilitarianism. For the view that what produces the maximum pleasure is right has for its bases the views (1) that what produces the maximum good is right, and (2) that pleasure is the only thing good in itself. If they were not assuming that what produces the maximum *good* is right, the utilitarians' attempt to show that pleasure is the only thing good in itself, which is in fact the point they take most pains to establish, would have been quite irrelevant to their attempt to prove that only what produces the maximum *pleasure* is right. If, therefore, it can be shown that productivity of the maximum good is not what makes all right actions right, we shall *a fortiori* have refuted hedonistic utilitarianism.

When a plain man fulfils a promise because he thinks he ought to do so, it seems clear that he does so with no thought of its total consequences, still less with any opinion that these are likely to be the best possible. He thinks in fact much more of the past than of the future. What makes him think it right to act in a certain way is the fact that he has promised to do so —that and, usually, nothing more. That his act will produce the best possible consequences is not his reason for calling it right. What lends colour to the theory we are examining, then, is not the actions (which form probably a great majority of our actions) in which some such reflection as 'I have promised' is the only reason we give ourselves for thinking a certain action right, but the exceptional cases in which the consequences of fulfilling a promise (for instance) would be so disastrous to others that we judge it right not to do so. It must of course be admitted that such cases exist. If I have promised to meet a friend at a particular time for some trivial purpose, I should certainly think myself justified in breaking my engagement if by doing so I could prevent a serious accident or bring relief to the victims of one. And the supporters of the view we are examining hold that my thinking so is due to my thinking that I shall bring more good into existence by the one action than by the other. A different account may, however, be given of the matter, an account which will, I believe, show itself to be the true one. It may be said that besides the duty of fulfilling promises I have and recognize a duty of relieving distress,[1] and that when I think it right to do the latter at the cost of not doing the former, it is not because I think I shall produce more good thereby but because I think it the duty which is in the circumstances more of a duty. This account surely corresponds much more closely with what we really think in such a situation. If, so far as I can see, I could bring equal amounts of good into being by fulfilling my promise and by helping some one to whom I had made no promise, I should not hesitate to regard the former as my duty. Yet on the view that what is right is right because it is productive of the most good I should not so regard it.

There are two theories, each in its way simple, that offer a solution of such cases of conscience. One is the view of Kant, that there are certain duties of perfect obligation, such as those of fulfilling promises, of paying debts, of telling the truth, which admit of no exception whatever in favour of duties of imperfect obligation, such as that of relieving distress. The other is the view of, for instance, Professor Moore and Dr. Rashdall, that there is only the duty of producing good, and

---

[1] These are not strictly speaking duties, but things that tend to be our duty, or *prima facie* duties. Cf. pp. 19–20.

that all 'conflicts of duties' should be resolved by asking 'by which action will most good be produced?' But it is more important that our theory fit the facts than that it be simple, and the account we have given above corresponds (it seems to me) better than either of the simpler theories with what we really think, viz. that normally promise-keeping, for example, should come before benevolence, but that when and only when the good to be produced by the benevolent act is very great and the promise comparatively trivial, the act of benevolence becomes our duty.

In fact the theory of 'ideal utilitarianism', if I may for brevity refer so to the theory of Professor Moore, seems to simplify unduly our relations to our fellows. It says, in effect, that the only morally significant relation in which my neighbours stand to me is that of being possible beneficiaries by my action.[1] They do stand in this relation to me, and this relation is morally significant. But they may also stand to me in the relation of promisee to promiser, of creditor to debtor, of wife to husband, of child to parent, of friend to friend, of fellow countryman to fellow countryman, and the like; and each of these relations is the foundation of a *prima facie* duty, which is more or less incumbent on me according to the circumstances of the case. When I am in a situation, as perhaps I always am, in which more than one of these *prima facie* duties is incumbent on me, what I have to do is to study the situation as fully as I can until I form the considered opinion (it is never more) that in the circumstances one of them is more incumbent than any other; then I am bound to think that to do this *prima facie* duty is my duty *sans phrase* in the situation.

I suggest '*prima facie* duty' or 'conditional duty' as a brief way of referring to the characteristic (quite distinct from that of being a duty proper) which an act has, in virtue of being of a certain kind (e.g. the keeping of a promise), of being an act which would be a duty proper if it were not at the same time of another kind which is morally significant. Whether an act

[1] Some will think it, apart from other considerations, a sufficient refutation of this view to point out that I also stand in that relation to myself, so that for this view the distinction of oneself from others is morally insignificant.

is a duty proper or actual duty depends on *all* the morally significant kinds it is an instance of. The phrase '*prima facie* duty' must be apologized for, since (1) it suggests that what we are speaking of is a certain kind of duty, whereas it is in fact not a duty, but something related in a special way to duty. Strictly speaking, we want not a phrase in which duty is qualified by an adjective, but a separate noun. (2) '*Prima facie* suggests that one is speaking only of an appearance which a moral situation presents at first sight, and which may turn out to be illusory; whereas what I am speaking of is an objective fact involved in the nature of the situation, or more strictly in an element of its nature, though not, as duty proper does, arising from its *whole* nature. * I can, however, think of no term which fully meets the case. 'Claim' has been suggested by Professor Prichard. The word 'claim' has the advantage of being quite a familiar one in this connexion, and it seems to cover much of the ground. It would be quite natural to say, 'a person to whom I have made a promise has a claim on me', and also, 'a person whose distress I could relieve (at the cost of breaking the promise) has a claim on me'. But (1) while 'claim' is appropriate from *their* point of view, we want a word to express the corresponding fact from the agent's point of view—the fact of his being subject to claims that can be made against him; and ordinary language provides us with no such correlative to 'claim'. And (2) (what is more important) 'claim' seems inevitably to suggest two persons, one of whom might make a claim on the other; and while this covers the ground of social duty, it is inappropriate in the case of that important part of duty which is the duty of cultivating a certain kind of character in oneself. It would be artificial, I think, and at any rate metaphorical, to say that one's character has a claim on oneself. *

There is nothing arbitrary about these *prima facie* duties. Each rests on a definite circumstance which cannot seriously be held to be without moral significance. Of *prima facie* duties I suggest, without claiming completeness or finality for it, the following division.[1]

---

[1] I should make it plain at this stage that I am *assuming* the correctness of some of our main convictions as to *prima facie* duties, or, more strictly, am claiming that we

(1) Some duties rest on previous acts of my own. These duties seem to include two kinds, (a) those resting on a promise or what may fairly be called an implicit promise, such as the implicit undertaking not to tell lies which seems to be implied in the act of entering into conversation (at any rate by civilized men), or of writing books that purport to be history and not fiction. These may be called the duties of fidelity. (b) Those resting on a previous wrongful act. These may be called the duties of reparation. (2) Some rest on previous acts of other men, i.e. services done by them to me. These may be loosely described as the duties of gratitude.[1] (3) Some rest on the fact or possibility of a distribution of pleasure or happiness (or of the means thereto) which is not in accordance with the merit of the persons concerned; in such cases there arises a duty to upset or prevent such a distribution. These are the duties of justice. (4) Some rest on the mere fact that there are other beings in the world whose condition we can make better in respect of virtue, or of intelligence, or of pleasure. These are the duties of beneficence. (5) Some rest on the fact that we can improve our own condition in respect of virtue or of intelligence. These are the duties of self-improvement. (6) I think that we should distinguish from (4) the duties that may be summed up under the title of 'not injuring others'. No doubt to injure others is incidentally to fail to do them good; but it seems to me clear that non-maleficence is apprehended as a duty distinct from that of beneficence, and as a duty of a more stringent character. It will be noticed that this alone among the types of duty has been stated in a negative way. An attempt might no doubt be made to state this duty, like the others, in a positive way. It might be said that it is really the duty to

know them to be true. To me it seems as self-evident as anything could be, that to make a promise, for instance, is to create a moral claim on us in someone else. Many readers will perhaps say that they do *not* know this to be true. If so, I certainly cannot prove it to them; I can only ask them to reflect again, in the hope that they will ultimately agree that they also know it to be true. The main moral convictions of the plain man seem to me to be, not opinions which it is for philosophy to prove or disprove, but knowledge from the start; and in my own case I seem to find little difficulty in distinguishing these essential convictions from other moral convictions which I also have, which are merely fallible opinions based on an imperfect study of the working for good or evil of certain institutions or types of action.

[1] For a needed correction of this statement, cf. pp. 22-3.

prevent ourselves from acting either from an inclination to harm others or from an inclination to seek our own pleasure, in doing which we should incidentally harm them. But on reflection it seems clear that the primary duty here is the duty not to harm others, this being a duty whether or not we have an inclination that if followed would lead to our harming them; and that when we have such an inclination the primary duty not to harm others gives rise to a consequential duty to resist the inclination. The recognition of this duty of non-maleficence is the first step on the way to the recognition of the duty of beneficence; and that accounts for the prominence of the commands 'thou shalt not kill', 'thou shalt not commit adultery', 'thou shalt not steal', 'thou shalt not bear false witness', in so early a code as the Decalogue. But even when we have come to recognize the duty of beneficence, it appears to me that the duty of non-maleficence is recognized as a distinct one, and as *prima facie* more binding. We should not in general consider it justifiable to kill one person in order to keep another alive, or to steal from one in order to give alms to another.

The essential defect of the 'ideal utilitarian' theory is that it ignores, or at least does not do full justice to, the highly personal character of duty. If the only duty is to produce the maximum of good, the question who is to have the good—whether it is myself, or my benefactor, or a person to whom I have made a promise to confer that good on him, or a mere fellow man to whom I stand in no such special relation—should make no difference to my having a duty to produce that good. But we are all in fact sure that it makes a vast difference.

One or two other comments must be made on this provisional list of the divisions of duty. (1) The nomenclature is not strictly correct. For by 'fidelity' or 'gratitude' we mean, strictly, certain states of motivation; and, as I have urged, it is not our duty to have certain motives, but to do certain acts. By 'fidelity', for instance, is meant, strictly, the disposition to fulfil promises and implicit promises *because we have made them*. We have no general word to cover the actual fulfilment of promises and implicit promises *irrespective of motive*; and I use 'fidelity', loosely but perhaps conveniently, to fill this gap. So too I use 'gratitude' for the returning of services, irrespective of motive. The term 'justice' is not so much confined, in ordinary usage, to a certain state of motivation, for we should often talk of a man as acting justly even when we did not think his motive was the wish to do what was just simply for the sake of doing so. Less apology is therefore needed for our use of 'justice' in this sense. And I have used the word 'beneficence' rather than 'benevolence', in order to emphasize the fact that it is our duty to do certain things, and not to do them from certain motives.

(2) If the objection be made, that this catalogue of the main types of duty is an unsystematic one resting on no logical principle, it may be replied, first, that it makes no claim to being ultimate. It is a *prima facie* classification of the duties which reflection on our moral convictions seems actually to reveal. And if these convictions are, as I would claim that they are, of the nature of knowledge, and if I have not misstated them, the list will be a list of authentic conditional duties, correct as far as it goes though not necessarily complete. The list of *goods* put forward by the rival theory is reached by exactly the same method—the only sound one in the circumstances—viz. that of direct reflection on what we really think. Loyalty to the facts is worth more than a symmetrical architectonic or a hastily reached simplicity. If further reflection discovers a perfect logical basis for this or for a better classification, so much the better.

(3) It may, again, be objected that our theory that there are these various and often conflicting types of *prima facie* duty leaves us with no principle upon which to discern what is our actual duty in particular circumstances. But this objection is not one which the rival theory is in a position to bring forward. For when we have to choose between the production of two heterogeneous goods, say knowledge and pleasure, the 'ideal utilitarian' theory can only fall back on an opinion, for which no logical basis can be offered, that one of the goods is the greater; and this is no better than a similar opinion that one of two duties is the more urgent. And again, when we consider the infinite variety of the effects of our actions in the way of

pleasure, it must surely be admitted that the claim which *hedonism* sometimes makes, that it offers a readily applicable criterion of right conduct, is quite illusory.

I am unwilling, however, to content myself with an *argumentum ad hominem*, and I would contend that in principle there is no reason to anticipate that every act that is our duty is so for one and the same reason. Why should two sets of circumstances, or one set of circumstances, *not* possess different characteristics, any one of which makes a certain act our *prima facie* duty? When I ask what it is that makes me in certain cases sure that I have a *prima facie* duty to do so and so, I find that it lies in the fact that I have made a promise; when I ask the same question in another case, I find the answer lies in the fact that I have done a wrong. And if on reflection I find (as I think I do) that neither of these reasons is reducible to the other, I must not on any *a priori* ground assume that such a reduction is possible.

An attempt may be made to arrange in a more systematic way the main types of duty which we have indicated. In the first place it seems self-evident that if there are things that are intrinsically good, it is *prima facie* a duty to bring them into existence rather than not to do so, and to bring as much of them into existence as possible. It will be argued in our fifth chapter that there are three main things that are intrinsically good— virtue, knowledge, and, with certain limitations, pleasure. And since a given virtuous disposition, for instance, is equally good whether it is realized in myself or in another, it seems to be my duty to bring it into existence whether in myself or in another. So too with a given piece of knowledge.

The case of pleasure is difficult; for while we clearly recognize a duty to produce pleasure for others, it is by no means so clear that we recognize a duty to produce pleasure for ourselves. This appears to arise from the following facts. The thought of an act as our duty is one that presupposes a certain amount of reflection about the act; and for that reason does not normally arise in connexion with acts towards which we are already impelled by another strong impulse. So far, the cause of our not thinking of the promotion of our own pleasure as a duty is analogous to the cause which usually prevents a highly sympathetic person from thinking of the promotion of the pleasure of others as a duty. He is impelled so strongly by direct interest in the well-being of others towards promoting their pleasure that he does not stop to ask whether it is his duty to promote it; and we are all impelled so strongly towards the promotion of our own pleasure that we do not stop to ask whether it is a duty or not. But there is a further reason why even when we stop to think about the matter it does not usually present itself as a duty: viz. that, since the performance of most of our duties involves the giving up of some pleasure that we desire, the doing of duty and the getting of pleasure for ourselves come by a natural association of ideas to be thought of as incompatible things. This association of ideas is in the main salutary in its operation, since it puts a check on what but for it would be much too strong, the tendency to pursue one's own pleasure without thought of other considerations. Yet if pleasure is good, it seems in the long run clear that it is right to get it for ourselves as well as to produce it for others, when this does not involve the failure to discharge some more stringent *prima facie* duty. The question is a very difficult one, but it seems that this conclusion can be denied only on one or other of three grounds: (1) that pleasure is not *prima facie* good (i.e. good when it is neither the actualization of a bad disposition nor undeserved), (2) that there is no *prima facie* duty to produce as much that is good as we can, or (3) that though there is a *prima facie* duty to produce other things that are good, there is no *prima facie* duty to produce pleasure which will be enjoyed by ourselves. I give reasons later [1] for not accepting the first contention. The second hardly admits of argument but seems to me plainly false. The third seems plausible only if we hold that an act that is pleasant or brings pleasure to ourselves must for that reason not be a duty; and this would lead to paradoxical consequences, such as that if a man enjoys giving pleasure to others or working for their moral improvement, it cannot be his duty to do so. Yet it seems to be a very stubborn fact, that in our ordinary consciousness we are not aware

[1] pp. 135-8.

of a duty to get pleasure for ourselves; and by way of partial explanation of this I may add that though, as I think, one's own pleasure is a good and there is a duty to produce it, it is only if we *think* of our own pleasure not as simply our own pleasure, but as an objective good, something that an impartial spectator would approve, that we can think of the getting it as a duty; and we do not habitually think of it in this way.*

If these contentions are right, what we have called the duty of beneficence and the duty of self-improvement rest on the same ground. No different principles of duty are involved in the two cases. If we feel a special responsibility for improving our own character rather than that of others, it is not because a special principle is involved, but because we are aware that the one is more under our control than the other. It was on this ground that Kant expressed the practical law of duty in the form 'seek to make yourself good and other people happy'. He was so persuaded of the internality of virtue that he regarded any attempt by one person to produce virtue in another as bound to produce, at most, only a counterfeit of virtue, the doing of externally right acts not from the true principle of virtuous action but out of regard to another person. It must be admitted that one man cannot compel another to be virtuous; compulsory virtue would just not be virtue. But experience clearly shows that Kant overshoots the mark when he contends that one man cannot do anything to *promote* virtue in another, to bring such influences to bear upon him that his own response to them is more likely to be virtuous than his response to other influences would have been. And our duty to do this is not different in kind from our duty to improve our own characters.

It is equally clear, and clear at an earlier stage of moral development, that if there are things that are bad in themselves we ought, *prima facie*, not to bring them upon others; and on this fact rests the duty of non-maleficence.

The duty of justice is particularly complicated, and the word is used to cover things which are really very different—things such as the payment of debts, the reparation of injuries done by oneself to another, and the bringing about of a distribution of happiness between other people in proportion to merit. I use the word to denote only the last of these three. In the fifth chapter I shall try to show that besides the three (comparatively) simple goods, virtue, knowledge, and pleasure, there is a more complex good, not reducible to these, consisting in the proportionment of happiness to virtue. The bringing of this about is a duty which we owe to all men alike, though it may be reinforced by special responsibilities that we have undertaken to particular men. This, therefore, with beneficence and self-improvement, comes under the general principle that we should produce as much good as possible, though the good here involved is different in kind from any other.

But besides this general obligation, there are special obligations. These may arise, in the first place, incidentally, from acts which were not essentially meant to create such an obligation, but which nevertheless create it. From the nature of the case such acts may be of two kinds—the infliction of injuries on others, and the acceptance of benefits from them. It seems clear that these put us under a special obligation to other men, and that only these acts can do so incidentally. From these arise the twin duties of reparation and gratitude.

And finally there are special obligations arising from acts the very intention of which, when they were done, was to put us under such an obligation. The name for such acts is 'promises'; the name is wide enough if we are willing to include under it implicit promises, i.e. modes of behaviour in which without explicit verbal promise we intentionally create an expectation that we can be counted on to behave in a certain way in the interest of another person.

These seem to be, in principle, all the ways in which *prima facie* duties arise. In actual experience they are compounded together in highly complex ways. Thus, for example, the duty of obeying the laws of one's country arises partly (as Socrates contends in the *Crito*) from the duty of gratitude for the benefits one has received from it; partly from the implicit promise to obey which seems to be involved in permanent residence in a country whose laws we know we are *expected* to obey, and still more clearly involved when we ourselves invoke the protection of its laws (this is the truth underlying the doctrine of the social contract); and partly (if we are fortunate in our country) from the fact that its laws are potent instruments for the general good.

Or again, the sense of a general obligation to bring about (so far as we can) a just apportionment of happiness to merit is often greatly reinforced by the fact that many of the existing injustices are due to a social and economic system which we have, not indeed created, but taken part in and assented to; the duty of justice is then reinforced by the duty of reparation.

It is necessary to say something by way of clearing up the relation between *prima facie* duties and the actual or absolute duty to do one particular act in particular circumstances. If, as almost all moralists except Kant are agreed, and as most plain men think, it is sometimes right to tell a lie or to break a promise, it must be maintained that there is a difference between *prima facie* duty and actual or absolute duty. When we think ourselves justified in breaking, and indeed morally obliged to break, a promise in order to relieve some one's distress, we do not for a moment cease to recognize a *prima facie* duty to keep our promise, and this leads us to feel, not indeed shame or repentance, but certainly compunction, for behaving as we do; we recognize, further, that it is our duty to make up somehow to the promisee for the breaking of the promise. We have to distinguish from the characteristic of being our duty that of tending to be our duty. Any act that we do contains various elements in virtue of which it falls under various categories. In virtue of being the breaking of a promise, for instance, it tends to be wrong; in virtue of being an instance of relieving distress it tends to be right. Tendency to be one's duty may be called a parti-resultant attribute, i.e. one which belongs to an act in virtue of some one component in its nature. *Being* one's duty is a toti-resultant attribute, one which belongs to an act in virtue of its whole nature and of nothing less than this.[1] This distinction between parti-resultant and toti-resultant attributes is one which we shall meet in another context also.[2]

Another instance of the same distinction may be found in the operation of natural laws. *Qua* subject to the force of

---

[1] But cf. the qualification in p. 33, n. 2.   [2] Cf. pp. 122-3.

gravitation towards some other body, each body tends to move in a particular direction with a particular velocity; but its actual movement depends on *all* the forces to which it is subject. It is only by recognizing this distinction that we can preserve the absoluteness of laws of nature, and only by recognizing a corresponding distinction that we can preserve the absoluteness of the general principles of morality. But an important difference between the two cases must be pointed out. When we say that in virtue of gravitation a body tends to move in a certain way, we are referring to a causal influence actually exercised on it by another body or other bodies. When we say that in virtue of being deliberately untrue a certain remark tends to be wrong, we are referring to no causal relation, to no relation that involves succession in time, but to such a relation as connects the various attributes of a mathematical figure. And if the word 'tendency' is thought to suggest too much a causal relation, it is better to talk of certain types of act as being *prima facie* right or wrong (or of different persons as having different and possibly conflicting claims upon us), than of their tending to be right or wrong.

Something should be said of the relation between our apprehension of the *prima facie* rightness of certain types of act and our mental attitude towards particular acts. It is proper to use the word 'apprehension' in the former case and not in the latter. That an act, *qua* fulfilling a promise, or *qua* effecting a just distribution of good, or *qua* returning services rendered, or *qua* promoting the good of others, or *qua* promoting the virtue or insight of the agent, is *prima facie* right, is self-evident; not in the sense that it is evident from the beginning of our lives, or as soon as we attend to the proposition for the first time, but in the sense that when we have reached sufficient mental maturity and have given sufficient attention to the proposition it is evident without any need of proof, or of evidence beyond itself. It is self-evident just as a mathematical axiom, or the validity of a form of inference, is evident. The moral order expressed in these propositions is just as much part of the fundamental nature of the universe (and, we may add, of any possible universe in which there were moral agents at all) as is the spatial or numerical structure expressed in the axioms of geometry or arithmetic. In our confidence that these propositions are true there is involved the same trust in our reason that is involved in our confidence in mathematics; and we should have no justification for trusting it in the latter sphere and distrusting it in the former. In both cases we are dealing with propositions that cannot be proved, but that just as certainly need no proof. *

Some of these general principles of *prima facie* duty may appear to be open to criticism. It may be thought, for example, that the principle of returning good for good is a falling off from the Christian principle, generally and rightly recognized as expressing the highest morality, of returning good for evil. To this it may be replied that I do not suggest that there is a principle commanding us to return good for good and forbidding us to return good for evil, and that I do suggest that there is a positive duty to seek the good of all men. What I maintain is that an act in which good is returned for good is recognized as *specially* binding on us just because it is of that character, and that *ceteris paribus* any one would think it his duty to help his benefactors rather than his enemies, if he could not do both; just as it is generally recognized that *ceteris paribus* we should pay our debts rather than give our money in charity, when we cannot do both. A benefactor is not only a man, calling for our effort on his behalf on that ground, but also our benefactor, calling for our *special* effort on *that* ground.

Our judgements about our actual duty in concrete situations have none of the certainty that attaches to our recognition of the general principles of duty. A statement is certain, i.e. is an expression of knowledge, only in one or other of two cases: when it is either self-evident, or a valid conclusion from self-evident premisses. And our judgements about our particular duties have neither of these characters. (1) They are not self-evident. Where a possible act is seen to have two characteristics, in virtue of one of which it is *prima facie* right, and in virtue of the other *prima facie* wrong, we are (I think) well aware that we are not certain whether we ought or ought not to do it; that whether we do it or not, we are taking a moral risk. We

come in the long run, after consideration, to think one duty
more pressing than the other, but we do not feel certain that
it is so. And though we do not always recognize that a possible
act has two such characteristics, and though there *may* be cases
in which it has not, we are never certain that any particular
possible act has not, and therefore never certain that it is right,
nor certain that it is wrong. For, to go no further in the analysis,
it is enough to point out that any particular act will in all
probability in the course of time contribute to the bringing
about of good or of evil for many human beings, and thus have
a *prima facie* rightness or wrongness of which we know nothing.
(2) Again, our judgements about our particular duties are not
logical conclusions from self-evident premisses. The only
possible premisses would be the general principles stating their
prima facie rightness or wrongness *qua* having the different
characteristics they do have; and even if we could (as we cannot)
apprehend the extent to which an act will tend on the one hand,
for example, to bring about advantages for our benefactors,
and on the other hand to bring about disadvantages for fellow
men who are not our benefactors, there is no principle by which
we can draw the conclusion that it is on the whole right or on
the whole wrong. In this respect the judgement as to the rightness of a particular act is just like the judgement as to the beauty
of a particular natural object or work of art. A poem is, for
instance, in respect of certain qualities beautiful and in respect
of certain others not beautiful; and our judgement as to the
degree of beauty it possesses on the whole is never reached by
logical reasoning from the apprehension of its particular beauties
or particular defects. Both in this and in the moral case we
have more or less probable opinions which are not logically
justified conclusions from the general principles that are recognized as self-evident.

There is therefore much truth in the description of the right
act as a fortunate act. If we cannot be certain that it is right, it
is our good fortune if the act we do is the right act. This consideration does not, however, make the doing of our duty a
mere matter of chance. There is a parallel here between the
doing of duty and the doing of what will be to our personal

advantage. We never *know* what act will in the long run be to our advantage. Yet it is certain that we are more likely in general to secure our advantage if we estimate to the best of our ability the probable tendencies of our actions in this respect, than if we act on caprice. And similarly we are more likely to do our duty if we reflect to the best of our ability on the *prima facie* rightness or wrongness of various possible acts in virtue of the characteristics we perceive them to have, than if we act without reflection. With this greater likelihood we must be content.

Many people would be inclined to say that the right act for me is not that whose general nature I have been describing, viz. that which if I were omniscient I should see to be my duty, but that which on all the evidence available to me I should think to be my duty. But suppose that from the state of partial knowledge in which I think act *A* to be my duty, I could pass to a state of perfect knowledge in which I saw act *B* to be my duty, should I not say 'act *B* was the right act for me to do'? I should no doubt add 'though I am not to be blamed for doing act *A*'. But in adding this, am I not passing from the question 'what is right' to the question 'what is morally good'? At the same time I am not making the *full* passage from the one notion to the other; for in order that the act should be morally good, or an act I am not to be blamed for doing, it must not merely be the act which it is reasonable for me to think my duty; it must also be done for that reason, or from some other morally good motive. Thus the conception of the right act as the act which it is reasonable for me to think my duty is an unsatisfactory compromise between the true notion of the right act and the notion of the morally good action.*

The general principles of duty are obviously not self-evident from the beginning of our lives. How do they come to be so? The answer is, that they come to be self-evident to us just as mathematical axioms do. We find by experience that this couple of matches and that couple make four matches, that this couple of balls on a wire and that couple make four balls: and by reflection on these and similar discoveries we come to see that it is of the nature of two and two to make four. In a precisely similar way, we see the *prima facie* rightness of an act which would be the fulfilment of a particular promise, and of another which would be the fulfilment of another promise, and when we have reached sufficient maturity to think in general terms, we apprehend *prima facie* rightness to belong to the nature of any fulfilment of promise. What comes first in time is the apprehension of the self-evident *prima facie* rightness of an individual act of a particular type. From this we come by reflection to apprehend the self-evident general principle of *prima facie* duty. From this, too, perhaps along with the apprehension of the self-evident *prima facie* rightness of the same act in virtue of its having another characteristic as well, and perhaps in spite of the apprehension of its *prima facie* wrongness in virtue of its having some third characteristic, we come to believe something not self-evident at all, but an object of probable opinion, viz. that this particular act is (not *prima facie* but) actually right.

In this respect there is an important difference between rightness and mathematical properties. A triangle which is isosceles necessarily has two of its angles equal, whatever other characteristics the triangle may have—whatever, for instance, be its area, or the size of its third angle. The equality of the two angles is a parti-resultant attribute.[1] And the same is true of all mathematical attributes. It is true, I may add, of *prima facie* rightness. But no act is ever, in virtue of falling under some general description, necessarily actually right; its rightness depends on its whole nature [2] and not on any element in it. The reason is that no mathematical object (no figure, for instance, or angle) ever has two characteristics that tend to give it opposite resultant characteristics, while moral acts often (as every one knows) and indeed always (as on reflection we must admit) have different characteristics that tend to make them at the same time *prima facie* right and *prima facie* wrong; there is

[1] Cf. pp. 28, 122–3.
[2] To avoid complicating unduly the statement of the general view I am putting forward, I have here rather overstated it. Any act is the origination of a great variety of things many of which make no difference to its rightness or wrongness. But there are always many elements in its nature (i. e. in what it is the origination of) that make a difference to its rightness or wrongness, and no element in its nature can be dismissed without consideration as indifferent.

probably no act, for instance, which does good to any one without doing harm to some one else, and *vice versa*.

Supposing it to be agreed, as I think on reflection it must, that no one *means* by 'right' just 'productive of the best possible consequences', or 'optimific', the attributes 'right' and 'optimific' might stand in either of two kinds of relation to each other. (1) They might be so related that we could apprehend *a priori*, either immediately or deductively, that any act that is optimific is right and any act that is right is optimific, as we can apprehend that any triangle that is equilateral is equiangular and *vice versa*. Professor Moore's view is, I think, that the coextensiveness of 'right' and 'optimific' is apprehended immediately.[1] He rejects the possibility of any proof of it. Or (2) the two attributes might be such that the question whether they are invariably connected had to be answered by means of an inductive inquiry. Now at first sight it might seem as if the constant connexion of the two attributes could be immediately apprehended. It might seem absurd to suggest that it could be right for any one to do an act which would produce consequences less good than those which would be produced by some other act in his power. Yet a little thought will convince us that this is not absurd. The type of case in which it is easiest to see that this is so is, perhaps, that in which one has made a promise. In such a case we all think that *prima facie* it is our duty to fulfil the promise irrespective of the precise goodness of the total consequences. And though we do not think it is necessarily our actual or absolute duty to do so, we are far from thinking that any, even the slightest, gain in the value of the total consequences will necessarily justify us in doing something else instead. Suppose, to simplify the case by abstraction, that the fulfilment of a promise to A would produce 1,000 units of good [2] for him, but that by doing some other act I could produce 1,001 units of good for B, to whom I have made no

[1] *Ethics*, 181.
[2] I am assuming that good is objectively quantitative (cf. pp. 142–4), but not that we can accurately assign an exact quantitative measure to it. Since it is of a definite amount, we can make the *supposition* that its amount is so-and-so, though we cannot with any confidence *assert* that it is.

promise, the other consequences of the two acts being of equal value; should we really think it self-evident that it was our duty to do the second act and not the first? I think not. We should, I fancy, hold that only a much greater disparity of value between the total consequences would justify us in failing to discharge our *prima facie* duty to *A*. After all, a promise is a promise, and is not to be treated so lightly as the theory we are examining would imply. What, exactly, a promise is, is not so easy to determine, but we are surely agreed that it constitutes a serious moral limitation to our freedom of action. To produce the 1,001 units of good for *B* rather than fulfil our promise to *A* would be to take, not perhaps our duty as philanthropists too seriously, but certainly our duty as makers of promises too lightly.

Or consider another phase of the same problem. If I have promised to confer on *A* a particular benefit containing 1,000 units of good, is it self-evident that if by doing some different act I could produce 1,001 units of good for *A* himself (the other consequences of the two acts being supposed equal in value), it would be right for me to do so? Again, I think not. Apart from my general *prima facie* duty to do *A* what good I can, I have another *prima facie* duty to do him the particular service I have promised to do him, and this is not to be set aside in consequence of a disparity of good of the order of 1,001 to 1,000, though a much greater disparity might justify me in so doing.

Or again, suppose that *A* is a very good and *B* a very bad man, should I then, even when I have made no promise, think it self-evidently right to produce 1,001 units of good for *B* rather than 1,000 for *A*? Surely not. I should be sensible of a *prima facie* duty of justice, i.e. of producing a distribution of goods in proportion to merit, which is not outweighed by such a slight disparity in the total goods to be produced.

Such instances—and they might easily be added to—make it clear that there is no self-evident connexion between the attributes 'right' and 'optimific'. The theory we are examining has a certain attractiveness when applied to our decision that a particular act is our duty (though I have tried to show that it does not agree with our actual moral judgements even here). But it is not even plausible when applied to our recognition of *prima facie* duty. For if it were self-evident that the right coincides with the optimific, it should be self-evident that what is *prima facie* right is *prima facie* optimific. But whereas we are certain that keeping a promise is *prima facie* right, we are not certain that it is *prima facie* optimific (though we are perhaps certain that it is *prima facie* bonific). Our certainty that it is *prima facie* right depends not on its consequences but on its being the fulfilment of a promise. The theory we are examining involves too much difference between the evident ground of our conviction about *prima facie* duty and the alleged ground of our conviction about actual duty.

The coextensiveness of the right and the optimific is, then, not self-evident. And I can see no way of proving it deductively; nor, so far as I know, has any one tried to do so. There remains the question whether it can be established inductively. Such an inquiry, to be conclusive, would have to be very thorough and extensive. We should have to take a large variety of the acts which we, to the best of our ability, judge to be right. We should have to trace as far as possible their consequences, not only for the persons directly affected but also for those indirectly affected, and to these no limit can be set. To make our inquiry thoroughly conclusive, we should have to do what we cannot do, viz. trace these consequences into an unending future. And even to make it reasonably conclusive, we should have to trace them far into the future. It is clear that the most we could possibly say is that a large variety of typical acts that are judged right appear, so far as we can trace their consequences, to produce more good than any other acts possible to the agents in the circumstances. And such a result falls far short of proving the constant connexion of the two attributes. But it is surely clear that no inductive inquiry justifying even this result has ever been carried through. The advocates of utilitarian systems have been so much persuaded either of the identity or of the self-evident connexion of the attributes 'right' and 'optimific' (or 'felicific') that they have not attempted even such an inductive inquiry as is possible.

And in view of the enormous complexity of the task and the inevitable inconclusiveness of the result, it is worth no one's while to make the attempt. What, after all, would be gained by it? If, as I have tried to show, for an act to be right and to be optimific are not the same thing, and an act's being optimific is not even the ground of its being right, then if we could ask ourselves (though the question is really unmeaning) which we ought to do, right acts because they are right or optimific acts because they are optimific, our answer must be 'the former'. If they are optimific as well as right, that is interesting but not morally important; if not, we still ought to do them (which is only another way of saying that they *are* the right acts), and the question whether they are optimific has no importance for moral theory.

There is one direction in which a fairly serious attempt has been made to show the connexion of the attributes 'right' and 'optimific'. One of the most evident facts of our moral consciousness is the sense which we have of the sanctity of promises, a sense which does not, on the face of it, involve the thought that one will be bringing more good into existence by fulfilling the promise than by breaking it. It is plain, I think, that in our normal thought we consider that the fact that we have made a promise is in itself sufficient to create a duty of keeping it, the sense of duty resting on remembrance of the past promise and not on thoughts of the future consequences of its fulfilment. Utilitarianism tries to show that this is not so, that the sanctity of promises rests on the good consequences of the fulfilment of them and the bad consequences of their non-fulfilment. It does so in this way: it points out that when you break a promise you not only fail to confer a certain advantage on your promisee but you diminish his confidence, and indirectly the confidence of others, in the fulfilment of promises. You thus strike a blow at one of the devices that have been found most useful in the relations between man and man—the device on which, for example, the whole system of commercial credit rests—and you tend to bring about a state of things wherein each man, being entirely unable to rely on the keeping of promises by others, will have to do everything for himself, to the enormous impoverishment of human well-being.

To put the matter otherwise, utilitarians say that when a promise ought to be kept it is because the total good to be produced by keeping it is greater than the total good to be produced by breaking it, the former including as its main element the maintenance and strengthening of general mutual confidence, and the latter being greatly diminished by a weakening of this confidence. They say, in fact, that the case I put some pages back [1] never arises—the case in which by fulfilling a promise I shall bring into being 1,000 units of good for my promisee, and by breaking it 1,001 units of good for some one else, the other effects of the two acts being of equal value. The other effects, they say, never are of equal value. By keeping my promise I am helping to strengthen the system of mutual confidence; by breaking it I am helping to weaken this; so that really the first act produces $1,000 + x$ units of good, and the second $1,001 - y$ units, and the difference between $+x$ and $-y$ is enough to outweigh the slight superiority in the *immediate* effects of the second act. In answer to this it may be pointed out that there must be *some* amount of good that exceeds the difference between $+x$ and $-y$ (i.e. exceeds $x+y$); say, $x+y+z$. Let us suppose the *immediate* good effects of the second act to be assessed not at 1,001 but at $1,000+x+y+z$. Then its *net* good effects are $1,000+x+z$, i.e. greater than those of the fulfilment of the promise; and the utilitarian is bound to say forthwith that the promise should be broken. Now, we may ask whether that is really the way we think about promises? Do we really think that the production of the slightest balance of good, no matter who will enjoy it, by the breach of a promise frees us from the obligation to keep our promise? We need not doubt that a system by which promises are made and kept is one that has great advantages for the general well-being. But that is not the whole truth. To make a promise is not merely to adapt an ingenious device for promoting the general well-being; it is to put oneself in a new relation to one person in particular, a relation which creates a specifically new *prima facie* duty to him, not reducible to the duty of promoting the general well-being of society. By all

[1] p. 34.

means let us try to foresee the net good effects of keeping one's promise and the net good effects of breaking it, but even if we assess the first at $1,000+x$ and the second at $1,000+x+z$, the question still remains whether it is not our duty to fulfil the promise. It may be suspected, too, that the effect of a single keeping or breaking of a promise in strengthening or weakening the fabric of mutual confidence is greatly exaggerated by the theory we are examining. And if we suppose two men dying together alone, do we think that the duty of one to fulfil before he dies a promise he has made to the other would be extinguished by the fact that neither act would have any effect on the general confidence? Any one who holds this may be suspected of not having reflected on what a promise is.

I conclude that the attributes 'right' and 'optimific' are not identical, and that we do not know either by intuition, by deduction, or by induction that they coincide in their application, still less that the latter is the foundation of the former. It must be added, however, that if we are ever under no special obligation such as that of fidelity to a promisee or of gratitude to a benefactor, we ought to do what will produce most good; and that even when we are under a special obligation the tendency of acts to promote general good is one of the main factors in determining whether they are right.

In what has preceded, a good deal of use has been made of 'what we really think' about moral questions; a certain theory has been rejected because it does not agree with what we really think. It might be said that this is in principle wrong; that we should not be content to expound what our present moral consciousness tells us but should aim at a criticism of our existing moral consciousness in the light of theory. Now I do not doubt that the moral consciousness of men has in detail undergone a good deal of modification as regards the things we think right, at the hands of moral theory. But if we are told, for instance, that we should give up our view that there is a special obligatoriness attaching to the keeping of promises because it is self-evident that the only duty is to produce as much good as possible, we have to ask ourselves whether we really, when we reflect, *are* convinced that this is self-evident, and whether we really *can* get rid of our view that promise-keeping has a bindingness independent of productiveness of maximum good. In my own experience I find that I cannot, in spite of a very genuine attempt to do so; and I venture to think that most people will find the same, and that just because they cannot lose the sense of special obligation, they cannot accept as self-evident, or even as true, the theory which would require them to do so. In fact it seems, on reflection, self-evident that a promise, simply as such, is something that *prima facie* ought to be kept, and it does *not*, on reflection, seem self-evident that production of maximum good is the only thing that makes an act obligatory. And to ask us to give up at the bidding of a theory our actual apprehension of what is right and what is wrong seems like asking people to repudiate their actual experience of beauty, at the bidding of a theory which says 'only that which satisfies such and such conditions can be beautiful'. If what I have called our actual apprehension is (as I would maintain that it is) truly an apprehension, i.e. an instance of knowledge, the request is nothing less than absurd.

I would maintain, in fact, that what we are apt to describe as 'what we think' about moral questions contains a considerable amount that we do not think but know, and that this forms the standard by reference to which the truth of any moral theory has to be tested, instead of having itself to be tested by reference to any theory. I hope that I have in what precedes indicated what in my view these elements of knowledge are that are involved in our ordinary moral consciousness.

It would be a mistake to found a natural science on 'what we really think', i.e. on what reasonably thoughtful and well-educated people think about the subjects of the science before they have studied them scientifically. For such opinions are interpretations, and often misinterpretations, of sense-experience; and the man of science must appeal from these to sense-experience itself, which furnishes his real data. In ethics no such appeal is possible. We have no more direct way of access to the facts about rightness and goodness and about what things are right or good, than by thinking about them;

the moral convictions of thoughtful and well-educated people
are the data of ethics just as sense-perceptions are the data of a
natural science. Just as some of the latter have to be rejected
as illusory, so have some of the former; but as the latter are
rejected only when they are in conflict with other more accurate
sense-perceptions, the former are rejected only when they are
in conflict with other convictions which stand better the test of
reflection. The existing body of moral convictions of the best
people is the cumulative product of the moral reflection of many
generations, which has developed an extremely delicate power
of appreciation of moral distinctions; and this the theorist
cannot afford to treat with anything other than the greatest
respect. The verdicts of the moral consciousness of the best
people are the foundation on which he must build; though he
must first compare them with one another and eliminate any
contradictions they may contain.

It is worth while to try to state more definitely the nature of
the acts that are right. We may try to state first what (if anything) is the universal nature of *all* acts that are right. It is
obvious that any of the acts that we do has countless effects,
directly or indirectly, on countless people, and the probability
is that any act, however right it be, will have adverse effects
(though these may be very trivial) on some innocent people.
Similarly, any wrong act will probably have beneficial effects
on some deserving people. Every act therefore, viewed in
some aspects, will be *prima facie* right, and viewed in others,
prima facie wrong, and right acts can be distinguished from
wrong acts only as being those which, of all those possible for
the agent in the circumstances, have the greatest balance of
prima facie rightness, in those respects in which they are *prima
facie* right, over their *prima facie* wrongness, in those respects
in which they are *prima facie* wrong—*prima facie* rightness
and wrongness being understood in the sense previously explained. For the estimation of the comparative stringency of
these *prima facie* obligations no general rules can, so far as I can
see, be laid down. We can only say that a great deal of stringency belongs to the duties of 'perfect obligation'—the duties

of keeping our promises, of repairing wrongs we have done, and of returning the equivalent of services we have received. For the rest, ἐν τῇ αἰσθήσει ἡ κρίσις.[1] This sense of our particular duty in particular circumstances, preceded and informed by the fullest reflection we can bestow on the act in all its bearings, is highly fallible, but it is the only guide we have to our duty.

When we turn to consider the nature of individual right acts, the first point to which attention should be called is that any act may be correctly described in an indefinite, and in principle infinite, number of ways. An act is the production of a change in the state of affairs (if we ignore, for simplicity's sake, the comparatively few cases in which it is the maintenance of an existing state of affairs; cases which, I think, raise no special difficulty). Now the only changes we can *directly* produce are changes in our own bodies or in our own minds. But these are not, as such, what as a rule we think it our duty to produce. Consider some comparatively simple act, such as telling the truth or fulfilling a promise. In the first case what I produce directly is movements of my vocal organs. But what I think it my duty to produce is a true view in some one else's mind about some fact, and between my movement of my vocal organs and this result there intervenes a series of physical events and events in his mind. Again, in the second case, I may have promised, for instance, to return a book to a friend. I may be able, by a series of movements of my legs and hands, to place it in his hands. But what I am just as likely to do, and to think I have done my duty in doing, is to send it by a messenger or to hand it to his servant or to send it by post; and in each of these cases what I *do* directly is worthless in itself and is connected by a series of intermediate links with what I do think it is my duty to bring about, viz. his receiving what I have promised to return to him. This being so, it *seems* as if what I *do* has no obligatoriness in itself and as if one or other of three accounts should be given of the matter, each of which makes rightness not belong to what I do, considered in its own nature.

(1) One of them would be that what is obligatory is not *doing* anything in the natural sense of producing any change

---

[1] 'The decision rests with perception'. Arist. *Nic. Eth.* 1109 b 23, 1126 b 4.

in the state of affairs, but *aiming at* something—at, for instance, my friend's reception of the book. But this account will not do. For (*a*) to aim at something is to act from a motive consisting of the wish to bring that thing about. But we have seen[1] that motive never forms part of the content of our duty; if anything is certain about morals, that, I think, is certain. And (*b*) if I have promised to return the book to my friend, I obviously do not fulfil my promise and do my duty merely by aiming at his receiving the book; I must see that he actually receives it. (2) A more plausible account is that which says I must do that which is likely to produce the result. But this account is open to the second of these objections, and probably also to the first. For in the first place, however likely my act may seem, even on careful consideration, and even however likely it may in fact be, to produce the result, if it does not produce it I have not done what I promised to do, i.e. have not done my duty. And secondly, when it is said that I ought to do what is likely to produce the result, what is *probably* meant is that I ought to do a certain thing as a result of the wish to produce a certain result, and of the thought that my act is likely to produce it; and this again introduces motive into the content of duty. (3) Much the most plausible of the three accounts is that which says, 'I ought to do that which will actually produce a certain result.' This escapes objection (*b*). Whether it escapes objection (*a*) or not depends on what exactly is meant. If it is meant that I ought to do a certain thing from the wish to produce a certain result and the thought that it will do so, the account is still open to objection (*a*). But if it is meant simply that I ought to do a certain thing, and that the reason why I ought to do it is that it will produce a certain result, objection (*a*) is avoided. Now this account in its second form is that which utilitarianism gives. It says what is right is certain acts, not certain acts motivated in a certain way; and it says that acts are never right by their own nature but by virtue of the goodness of their actual results. And this account is, I think, clearly nearer the truth than one which makes the rightness of an act depend on the goodness of either the *intended* or the *likely* results.

[1] pp. 5–6.

Nevertheless, this account appears not to be the true one. For it implies that what we consider right or our duty is what we do *directly*. It is this, e.g. the packing up and posting of the book, that derives its moral significance not from its own nature but from its consequences. But this is *not* what we should describe, strictly, as our duty; our duty is to fulfil our promise, i.e. to put the book into our friend's possession. This we consider obligatory in its own nature, just because it is a fulfilment of promise, and not because of *its* consequences. But, it might be replied by the utilitarian, I do not do this; I only do something that leads up to this, and what I do has no moral significance in itself but only because of its consequences. In answer to this, however, we may point out that a cause produces not only its immediate, but also its remote consequences, and the latter no less than the former. I, therefore, not only produce the immediate movements of parts of my body but also my friend's reception of the book, which results from these. Or, if this be objected to on the grounds that I can hardly be said to have produced my friend's reception of the book when I have packed and posted it, owing to the time that has still to elapse before he receives it, and that to say I have produced the result hardly does justice to the part played by the Post Office, we may at least say that I have *secured* my friend's reception of the book. What I do is as truly describable in this way as by saying that it is the packing and posting of a book. (It is equally truly describable in many other ways; e.g. I have provided a few moments' employment for Post Office officials. But this is irrelevant to the argument.) And if we ask ourselves whether it is *qua* the packing and posting of a book, or *qua* the securing of my friend's getting what I have promised to return to him, that my action is right, it is clear that it is in the second capacity that it is right; and in this capacity, the only capacity in which it is right, it is right by its own nature and not because of its consequences.

This account may no doubt be objected to, on the ground that we are ignoring the freedom of will of the other agents— the sorter and the postman, for instance—who are equally responsible for the result. Society, it may be said, is not like a machine, in which event follows event by rigorous necessity. Some one may, for instance, in the exercise of his freedom of will, steal the book on the way. But it is to be observed that I have excluded that case, and any similar case. I am dealing with the case in which I secure my friend's receiving the book; and if he does not receive it I have not secured his receiving it. If on the other hand the book reaches its destination, that alone shows that, the system of things being what it is, the trains by which the book travels and the railway lines along which it travels being such as they are and subject to the laws they are subject to, the postal officials who handle it being such as they are, having the motives they have and being subject to the psychological laws they are subject to, my posting the book was the one further thing which was sufficient to procure my friend's receiving it. If it had not been sufficient, the result would not have followed. The attainment of the result proves the sufficiency of the means. The objection in fact rests on the supposition that there can be unmotived action, i.e. an event without a cause, and may be refuted by reflection on the universality of the law of causation.

It is equally true that non-attainment of the result proves the insufficiency of the means. If the book had been destroyed in a railway accident or stolen by a dishonest postman, that would prove that my immediate act was not sufficient to produce the desired result. We get the curious consequence that however carelessly I pack or dispatch the book, if it comes to hand I have done my duty, and however carefully I have acted, if the book does not come to hand I have not done my duty. Success and failure are the only test, and a sufficient test, of the performance of duty. Of course, I should deserve more praise in the second case than in the first; but that is an entirely different question; we must not mix up the question of right and wrong with that of the morally good and the morally bad. And that our conclusion is not as strange as at first sight it might seem is shown by the fact that if the carelessly dispatched book comes to hand, it is not my duty to send another copy, while if the carefully dispatched book does not come to hand I must send another copy to replace it. In the first case I have not my duty still to do, which shows that I have done it; in the second I have it still to do, which shows that I have not done it.

We have reached the result that my act is right *qua* being an ensuring of one of the particular states of affairs of which it is an ensuring, viz., in the case we have taken, of my friend's receiving the book I have promised to return to him. But this answer requires some correction; for it refers only to the *prima facie* rightness of my act. If to be a fulfilment of promise were a sufficient ground of the rightness of an act, all fulfilments of promises would be right, whereas it seems clear that there are cases in which some other *prima facie* duty overrides the *prima facie* duty of fulfilling a promise. The more correct answer would be that the ground of the actual rightness of the act is that, of all acts possible for the agent in the circumstances, it is that whose *prima facie* rightness in the respects in which it is *prima facie* right most outweighs its *prima facie* wrongness in any respects in which it is *prima facie* wrong. But since its *prima facie* rightness is mainly due to its being a fulfilment of promise, we may call its being so the salient element in the ground of its rightness.

Subject to this qualification, then, it is as being the production (or if we prefer the word, the securing or ensuring) of the reception by my friend of what I have promised him (or in other words as the fulfilment of my promise) that my act is right. It is not right as a packing and posting of a book. The packing and posting of the book is only incidentally right, right only because it is a fulfilment of promise, which is what is directly or essentially right.

Our duty, then, is not to do certain things which will produce certain results. Our acts, at any rate our acts of special obligation, are not right because they will produce certain results—which is the view common to all forms of utilitarianism. To say that is to say that in the case in question what is essentially right is to pack and post a book, whereas what is essentially right is to secure the possession by my friend of what I have promised to return to him. An act is not right because it, being one thing, produces good results different from itself; it is right because it is itself the production of a certain state of affairs. Such production is right in itself, apart from any consequence.

But, it might be said, this analysis applies only to acts of special obligation; the utilitarian account still holds good for the acts in which we are not under a special obligation to any person or set of persons but only under that of augmenting the general good. Now merely to have established that there *are* special obligations to do certain things irrespective of their consequences would be already to have made a considerable breach in the utilitarian walls; for according to utilitarianism there is no such thing, there is only the single obligation to promote the general good. But, further, on reflection it is clear that just as (in the case we have taken) my act is not only the packing and posting of a book but the fulfilling of a promise, and just as it is in the latter capacity and not in the former that it is my duty, so an act whereby I augment the general good is not only, let us say, the writing of a begging letter on behalf of a hospital, but the producing (or ensuring) of whatever good ensues therefrom, and it is in the latter capacity and not in the former that it is right, if it *is* right. That which is right is right not because it is an act, one thing, which will produce another thing, an increase of the general welfare, but because it is itself the producing of an increase in the general welfare. Or, to qualify this in the necessary way, its being the production of an increase in the general welfare is the salient element in the ground of its rightness. Just as before we were led to recognize the *prima facie* rightness of the fulfilment of promises, we are now led to recognize the *prima facie* rightness of promoting the general welfare. In both cases we have to recognize the *intrinsic* rightness of a certain type of act, not depending on its consequences but on its own nature.

48

APPENDIX I

RIGHTS

A general discussion of right or duty would hardly be complete without some discussion, even if only a brief one, of the closely related subject of rights. It is commonly said that rights and duties are correlative, and it is worth while to inquire whether and, if at all, in what sense this is true. The statement may stand for any one, or any combination, of the following logically independent statements:

(1) A right of *A* against *B* implies a duty of *B* to *A*.
(2) A duty of *B* to *A* implies a right of *A* against *B*.
(3) A right of *A* against *B* implies a duty of *A* to *B*.
(4) A duty of *A* to *B* implies a right of *A* against *B*.

What is asserted in (1) is that *A*'s having a right to have a certain individual act done to him by *B* implies a duty for *B* to do *that* act to *A*; (2) asserts the converse implication; what is meant by (3) is that *A*'s having a right to have a certain act done to him by *B* implies a duty for *A* to do *another* act to *B*, which act may be either a similar act (as where the right of having the truth told to one implies the duty of telling the truth) or a different sort of act (as where the right to obedience implies the duty of governing well); (4) asserts the converse implication.

Of these four propositions the first appears to be unquestionably true; a right in one being against another is a right to treat or be treated by that other in a certain way, and this plainly implies a duty for the other to behave in a certain way. But there is a certain consideration which throws doubt on the other three propositions. This arises from the fact that we have duties to animals and to infants. The latter case is complicated by the fact that infants, while they are not (so we commonly believe) actual moral agents, are potential moral agents, so that the duty of parents, for instance, to support them may be said to be counterbalanced by a duty which is not incumbent on the infants at the time but will be incumbent on them later, to obey and care for their parents. We had better therefore take the less complicated case of animals, which we commonly suppose not to be even potential moral agents.

It may of course be denied that we have duties to animals. The view held by some writers is that we have duties concerning animals but not to them, the theory being that we have a duty to behave humanely to our fellow men, and that we should behave humanely to animals simply for fear of creating a disposition in ourselves which will make us tend to be cruel to our fellow men. Professor D. G. Ritchie, for instance, implies that we have not a duty to animals except in a sense like that in which the owner of an historic house may be said to have a duty to the house.[1] Now the latter sense is, I suppose, purely metaphorical. We may in a fanciful mood think of a noble house as if it were a conscious being having feelings which we are bound to respect. But we do not really think that it has them. I suppose that the duty of the owner of an historic house is essentially a duty to his contemporaries and to posterity; and he may also think it is a duty to his ancestors. On the other hand, if we think we ought to behave in a certain way to animals, it is out of consideration primarily for *their* feelings that we think we ought to behave so; we do not think of them merely as a practising-ground for virtue. It is because we think their pain a bad thing that we think we should not gratuitously cause it. And I suppose that to say we have a duty to so-and-so is the same thing as to say that we have a duty, grounded on facts relating to them, to behave in a certain way towards them.

Now if we have a duty to animals, and they have not a duty to us (which seems clear, since they are not moral agents), the first and last of our four propositions cannot both be true, since (4) implies that a duty of men to animals involves a right of men against animals, and (1) implies that this involves a duty of animals to men, and therefore (4) and (1) together imply that a duty of men to animals involves a duty of animals to men. And since the first proposition is clearly true, the fourth must be false; it cannot be true that a duty of A to B necessarily involves a right of A against B. Similarly, the second and third propositions cannot both be true; for (2) and (3) taken together

[1] *Natural Rights*, 108.

imply that a duty of men to animals involves a duty of animals to men. But here it is not so clear which of the two propositions is true; for it is not clear whether we should say that though we have a duty to animals they have no right against us, or that though they have a right against us they have no duty to us. If we take the first view, we are implying that in order to have rights, just as much as in order to have duties, it is necessary to be a moral agent. If we take the second view, we are implying that while only moral agents have duties, the possession of a nature capable of feeling pleasure and pain is all that is needed in order to have rights. It is not at all clear which is the true view. On the whole, since we mean by a right something that can be justly claimed, we should probably say that animals have not rights, not because the claim to humane treatment would not be just if it were made, but because they cannot make it. But the doubt which we here find about the application of the term 'rights' is characteristic of the term. There are other ways too in which its application is doubtful. Even if we hold that it is our duty not merely to do what is just to others but to promote their welfare beyond what justice requires, it is not at all clear that we should say they have a right to beneficent treatment over and above what is just. We have a tendency to think that not every duty incumbent on one person involves a right in another.

This characteristic of our way of thinking about rights has been fastened upon by theory. Green, for instance, divides the whole region of duty into three parts: (1) moral duties which involve no rights on the other side, (2) obligations involving such rights, both obligations and rights being included in the *jus naturae* and being such as *should* be legally recognized, (3) legal obligations involving legal rights on the other side.[1] He describes the rights in class (2)—what I will for brevity call moral rights—as sharing with legal rights the characteristic of depending for their existence on some form of general recognition. The recognition in the latter case consists in the making of a law; in the former it consists simply in a general state of public opinion. Now it is plainly wrong to describe either

---

[1] *Principles of Political Obligation*, §§ 10, 11.

legal or moral rights as depending for their existence on their recognition, for to recognize a thing (in the sense in which 'recognize' is here used) is to recognize it as existing already. The promulgation of a law is not the recognition of a legal right, but the creation of it, though it may imply the recognition of an already existing moral right. And to make the existence of a *moral* right depend on its being recognized is equally mistaken. It would imply that slaves, for instance, acquired the moral right to be free only at the moment when a majority of mankind, or of some particular community, formed the opinion that they ought to be free, i.e. when the particular person whose conversion to this view changed a minority into a majority changed his mind. Such a view, of course, cannot be consistently maintained, and we find Green implying in successive sections that social recognition is indispensable to the existence of rights,[1] and that the slave has a right to citizenship though this right is not recognized by society.[2] In the latter passage we see the true Green, the passionate lover of liberty, reacting against the theory of the previous page. Some may think that slavery is not wrong; but every one will admit that there are certain forms of treatment of others which are wrong and which the sufferer has the right to have removed, whether this right is recognized by society or not.

There is, however, to be found in Green another view which is less clearly false. According to this, the existence of a right is made to depend not on the recognition of *it* but on the recognition of a power in the person in question to seek an end common to all the citizens of a community.[3] This avoids the patent error of making the existence of a right depend on its being recognized to exist. Yet like the former view it makes a moral right depend not on the nature of a given person and his relations to his fellows, but on what people think about them, i.e. on what a majority of the community think about them. But

[1] 'A claim to which reality is given by social recognition, and thus implicitly a right' (§ 139). Cf. 'This recognition of a power, in some way or other, as that which should be, is always necessary to render it a right' (§ 23). 'Rights are made by recognition. There is no right "but thinking makes it so" ' (§ 136).

[2] § 140 implies that the slave's right to citizenship is founded on his possessing a common human consciousness with the citizens of the state.

[3] Cf. e.g. §§ 25, 26.

though the existence of *legal* rights depends on the degree of enlightenment of the community, the existence of moral rights plainly does not, but on the nature and relations of the persons concerned.

Green's theory seems to have arisen as follows. He starts his historical survey with Hobbes and Spinoza, both of whom identify right with power. A *legal* right *may* be identified with a certain kind of power; it is the power of getting certain things not by one's own brute force but by the aid of the law. Green seems to have tried to get a theory of moral rights by making a similar amendment of the bare identification of right with power; and he accordingly identifies them with the power of getting certain things not by one's own brute force nor by the aid of the law but by the aid of public opinion; instead of saying, what is surely evident, that a moral right is not a power at all. Yet there are elements in his account which point to a truer theory; e.g. 'a "right" is an ideal attribution ("ideal" in the sense of not being sensibly verifiable)'.[1] Now whether a given society recognizes a particular right is, I take it, sensibly verifiable in the sense in which Green here insists that a right is not. What is not sensibly verifiable is whether the society is justified in recognizing the right, and this depends on whether the right is there antecedently to society's recognition of it. Thus the insistence that a right is not sensibly verifiable points to an objective theory of rights; but unfortunately Green follows this clue no farther.

If we eliminate the possibility of holding that animals have rights, by saying that only that which has a moral nature can have a right, our main doubt with regard to the correlation of rights and duties is on the question whether there is a right to beneficence. It is obvious that a man has a right to just treatment, and it is commonly agreed that he has a right to have promises made to him fulfilled; it is less generally agreed that he has a right to beneficent treatment, even when it is admitted that it is our duty to treat him beneficently.

Some would even say that to treat others beneficently is to go beyond our duty. But probably this statement rests on a

[1] § 38.

mere confusion. We usually oppose justice to *benevolence*. But while treating a man justly is commonly understood to mean doing certain things to him (paying our debts to him, and the like), irrespective of the spirit in which we do them, treating him benevolently obviously means doing certain things to him from goodwill. And it is rightly felt that there is a great difference between the two things, and it is found natural to say that the one implies, and the other does not, a right on the other side, and (by some people) even to say that the one is a duty and the other is not. But if we will distinguish between doing what is just and doing it in the spirit of justice, and between doing what is beneficent and doing it in the spirit of beneficence, then (in accordance with the principle that it is always acts, and not acts from a certain motive, that are our duty) it is clear that it is not our duty to act in the spirit of justice, any more than in the spirit of beneficence, and that it *is* our duty to do what is beneficent, as it is our duty to do what is just.

If we are clear on this point, our main objection to saying that the other person has a right to beneficence disappears. I do not say that our whole objection disappears; for there hangs about the notion of a 'right' the notion of its being not only something which one person should in decency respect but also something which the other person can in decency claim, and we feel that there is something indecent in the making of a *claim* to beneficence.

These doubts about the application of the term 'right' appear to spring from the fact that 'right' (the noun) does not stand for a purely moral notion. It began, I suppose, by standing for a legal notion, and its usage has broadened out so as to include certain things that cannot be claimed at law; but its usage has not yet broadened out so much as to become completely correlative to duty. Once we start on the process of broadening it out, however, there seems to be no secure resting-place short of this.

Returning now to the four propositions about the correlativity of duties and rights, it seems that with regard to the second proposition, 'A duty of *B* to *A* implies a right of *A* against *B*' (which has latterly been the subject of our discussion), we should say (1) that this is not true when *A* is not a moral agent, and (2) that it is true when *A* is a moral agent (even if the duty be the duty of beneficent action). And since our only doubt about the third proposition, 'A right of *A* against *B* implies a duty of *A* to *B*', arises from our doubt whether animals have not rights, if we agree that animals have not rights we need not doubt the truth of this proposition. It is this proposition, above all, that has been maintained by those who have insisted on the correlativity of rights and duties; for this was maintained essentially against the belief that men have 'natural rights' in a state of nature in which they have no duties.

A further problem, however, awaits us, viz. whether a failure to do one's duty involves a corresponding loss of right. Or rather, as we have found the meaning of 'rights' more doubtful than that of 'duties', it will be more profitable to omit any reference to rights, and put our question in the form, 'if *A* fails in his duty to *B*, does that put an end to *B*'s duty to *A*?' In some cases we seem to be clear that this is so. If a tradesman sends me goods inferior to those I chose in his shop, I am not morally, any more than legally, bound to pay him the full price; I may return the goods and pay nothing, or (with his consent) keep them and pay a lower price. And in general any duty arising out of a contract is cancelled by non-fulfilment of the corresponding duty on the other side. In other cases we are not so clear. It is not so generally agreed, for instance, that if *A* tells lies to *B*, *B* is justified in telling lies to *A*. Two blacks, we say in such a case, do not make a white. Yet the peculiar stringency of the duty of veracity seems to spring from an implicit understanding that language shall be used to convey the real opinions of the speakers, and it would seem that a failure to carry out the understanding on one side makes it no longer binding on the other; and we should have small patience with an habitual liar who insisted on strict veracity in others. It must be admitted that a man who has deceived me has destroyed what would have been the main reason for its being my duty to tell him the truth. But we should probably hesitate to say that by his breach of the implicit understanding my duty to tell him the truth has been entirely destroyed, as by the tradesman's breach of contract my duty to pay him has been destroyed. Various reasons help to account for this. For one thing, it is likely that by deceiving a liar I may indirectly deceive innocent people; for another, the consequences for my own character are likely to be particularly dangerous. But the main reason probably lies elsewhere. Before the contract was made between my tradesman and me, there was no duty incumbent on me of paying him this sum of money. I had a general duty to promote the good of all men, but there was no obvious reason for supposing that this could be best done by transferring this sum of money to him. But even before the implicit undertaking to tell the truth was established I had a duty not to tell lies, since to tell lies is *prima facie* to do a positive injury to another person. Since this duty does not rest on contract, it is not abolished by the breach of contract, and therefore while a person who has been deceived by another is justified in refusing to answer his questions, he is not justified in telling him lies. Yet that this forms only a small part of the stringency of the duty of truthfulness may be inferred from the leniency with which we should judge deceit, in a case in which no implicit undertaking to tell the truth has been established, e.g. when a civilized man deceives a savage whom he has just met for the first time, or *vice versa*, or when one of two savages belonging to different tribes deceives the other. Deceit is much more venial in such a case, because the offender has no reason to suppose that the other is not deceiving, or going to deceive, *him*.

Taking, then, the obvious division between duties arising out of contract and those that arise otherwise, we must say that while the former are cancelled by breach of the contract on the other side, the latter are not cancelled by the bad behaviour of the other person. It would also seem, from a consideration of our actual moral judgements, that the former type of duty is the more stringent of the two.

Now the distinction between the rights corresponding to duties that arise out of contract, and the rights corresponding to other duties, may be quite suitably expressed as a distinction between contractual and natural rights, and the notion of natural rights as a distinct class may thus be vindicated, if it be cut free from the belief which has been so often bound up with it, that there are rights in a state of nature, i.e. in a state in which there are no duties. Such a belief is made possible for Hobbes only by a complete confusion between rights and powers, amounting to an express identification of the two.

APPENDIX II

PUNISHMENT

In connexion with the discussion of rights it is proper to consider a question which has always interested and usually puzzled moralists, and which forms a crucial example for the testing of moral theories—the question of punishment. A utilitarian theory, whether of the hedonistic or of the 'ideal' kind, if it justifies punishment at all, is bound to justify it solely on the ground of the effects it produces. The suffering of pain by the person who is punished is thought to be in itself a bad thing, and the bringing of this bad thing into the world is held to need justification, and to receive it only from the fact that the effects are likely to be so much better than those that would follow from his non-punishment as to outweigh the evil of his pain. The effects usually pointed to are those of deterrence and of reformation. In principle, then, the punishment of a guilty person is treated by utilitarians as not different in kind from the imposition of inconvenience, say by quarantine regulations, on innocent individuals for the good of the community. Or again, if a state found to be prevalent some injury to itself or to its members that had not been legislated against, and proceeded to punish the offenders, its action would in principle be justified by utilitarians in the same way as its punishment of offenders against the law is justified by them, viz. by the good of the community. No doubt the state would have greater difficulty in justifying its action, for such action would produce bad consequences which the punishment of law-breakers does not. But the difference would be only in degree. Nay more, a govern-

ment which found some offence against the law prevalent, and
in its inability to find the offenders punished innocent people
on the strength of manufactured evidence, would still be able
to justify its action on the same general principle as before.
Plain men, and even perhaps most people who have reflected
on moral questions, are likely to revolt against a theory which
involves such consequences, and to exclaim that there is all the
difference in the world between such action and the punishment of offenders against the law. They feel the injustice of
such action by the state, and are ready to say, in the words
imputed to them by Mr. Bradley: 'Punishment is punishment,
only when it is deserved. We pay the penalty because we owe
it, and for no other reason; and if punishment is inflicted for
any other reason whatever than because it is merited by wrong,
it is a gross immorality, a crying injustice, an abominable crime,
and not what it pretends to be. We may have regard for whatever considerations we please—our own convenience, the good
of society, the benefit of the offender; we are fools, and worse,
if we fail to do so. Having once the right to punish, we may
modify the punishment according to the useful and the pleasant;
but these are external to the matter, they cannot give us a right
to punish, and nothing can do that but criminal desert.' [1]
    There is one form of utilitarian view which differs in an
important respect from that above ascribed to utilitarians.
Professor Moore admits the possibility, which follows from
his doctrine of organic unities, that punishment may not need
to be justified merely by its *after*-effects. He points out [2] that
it may well be the case that though crime is one bad thing and
pain another, the union of the two in the same person may be
a less evil than crime unpunished, and might even be a positive
good. And to this extent, while remaining perfectly consistent
with his own type of utilitarianism, he joins hands with intuitionists, most of whom, at any rate, would probably hold that
the combination of crime and punishment is a lesser evil than
unpunished crime.
    Most intuitionists would perhaps take the view that there is
a fundamental and underivative duty to reward the virtuous

[1] *Ethical Studies*, ed. 2, 26-7.   [2] *Principia Ethica*, 214.

and to punish the vicious. I am inclined to diverge from this view. Two things seem to me to be clear: that we have a *prima facie* duty to do this, and that a state of affairs in which the good are happy and the bad unhappy is better than one in which the good are unhappy and the bad happy. Now if the first of these is an underivative fact, the two facts are logically unconnected. For it can be an underivative fact only if the intuitionist view is true, and if that view is true the superiority of the one state of affairs over the other cannot follow from the duty of producing it, since on the intuitionist view there are duties other than the duty of producing good. But an intuitionist may with propriety perform the reverse derivation; he may derive the *prima facie* duty of reward and punishment from the superiority of the state of affairs produced, since he may—and, as I think, must—admit that if a state of affairs is better than its alternatives there is a *prima facie* duty to produce it if we can. The duty of reward and punishment seems to me to be in this way derivative. It can be subsumed under the duty of producing as much good as we can; though it must be remembered that the good to be produced in this case is very different from the other goods we recognize (say virtue, knowledge, and pleasure), consisting as it does in a certain relative arrangement of virtue, vice, pleasure, and pain.

But if we hold that there is this duty, it must be admitted that it is one which it is very difficult for us to see our way to performing, since we know so little about the degrees of virtue and vice, and of happiness and unhappiness, as they occur in our fellow men. And in particular there are two grave objections to holding that the principle of punishing the vicious, for the sake of doing so, is that on which the state should proceed in its bestowal of punishments.

(1) What we perceive to be good is a condition of things in which the total pleasure enjoyed by each person in his life as a whole is proportional to his virtue similarly taken as a whole. Now it is by no means clear that we should help to bring about this end by punishing particular offences in proportion to their moral badness. Any attempt to bring about such a state of affairs should take account of the whole character of the persons

involved, as manifested in their life taken as a whole, and of the happiness enjoyed by them throughout their life taken as a whole, and it should similarly take account of the virtue taken as a whole, and of the happiness taken as a whole, of each of the other members of the community, and should seek to bring about the required adjustments. In the absence of such a view of the whole facts, the criminals that a retributive theory of state punishment would call on us to punish for the sake of doing so may well be persons who are more sinned against than sinning, and may be, quite apart from our intervention, already enjoying less happiness than a perfectly fair distribution would allow them. The offences which the state legislates against are only a small part of the wrong acts which are being done every day, and a system which punishes not all wrong acts, but only those which have been forbidden by law, and does not attempt to reward all good acts—such an occasional and almost haphazard system of intervention does not hold out any good hope of promoting the perfect proportionment of happiness to virtue. Nor would it be in the least practicable for the state to attempt the thorough review of the merit and the happiness of all its members, which alone would afford a good hope of securing this end.

(2) Even if it were practicable, it is by no means clear that it is the business of the state to aim at this end. Such a view belongs, I think, to an outworn view of the state, one which identifies the state with the whole organization of the community. In contrast to this, we have come to look upon the state as the organization of the community for a particular purpose, that of the protection of the most important rights of individuals, those without which a reasonably secure and comfortable life is impossible; and to leave the promotion of other good ends to the efforts of individuals and of other organizations, such as churches, trade unions, learned and artistic societies, clubs. Now it cannot, I think, be maintained that the apportionment of happiness to merit is one of the essential conditions to the living of a reasonably secure and comfortable life. Life has gone on for centuries being lived with reasonable security and comfort though states have never achieved or

even attempted with any degree of resolution to effect this apportionment. And in fact for the state to make such an attempt would seriously interfere with its discharge of its proper work. Its proper work is that of protecting rights. Now rights are (as we have seen) rights to be treated in certain ways and not to be treated in certain ways from certain motives; what the state has to take account of, therefore, is not morally bad actions, but wrong acts, and it has to take account of them in such a way as to diminish the chance of their repetition. And this attempt would only be interfered with if the state were at the same time trying to effect a proportionment of happiness to moral worth in its members. The latter task, involving as it would a complete review of the merit and happiness of all its members, would involve leaving the punishment for each offence undetermined by law, and to be determined in the light of all the circumstances of each case; and punishment so completely undetermined in advance would be quite ineffective as a protector of rights.

But to hold that the state has no duty of retributive punishment is not necessarily to adopt a utilitarian view of punishment. It seems possible to give an account of the matter which retains elements in punishment other than that of expediency, without asserting that the state has any duty properly defined as the duty of punishing moral guilt. The essential duty of the state is to protect the most fundamental rights of individuals. Now, rights of any human being are correlative to duties incumbent on the owner of rights, or, to put it otherwise, to rights owned by those against whom he has rights; and the main element in any one's right to life or liberty or property is extinguished by his failure to respect the corresponding right in others.[1] There is thus a distinction in kind which we all in fact recognize, but which utilitarianism cannot admit, between the punishment of a person who has invaded the rights of others and the infliction of pain or restraint on one who has not. The state ought, in its effort to maintain the rights of innocent persons, to take what steps are necessary to prevent violations of these rights; and the offender, by violating the life or liberty or property of

[1] Cf. pp. 54-5.

another, has lost his own right to have his life, liberty, or
property respected, so that the state has no *prima facie* duty
to spare him, as it has a *prima facie* duty to spare the innocent.
It is morally at liberty to injure him as he has injured others,
or to inflict any lesser injury on him, or to spare him, exactly as
consideration both of the good of the community and of his
own good requires. If, on the other hand, a man has respected
the rights of others, there is a strong and distinctive objection
to the state's inflicting any penalty on him with a view to the
good of the community or even to his own good. The interests
of the society may sometimes be so deeply involved as to make it
right to punish an innocent man 'that the whole nation perish
not'. But then the *prima facie* duty of consulting the general
interest has proved more obligatory than the perfectly distinct
prima facie duty of respecting the rights of those who have
respected the rights of others.

This is, I believe, how most thoughtful people feel about
the affixing of penalties to the invasion of the rights of others.
They may have lost any sense they or their ancestors had that
the state should inflict retributive punishment for the sake of
doing so, but they feel that there is nevertheless a difference
of kind between the community's right to punish people for
offences against others, and any right it may have to inconvenience or injure innocent people in the public interest. This
arises simply from the fact that the state has a *prima facie* duty
not to do the latter and no such duty not to do the former.

We can, I think, help ourselves towards an understanding of
the problem by distinguishing two stages which are not usually
kept apart in discussions of it. The infliction of punishment by
the state does not, or should not, come like a bolt from the blue.
It is preceded by the making of a law in which a penalty is
affixed to a crime; or by the custom of the community and the
decisions of judges a common law gradually grows up in which
a penalty is so affixed. We must, I think, distinguish this stage,
that of the affixing of the penalty, from that of its infliction, and
we may ask on what principles the state or its officials should act
at each stage.

At the earlier stage a large place must be left for considerations of expediency. We do not claim that laws should be made against all moral offences, or even against all offences by men against their neighbours. Legislators should consider such questions as whether a given law would be enforced if it were made, and whether a certain type of offence is important enough to make it worth while to set the elaborate machinery of the law at work against it, or is better left to be punished by the injured person or by public opinion. But even at this stage there is one respect in which the notion of justice, as something quite distinct from expediency, plays a part in our thoughts about the matter. We feel sure that if a law is framed against a certain type of offence the punishment should be proportional to the offence. However strong the temptation to commit a certain type of offence may be, and however severe the punishment would therefore have to be in order to be a successful deterrent, we feel certain that it is unjust that very severe penalties should be affixed to very slight offences. It is difficult, no doubt, to define the nature of the relation which the punishment should bear to the crime. We do not see any *direct* moral relation to exist between wrong-doing and suffering so that we may say directly, such and such an offence deserves so much suffering, neither more nor less. But we do think that the injury to be inflicted on the offender should be not much greater than that which he has inflicted on another. Ideally, from this point of view, it should be no greater. For he has lost his *prima facie* rights to life, liberty, or property, only in so far as these rested on an explicit or implicit undertaking to respect the corresponding rights in others, and in so far as he has failed to respect those rights. But laws must be stated in general terms, to cover a variety of cases, and they cannot in advance affix punishments which shall never be greater than the injury inflicted by the wrong-doer. We are therefore content with an approximation to what is precisely just. At the same time we recognize that this, while it is a *prima facie* duty, is not the only *prima facie* duty of the legislator; and that, as in the selection of offences to be legislated against, so in the fixing of the penalty, he must consider expediency, and may make the penalty more or less severe as it dictates. His action should, in fact, be guided by regard to the *prima facie* duty of injuring wrong-doers only to the extent that they have injured others, and also to the *prima facie* duty of promoting the general interest. And I think that we quite clearly recognize these as distinct and specifically different elements in the moral situation. To say this is not to adopt a compromise between the intuitionist and the utilitarian view; for it can fairly be claimed that one of the duties we apprehend intuitively is that of promoting the general interest so far as we can.

When the law has been promulgated and an offence against it committed, a new set of considerations emerges. The administrator of the law has not to consider what is the just punishment for the offence, nor what is the expedient punishment, except when the law has allowed a scale of penalties within which he can choose. When that is the case, he has still to have regard to the same considerations as arose at the earlier stage. But that, when the penalty fixed by law is determinate, this and no other should be inflicted, and that, when a scale of penalties is allowed, no penalty above or below the scale should be inflicted, depends on a *prima facie* duty that did not come in at the earlier stage, viz. that of fidelity to promise. Directly, the law is not a promise: it is a threat to the guilty, and a threat is not a promise. The one is an undertaking to do or give to the promisee something mutually understood to be advantageous to him; the other, an announcement of intention to do to him something mutually understood to be disadvantageous to him. Punishment is sometimes justified on the ground that to fail to punish is to break faith with the offender. It is said that he has a right to be punished, and that not to punish him is not to treat him with due respect as a moral agent responsible for his actions, but as if he could not have helped doing them. This is, however, not a point of view likely to be adopted by a criminal who escapes punishment, and seems to be a somewhat artificial way of looking at the matter, and to ignore the difference between a threat and a promise.

But while the law is not a promise to the criminal, it is a promise to the injured person and his friends, and to society.

It promises to the former, in certain cases, compensation, and always the satisfaction of knowing that the offender has not gone scot-free, and it promises to the latter this satisfaction and the degree of protection against further offences which punishment gives. At the same time the whole system of law is a promise to the members of the community that if they do not commit any of the prohibited acts they will not be punished.

Thus to our sense that *prima facie* the state has a right to punish the guilty, over and above the right which it has, in the last resort, of inflicting injury on any of its members when the public interest sufficiently demands it, there is added the sense that promises should *prima facie* be kept; and it is the combination of these considerations that accounts for the moral satisfaction that is felt by the community when the guilty are punished, and the moral indignation that is felt when the guilty are not punished, and still more when the innocent are. There may be cases in which the *prima facie* duty of punishing the guilty, and even that of not punishing the innocent, may have to give way to that of promoting the public interest. But these are not cases of a wider expediency overriding a narrower, but of one *prima facie* duty being more obligatory than two others different in kind from it and from one another.

III

THE MEANING OF 'GOOD'

A STUDY of the meaning of 'good' and of the nature of
goodness should begin by recognizing that there is a wide
diversity of senses in which the word is used. The first distinction, perhaps, to be drawn is that between (*A*) the adjunctive
or attributive use of the word, as when we speak of a good
runner or of a good poem, and (*B*) the predicative use of it, as
when it is said that knowledge is good or that pleasure is good.
It is evident that in ordinary usage the first meaning—that of
'good of its kind'—is much the commoner; it appears also to
be the earlier.[1] Within the attributive use of the word we may
distinguish (1) its application to persons, and (2) its application
to things. In case (1) the root idea expressed by 'good' seems
to be that of success or efficiency. We ascribe to some one a
certain endeavour, and describe him as a good so-and-so if we
think him comparatively successful in this endeavour. It might
be thought that in certain cases (e. g. 'a good singer', 'a good
doctor') another idea is in our minds, viz. that the person in
question ministers to our pleasure, or to our health—in general
to the satisfaction of some desire of ours. But our pleasure or
our health comes in only incidentally in such cases; it comes in
just because the endeavour we are imputing to the person in
question is the endeavour to give us pleasure or to improve
our health. It does not, therefore, it would appear, form part of
the general connotation of 'good' when thus used. We can in
this same sense call a man 'a good liar', not because he contributes to the satisfaction of any of our desires, but because we
think him successful in what he sets out to do.

In case (2) there appear to be various elements included in
what we mean by 'good'. We seem to mean in the first place
(*a*) 'ministering to some particular human interest'. A good
knife is essentially one that can be successfully used for cutting,
a good poem one that arouses aesthetic pleasure in us. But
there is also here (*b*) the notion that the thing in question is one

[1] *N.E.D.*, s.v. 'Good'.

in which the maker of it has successfully achieved his purpose —a notion which might be called the 'passive' counterpart of the notion explained under (1). As a rule both the notions (*a*) and (*b*) appear to be involved in our application of 'good' to anything other than persons; but sometimes the one and sometimes the other predominates. There is, however, (*c*) a third element, less seriously intended, in our application of 'good' to non-persons. When we speak of a good lie or of a good sunset we are half-personalizing lies and sunsets and thinking of this particular lie or sunset as succeeding in that which all lies or sunsets are trying to achieve; i. e. we are, not quite seriously, transferring to non-persons the meaning of 'good' appropriate to persons.

Further, we have to note that 'good' in its application to persons has a special sense in which it stands for moral excellence. This is the case whether we emphasize the adjective or the noun in the phrase 'a good man'. Both 'a *good* man', as opposed to a strong, clever, handsome, &c., man, and 'a good *man*', as opposed to a good poet, plumber, scholar, &c., stand for moral excellence. The tendency to limit 'good' to the meaning 'morally good' seems not to be involved in the original connotation of the word, which is originally expressive of indefinite commendation.[1] The limitation seems to me to have arisen in the following way. Mankind has, in an unsystematic way, reflected a good deal on the question, what things are good in themselves, intrinsically good, and has come to think that certain dispositions (of which the most conspicuous are conscientiousness and benevolence) are the things that are most certainly and in the highest degree good in themselves; and it has tended more and more to adapt the adjunctive use of the word to the predicative use, and apply it *par excellence* to men characterized by such dispositions.

It is to be noted that 'good' in the sense of 'good of its kind' is doubly relative. It is in the first place relative to the kind— to what the kind is aiming at (when the word is applied to

---

[1] Cf. the *N.E.D.*'s primary definition of the word: 'The most general adjective of commendation, implying the existence in a high, or at least satisfactory, degree of characteristic qualities which are either admirable in themselves or useful for some purpose.'

persons) or to the activity which produces the kind or to the interest which the kind subserves (when the word is applied to things). When we call a person or a thing 'a good so-and-so' we do not imply that it is necessarily good in any respect other than that expressed in the noun. What is a good x may be a bad y or z. And 'good of its kind' is relative in a further sense, viz. that it is comparative. We have in mind what we suppose to be a rough average of the excellence of the members of the kind, and we call anything better than this good and anything worse than it bad, not implying that there is any fixed neutral point at which what is good ends and what is bad begins. 'Good' in this usage means 'better than the average' or perhaps 'considerably better than the average', and 'bad' 'worse than the average' or 'considerably worse than the average'. Whether 'good' is used with reference to successful endeavour or to utility, we do not imply, nor usually suppose, that there is a definite line between success and failure, or between utility and inutility, and that the things we call good are in any other than a comparative sense good, or those we call bad in any other than a comparative sense bad.

Finally we may note that 'good' in the sense of 'good of its kind' may be applied not only to an individual which is a good instance of its species, but also to a species which is a good species of its genus. We may say not only 'that is a good sonnet', but 'the sonnet is a good poetical form'.

We may turn now to the predicative use of 'good'. But it must be noted that the grammatical difference is not a sure clue to the difference of usage. Often when we say 'x is good' we mean that it is a good so-and-so, and the universe of discourse makes it clear what noun is to be understood. What I wish to call attention to now is the cases in which there is no such implication, as when it is said that 'courage is good' or 'pleasure is good'. In such a usage, 'good' is not relative in either of the senses just pointed out. We do not mean that courage or pleasure is a successful or useful instance of a species, or species of a genus, nor do we mean that it is merely comparatively good, rising above the average of its kind. In both these respects 'good' in this usage is an absolute term.

Within this usage, however, several varieties have to be distinguished. (1) In the first place, 'good' may here still mean 'useful'. A hedonist may call virtue good, though he means only that it is conducive to pleasure. But while in calling a thing good of its kind (when this refers to usefulness) we mean simply that it conduces to the end things of its kind are meant to conduce to (so that we may call a particular poison gas a good poison gas, whatever we may think of the value of the ends subserved by poison gases), in calling a thing good absolutely (though still in the sense that it is useful) we mean that it is a means to an end which is good; i.e. 'good' in this usage is a complex notion implying both a causal relation between the thing judged good and a certain effect, and the goodness of the effect. Thus this usage points directly to another (2), viz. that in which 'good' means 'intrinsically good'. I use this phrase rather than 'good as an end', because the latter phrase taken strictly would imply that the things referred to are good only when desired, and therefore only when non-existent. But that which is intrinsically good is not good only when it is desired. If it is a thing good to be desired when not yet existent, it is also a thing to be approved when it exists and to be regretted when it has perished, and its goodness is no more closely connected with the first of these attitudes than with the other two. The intrinsically good is best defined as that which is good apart from any of the results it produces.

(3) There is a sense of 'good' which Professor Moore has distinguished from that conveyed by the expression 'intrinsically good', as a narrower sense than this. He points out[1] that hedonistic utilitarianism 'does *not* assert that pleasure is the only thing *intrinsically* good, and pain the only thing *intrinsically* evil. On the contrary, it asserts that any whole which *contains* an excess of pleasure over pain is intrinsically good, no matter how much else it may contain besides; and similarly that any whole which contains an excess of pain over pleasure is intrinsically bad.' What that theory asserts is that pleasure is the only thing 'ultimately good' or 'good for its own sake'. Both 'intrinsically good' and 'ultimately good' imply that the

[1] *Ethics*, 73.

thing in question would be good, even if it existed quite alone.
'We may, in short, divide intrinsically good things into two
classes: namely (1) those which, while as wholes they are intrinsically good, nevertheless contain some parts which are not
intrinsically good; and (2) those which either have no parts at
all, or, if they have any, have none but what are themselves
intrinsically good.' And he uses 'ultimately good' to denote
the second of these classes. 'Good throughout' would express
more obviously the same meaning.

The distinction is an important one. A whole, for instance,
which contains good elements and indifferent ones, but none
that are bad, is good 'apart from its consequences' and 'would
be good even if it existed quite alone', and is thus intrinsically
good, in the sense defined. But if the indifferent elements not
only are themselves indifferent but do not contribute to the
goodness of the whole, the whole is good not for its own sake
but for the sake of its good elements, and is thus not ultimately
good, in the sense defined. It might seem as if the distinction
answered to Aristotle's distinction between that which has a
certain attribute strictly *qua* itself (ᾗ αὐτό), and that which has
it in virtue of an element of itself (κατὰ μέρος); while the
wider distinction between the intrinsically good and the good
as a means answers roughly to Aristotle's wider distinction
between that which has an attribute in virtue of itself and that
which has it in virtue of a concomitant (καθ' αὐτό and κατὰ
συμβεβηκός). But Professor Moore would not accept this
identification, for his well-known doctrine of organic unities
states that elements in themselves indifferent or bad may yet
contribute to the goodness of a whole in which they occur.
Thus a whole containing, say, one good and one indifferent
element may have a goodness greater than that of its good
element, and is then not simply good 'in virtue of a part of
itself', while nevertheless it is not 'ultimately good'.

The importance of this doctrine is difficult to assess; for it
must be admitted that clear instances of 'organic unities' in this
sense are rather hard to discover. At first sight, one would say
that the clearest examples are to be found in the regions of
aesthetic and of economic value. (*a*) In the aesthetic region,

it is a familiar fact that some detail of a poem, say, or of a picture, which if it stood alone would have little or no aesthetic value, yet contributes greatly to the effectiveness of the whole. But if the view to be suggested later[1] is true, that beauty is not a form of intrinsic value, but only the power in an object of evoking something that has value, the aesthetic experience, then a beautiful object is not a case in point since the only value that it or any of its parts has is an instrumental value. (*b*) In the economic region, it is a familiar fact that a pair of boots is worth more than twice as much as a single boot, and an assembled machine much more than the parts when unassembled. But here the values in question are still more obviously instrumental, not intrinsic, and therefore not an illustration of the doctrine.

Professor Moore's examples are not very convincing. Take for instance his first illustration.[2] 'It seems to be true that to be conscious of a beautiful object is a thing of great intrinsic value; whereas the same object, if no one be conscious of it, has certainly comparatively little value, and is commonly held to have none at all. But the consciousness of a beautiful object is certainly a whole of some sort in which we can distinguish as parts the object on the one hand and the being conscious on the other. Now this latter factor occurs as part of a different whole, whenever we are conscious of anything; and it would seem that some of these wholes have at all events very little value, and may even be indifferent or positively bad. Yet we cannot always attribute the slightness of their value to any positive demerit in the object which differentiates them from the consciousness of beauty; the object itself may approach as near as possible to absolute neutrality. Since, therefore, mere consciousness does not always confer great value upon the whole of which it forms a part, even though its object may have no great demerit, we cannot attribute the great superiority of the consciousness of a beautiful thing over the beautiful thing itself to the mere addition of the value of consciousness to that of the beautiful thing. Whatever the intrinsic merit of consciousness may be, it does not give to the whole of which it

---

[1] pp. 127-31.   [2] *Principia Ethica*, 28-9.

forms a part a value proportioned to the sum of its value and that of its object.' This analysis can surely not be accepted. Consciousness, by which I think Professor Moore means apprehension, is a state of a mind, and does not include its object (say, a body) as a part of itself. The only whole which could be said to include consciousness plus its object is the whole (if it can be called a whole) consisting of the object plus the consciousness of it. The true analysis of the consciousness of a beautiful object, it would seem, is not into consciousness plus the beautiful object, but into (*a*) its being an instance of consciousness in general, and (*b*) its being an instance of consciousness of something beautiful. And it seems to owe its whole value to the second of the facts named.

Or again take another of Professor Moore's examples.[1] 'If we compare the value of a certain amount of pleasure, *existing absolutely by itself*, with the value of certain "enjoyments", containing an equal amount of pleasure, it may become apparent that the "enjoyment" is much better than the pleasure, and also, in some cases, much worse. In such a case it is plain that the "enjoyment" does *not* owe its value *solely* to the pleasure it contains, although it might easily have appeared to do so, when we only considered the other constituents of the enjoyment, and seemed to see that, without the pleasure, they would have had no value. It is now apparent, on the contrary, that the whole "enjoyment" owes its value quite equally to the presence of the other constituents, *even though* it may be true that the pleasure is the only constituent having any value by itself.' The situation here is that there are pleasurable states of mind (e. g. enjoyments of beauty) which are judged to have more intrinsic value than equally pleasurable states which were merely pleasurable states could have. And Professor Moore seems willing to admit that the element other than pleasantness in the first kind of states of mind may have no value, or a value less than the excess value of these states over the merely pleasurable ones. If this be so, the case would certainly illustrate the doctrine of organic unities. But it seems at least arguable that the element, other than pleasure, in the complex state—the element

[1] *Principia Ethica*, 188.

of insight, or whatever we may prefer to call it—has great intrinsic value, enough to account entirely for the superior value of the whole in which it is an element. And if so, the case will not illustrate the doctrine of organic unities.

There seems, however, to be at least one case which illustrates the doctrine. Few people would hesitate to say that a state of affairs in which A is good and happy and B bad and unhappy is better than one in which A is good and unhappy and B bad and happy, even if A is equally good in both cases, B equally bad in both cases, A precisely as happy in the first case as B is in the second, and B precisely as unhappy in the first case as A is in the second. The surplus value of the first whole arises not from the value of its elements but from the co-presence of goodness and happiness in one single person, and of badness and unhappiness in another. And it is probable that the principle has other applications, though it is hard to be sure of these in detail.

The importance of the doctrine so far as its application goes is somewhat doubtful. But its truth in the abstract seems unquestionable. We have no right to assume that the value of a whole is precisely equal to the sum of the values of its elements taken separately. It may owe some of its value to the co-presence of certain of its elements in certain relations to one another; and this co-presence of its elements cannot fairly be called another element and thus taken to justify us in saying that the value of the whole is the sum of the values of its elements.

In view of his doctrine of organic unities, Professor Moore holds that there is yet another sense of good, (4), that must be recognized. 'When we say that a thing is "good" we may mean either (1) that it is intrinsically good or (2)[1] that it adds to the value of many intrinsically good wholes or (3) that it is useful or has good effects.'[2] The second of these three meanings is properly distinguished both from the meaning 'intrinsically good' and from the meaning 'instrumentally good', and might be called 'contributively good'. But it may be doubted if it is a sense in which the word 'good' is often actually used.

----

[1] = Our (4).   [2] *Ethics*, 250.

For when a whole $A+B$ is thought to be intrinsically good, its goodness is usually taken to be either equal to that of one of its elements A, B not being good in any sense (except perhaps the instrumental sense), or if the goodness of the whole is taken to be greater than that of A, an *intrinsic* goodness accounting for the excess goodness of the whole is ascribed to B. In fact, in so far as the clear recognition of the principle of organic unities is novel, this fourth sense of 'good' cannot have been any one of the ordinary *meanings* of good, though many of the things that have been called good may in fact have been good only in this sense.

It is, I think, clear that it is the predicative rather than the attributive senses of 'good' that are most important for philosophy. And of the predicative senses, the first or instrumental is clearly a complex notion including (a) the notion of a causal relation between something and something else, and (b) the notion of the intrinsic goodness of the effect. It contains nothing but these two elements. And of these two, it would be foreign to our purpose to embark upon a discussion of causality. We are left therefore with the notions of the intrinsically good, the ultimately good, and the contributively good. Further, feeling uncertain about the application in fact (though I do not doubt the truth) of the principle of organic unities, I regard the things that are intrinsically but not ultimately good as owing, generally speaking, their value to those elements in them that *are* ultimately good; as being good, in fact, 'in virtue of a part of themselves', the other parts of them being irrelevant to their goodness. In ethics we have to take account of wholes that are intrinsically but not ultimately good. For it is certain that when we act we produce, along with any intrinsically good or bad results that we produce, many others that are neither (e. g. states of bodies). What we have to choose between the production of is not states of affairs all of whose elements are intrinsically good or intrinsically bad, but states of affairs many of whose elements are neither. But these elements will (except in so far as they may be contributively good) afford us no reason for choosing to produce one such whole state rather than another. And similarly in the parts that are intrinsically but not ultimately good, the sub-parts that are not intrinsically good will afford us no reason for trying to produce such parts. What we must concentrate our attention upon is the elements that are ultimately good; the others must be treated as mere inevitable accompaniments of these. The notion of the ultimately good—the notion, that is to say, of that which is good strictly for its own sake and neither for the sake of its results nor for the sake of an element in itself—is thus the central and fundamental one.

But whatever is ultimately good is also intrinsically good, i. e. is good apart from its consequences, or would be good even if it were quite alone. We must make sure therefore that we understand (as well as we can) the nature of intrinsic goodness. And if we can once understand this, there will be little to add about the further feature which distinguishes the ultimately from the merely intrinsically good. We have simply to add that the ultimately good as distinct from the merely intrinsically good contains no element that is not intrinsically good.

IV

THE NATURE OF GOODNESS

IT is round the question of the intrinsically good that the chief controversies about the nature of goodness or of value revolve. For most theories of value may be divided into those which treat it as a quality and those which treat it as a relation between that which has value and something else—which is usually but not always said to be some state of a mind, such as that of being pleased by the object or desiring it or approving of it or finding its desire satisfied by it. And it seems clear that any view which treats goodness as a relation between that which is good and something else denies that anything is intrinsically good, since by calling a thing intrinsically good we mean that it would be good even if nothing else existed. One of the advocates of a relational view of value, Professor Perry, seeks to maintain that a relational view does not involve the denial of intrinsic value, which he evidently thinks would be a consequence hostile if not fatal to his view. 'A . . . serious objection' to his theory, he says,[1] 'is based upon the nature of *intrinsic* value. We judge a thing to be intrinsically good "where we judge, concerning a particular state of things, that it would be worth while—would be 'a good thing'—that that state of things should exist, *even if nothing else were to exist besides*, either at the same time or afterwards".'[2] If a thing derives value from its relation to an interest taken in it, it would seem impossible that anything whatsoever should possess value in itself. But in that case value would seem always to be borrowed, and never owned; value would shine by a reflected glory having no original source.

'The question', he continues, 'turns upon the fact that any predicate may be judged synthetically or analytically. Suppose that "good" were to be regarded as a simple quality like yellow. It would then be possible to judge either synthetically, that the primrose was fair or yellow; or, analytically, that the fair,

---

[1] *A General Theory of Value*, 132.   [2] G. E. Moore, *Ethics*, 162.

yellow primrose was fair or yellow. Only the fair, yellow primrose would be fair and yellow "even if nothing were to exist besides". But the logic of the situation is not in the least altered if a relational predicate is substituted for a simple quality; indeed it is quite possible to regard a quality as a monadic (a single term) relation. Tangential, for example, is a relational predicate; since a line is a tangent only by virtue of the peculiar relation of single-point contact with another line or surface. Let R^t represent this peculiar relation, and A, B, two lines. One can then judge either synthetically, that $(A)\ R^t(B)$; or, analytically, that $(A)\ R^t\ (B)$ is R^t. Similarly, let S represent an interested subject, O an object, and R^i the peculiar relation of interest taken and received. We can then judge either synthetically, that $(O)\ R^i\ (S)$; or, analytically, that $(O)\ R^i\ (S)$ is R^i. In other words, one can say either that O is desired by S, or that O-desired-by-S is a case of the general character "desired".'

I assume, as it seems necessary to assume in order to make the example relevant, that 'fair' here = 'beautiful', and that beauty is taken as a species of goodness. Professor Perry is evidently taking 'yellow' to be a simple, non-relational quality, and holding 'good' to be a relational one, viz. = 'object of interest to some one' (loosely represented by 'desired-by-S'). I am in doubt about the meaning of 'only' in the sentence 'Only the fair, yellow primrose would be fair and yellow "even if nothing were to exist besides".' (1) 'Only' may mean 'yet'. If so, Professor Perry is admitting that the fair yellow primrose would be yellow, and would be beautiful if beauty were a non-relational quality, even if there were nothing else in the world. And if this be so, that constitutes a vital difference between such attributes, which would attach to their subject even if there were nothing else in the world, and attributes such as 'desired-by-S', which certainly would not attach to O unless S existed as well. (2) More probably, I think, 'only' means 'alone'; i. e. Professor Perry is saying that in contrast with the fair yellow primrose, the *primrose* would not be fair and yellow if nothing else were to exist, just as O would not be desired by S if S did not exist as well as O.

Now it is true that the primrose could not be fair or yellow if nothing but it existed. It could not be fair if its fairness did not exist, nor yellow if its yellowness did not. But it is equally true that the *fair yellow primrose* (which Professor Perry contrasts with the *primrose* in this respect) could not be fair or yellow if its fairness or its yellowness did not exist; and its fairness and its yellowness are quite as different from the fair yellow primrose as they are from the primrose, so that there is no difference between the primrose and the fair yellow primrose in this respect. But if yellowness, or fairness, is a non-relational quality of the primrose, the primrose might be yellow or fair though nothing but the primrose *and its attribute* of being yellow or fair existed. On the other hand, if goodness is a relational quality (say = object of interest to some one), nothing could be good unless, besides it and its attribute of 'being an object of interest to some one', something else existed, viz. a person to whom it is an object of interest. The essential difference would remain, that non-relational attributes can be possessed by subjects though nothing but the subjects and the attributes exist; while relational attributes can be possessed by subjects only if something besides both the subjects and the attributes exists, viz. the things that form the other terms of the relations. Thus if the definition of an intrinsic attribute as one which its subject would possess if nothing other than the subject existed, be amended into the form 'an intrinsic attribute is one which the subject would possess even if nothing but the subject and the attribute existed', it is evident that non-relational attributes are intrinsic and that relational attributes cannot be so. If 'good', then, be defined as Professor Perry defines it, nothing can be intrinsically good. And his attempt to get over the difficulty of the apparent necessity (for a relational view of value) of denying that anything has intrinsic value, by means of the distinction between analytic and synthetic judgements, comes to nothing. 'O-desired-by-S' is not a different object which can truly be said to possess intrinsic value when it is denied that any O apart from being desired has intrinsic value. 'O-desired-by-S is good' is simply another way of saying 'any O has value not in itself but by virtue of the co-existence with it, and in a certain relation to it, of S'. And to say this is to deny intrinsic value to anything. And similarly any other view which identifies goodness with or makes it depend upon a relation between that which is good and something else, denies the existence of intrinsic value.

The theories which identify goodness with some relation are bound to think of this either (I) as a relation between that which is good and some or all of its elements, *or* (II) as a relation between some or all of its elements, *or* (III) as a relation between it or some or all of its elements and something else.

Out of the many theories about the nature of goodness, I am unable to think of any which belongs to type (I), and this type need not, perhaps, be examined. There have been theories of type (II), viz. those that identify the good with the harmonious or coherent. With reference to any such view, the question must first be asked whether it is meant (*a*) that goodness just is coherence, or (*b*) that what is good is good because it is coherent. Only the first of these views is strictly relevant here, where we are inquiring what goodness *is*. The second view does not answer this question; it leaves still open the question what is the nature of the attribute goodness which coherent things are said to have because they are coherent. Now the first view seems to be clearly false. It is surely clear that, however close a connexion there may be between coherence and goodness, we never *mean*, when we call a thing good, that it is coherent. If this were what we meant, 'the coherent, and only the coherent, is good' would be a mere tautology, since it would be equivalent to 'the coherent, and only the coherent, is coherent'; but it is evidently not a mere tautology, but a proposition which if true is very important. The theory then, if it is to have any plausibility, must be understood in the second form; and in this form it is no answer to the question we are asking, what is goodness.

It may be well, however, to offer some comments on the theory in its second form, even if this is not strictly relevant to the present stage of our inquiry. In the first place it may be remarked that any such theory seems to start with the presumption that there is some single attribute, other than goodness,

that makes all good things good, and that the only question is
what this attribute is. Now I agree that goodness is a consequential attribute; that anything that is good must be good
either by virtue of its whole nature apart from its goodness, or
by virtue of something in its nature other than goodness. This
seems to me a very important fact about goodness, and one
that marks it off from most other attributes.[1] But I cannot
agree that the presumption is that there is any *one* characteristic
by virtue of which all the things that are good are good. If
conscientiousness and benevolence, for instance, are both good,
it is just as likely, initially, that conscientiousness is good
because it is conscientiousness, and benevolence good because
it is benevolence. Still, this must not be assumed to be the case,
any more than the opposite view must be assumed. We must
be prepared to consider on its merits any suggested general
ground of goodness. But when I ask myself whether conscientiousness, or benevolence, for instance, can be held to be good
by virtue of the coherence of its elements, I have to ask what
the supposed elements are, and in what respect they are supposed to cohere, and to these questions I find no clear answer
given by those who hold the theory. It would be more plausible
(though not, I think, true) to say that the goodness of conscientious or benevolent action depends on its coherence with
something outside it, e. g. with the whole system of purposes of
the agent, or of the society he lives in. But such a theory would
belong not to type (II), which we are examining, but to type
(III). Or again, suppose that one judges a particular pleasure
to be good, is it not clear that even if most and possibly all
pleasures are complex, it is not on account of its being a complex united by the relation of coherence, but on account of its
having the felt character of pleasantness, that it is judged to be
good?

When we turn to type (III), we find that the relation which
is identified with goodness (or else held to be what makes good
things good) is sometimes held to be necessarily a relation to a
mind, while sometimes this limitation is not imposed. I take
as a typical view of the latter kind one of which I owe my

[1] Cf. pp. 121-2.

knowledge to an article by Professor Urban.[1] Professor Sheldon, as reported by Professor Urban, holds that value is 'fulfilment of any tendency whatever'. The essential objection to
this theory seems to me to be this. Empty 'tendency' of any
reference to the aims of conscious beings (which it is the special
point of this theory to do), and what meaning is left for 'fulfilment of any tendency'? What is left is the notion of a thing's
being under the influence of a certain force, and of its actually
passing into the state it would pass into if acted on by that force
alone. And who will say that this purely physical circumstance
is either identical or even coextensive with value?

To this Professor Sheldon (as reported by Professor Urban)
answers: 'Good is no doubt a different notion from fulfilment,
and therefore appears to contain something not authorized in
the content of the latter notion. But that is because good or
value is the relation between the fulfilment (or furthering) and
the tendency, a relation uniquely and sufficiently determined
by the two.'[2] To this it seems to me enough to reply that this
relation can exist, as much as anywhere else, in the case of
bodies acted on by physical forces, where no one would dream
of applying the notion of good or value. If we *must* have a
relational theory of value, there seems to be much more plausibility in the 'psychological' than in the 'ontological' form of
the theory.

The 'psychological' theories as a rule take the form of holding that a thing's being good means either (*A*) that some person
or persons have some feeling towards it, or (*B*) that some person or persons think it to be good; and such views, or rather
those of the first type, have some initial attractiveness. (*A*) Our
judgements that certain things are good are in fact constantly
accompanied by feelings towards them—feelings of pleasure,
and of regret for their absence; and this fact is apt to lead to one
or other of two views, or more often perhaps to a mixture of
the two. One view is that by being objects of some such feeling
(let us say, adopting Professor Perry's comprehensive phrase,
by being 'objects of interest') things acquire a further character,
that of value. The other is that to have value is just to be an

---

object of interest, and nothing more. I am rather in doubt how to classify the view put forward in *A General Theory of Value* by Professor Perry himself. Passages could be found in his book to support the interpretation of him as holding the first view; e. g. those in which value is described as *dependent* on interest. But on the whole it seems pretty clear that it is the second view he wishes to maintain. 'The view', he says,[1] 'may otherwise be formulated in the equation: x is valuable $=$ interest is taken in x'; and immediately after, 'Value is thus a specific relation into which things possessing any ontological status whatsoever, whether real or imaginary, may enter with interested subjects' —i. e. the relation of being objects of interest to them. Again,[2] 'Thus the question' (the question to which he provides an answer) 'is the question, In what consists' (*not*, On what depends) 'value in the generic sense?'

If the *first* interpretation be the true one, there remain difficult questions to which he provides no answer. If value is something not consisting in, but depending on, being an object of interest, what is value itself, and what is the nature of the relation vaguely described as dependence? Is the relation a causal one, or a logical one, and if neither of these, what is it? To these no answer is suggested. But these questions need not be pressed, for I fancy that Professor Perry would accept the *second* interpretation as the true account of his view.

On this second interpretation, the theory is that 'good' and 'object of interest' are just different ways of expressing exactly the same notion. But it is surely clear that this is not true. It is surely clear that when we call something good we are thinking of it as possessing in itself a certain attribute and are not thinking of it as necessarily having an interest taken in it. If when we attend to something we are impelled to describe it as good, it is surely not impossible to think that, though of course we can only discover its goodness by attending to it, it had its goodness before we attended to it and would have had it if we had not attended to it. And again it is evidently possible to think that some of the things in which an interest has been taken have nevertheless been bad. But if 'good' and 'object of

---

[1] *A General Theory of Value*, 116.   [2] Ib. 118.

interest' meant exactly the same, it would be impossible to think either of these two things which it clearly is possible to think. The view, therefore, that 'good' and 'object of interest' stand for the same notion must be given up. What the relational theory must maintain, if it is to be plausible, must be something different; it must be that whereas most people think that certain things have a characteristic, goodness, distinct from that of being objects of interest, nothing has any such characteristic. And then the question arises, what could have led mankind to form this quite superfluous notion to which nothing in reality corresponds? It is not as if the notion of goodness were a complex notion formed, like such notions as that of 'centaur', by a play of fancy in which characteristics found separate in reality are imagined to coexist; for there are no characteristics of which 'good' can be said to be a compound. We may, however, not merely ask how the notion could have come into being if it were not the apprehension of a reality.[1] We may claim that we are directly aware that conscientious action, for example, has a value of its own, not identical with or even dependent upon our or any one else's taking an interest in it. Our reason informs us of this as surely as it informs us of anything, and to distrust reason here is in principle to distrust its power of ever knowing reality.

Another fatal objection to any theory which identifies good with being an object of interest, or of any particular type of feeling, becomes apparent when we ask by whom the interest or the feeling is supposed to be felt. Some answers escape some objections and others escape others, but each possible answer is exposed to at least one fatal objection of its own. This ground has been very fully covered by Professor Moore in an examination of the corresponding theories about 'right',[2] and both in the case of 'right' and in the case of 'good' his line of argument seems to me unanswerable. Theories of this type are divisible into those which identify goodness with the presence of some feeling (1) in at least one person, no matter who he is, (2) in the person who judges an object to be good, (3) in a majority

---

[1] Cf. Cook Wilson's argument against the possibility of a fictitious 'simple idea', *Statement and Inference*, ii. 511–21.   [2] *Ethics*, chs. 3 and 4.

of persons of some class or other—say persons belonging to a particular stage in the history of civilization, (4) in a majority of mankind, or (5) in all mankind. To (1) there seem to be four objections. (*a*) It surely can hardly be denied that, whatever feeling we select as the feeling involved—whether for instance this be taken to be pleasure, or approval—a man may doubt whether a certain thing is good, even when he does not doubt that some one or other has had such a feeling towards it. (*b*) If what I mean when I call something good is that some one or other has a certain feeling towards it, and if what any other person means when he calls it bad is that some one or other has an opposite feeling towards it, we should not be at variance, because both propositions might be true. Yet if anything is clear, it is that we do suppose ourselves to be making incompatible statements about the object. (*c*) If something, without changing its nature, at some moment aroused for the first time the feeling in question in some mind, we should clearly judge not that the object had then first become good, but that its goodness had then first been apprehended. And (*d*) it might be enough to ask whether any one finds it even possible to think that goodness could be brought into being by the feeling of *some one or other*, no matter how vicious or stupid or ignorant he might be. It seems clear that by goodness we mean something at any rate more objective than that.

To the theory in form (2) the primary objection is identical with objection (*b*) above. If all I mean by saying that an object is good were that it arouses a certain feeling in me, and all you mean by saying that it is not good, or is bad, were that it does not arouse that feeling, or arouses an opposite feeling, in you, we should not be at variance, for we might both be right. And objection (*c*) applies with just as much force to this theory as to the previous one.

To the theory in form (3) it may be objected (*a*) that it will follow that two people who claim to be representing the feelings of majorities of different sets of persons will never be at variance if they pronounce the same thing respectively good and bad. Yet it is clear that even when two men belong to different sets of persons, the feelings of a majority of which they would on this view be claiming to represent, they believe themselves to be making incompatible statements when they call something respectively good and bad. Clearly therefore what they claim to be expressing is not the feelings of different majorities. But further (*b*) it is surely plain that there are cases in which a man thinks something good, without thinking that there is a majority of any class of men who have a certain feeling towards it. Even if we think that a majority of persons at our own stage of civilization, for instance, would have feelings like ours if they attended to the object, we may feel sure that they have not attended to it and therefore have not the feeling in question towards it.

The theory in form (4) is not open to the *first* objection made to the previous theory. For any one who thought that a majority of mankind had a certain feeling towards an object *would* be at variance with any one who thought that they had not this feeling, or had an opposite feeling. But objection (*b*) to theory (3) applies with redoubled force to theory (4).

And finally, to theory (5) it applies with even greater force.

(*B*) The second and remaining type of what I may call purely subjective theories of good is that which holds that for me to think an object good is to think that (1) some one or other, or (2) I, or (3) a majority of some set of men, or (4) a majority of mankind, or (5) all mankind, *think* it good. It is unnecessary and would be tedious to examine these theories as fully as we have examined those of type (*A*). It is enough to point out that corresponding objections are equally fatal to them, and to add a new objection fatal to all theories of type (*B*).

The objections to *A* 1 apply equally to *B* 1
  ,,   ,,   ,, *A* 2   ,,   ,,   ,, *B* 2
  ,,   ,,   ,, *A* 3   ,,   ,,   ,, *B* 3
  ,,   ,,   ,, *A* 4   ,,   ,,   ,, *B* 4
  ,,   ,,   ,, *A* 5   ,,   ,,   ,, *B* 5

But apart from these objections to special forms of theory (*B*), the whole theory has one absurdity common to all its forms. It is perfectly evident that the meaning of '*X* is good' cannot be identical with the meaning of 'some one (or I, or a majority of some class of men, &c.) thinks that X is good', since it *is* identical with the meaning of only one element in the latter phrase. Or, to put the same objection otherwise, to say that S thinks X good leaves it an open question whether X *is* good. For opinion has the characteristic, which feeling has not, of being either true or false. If S thinks falsely that X is good, then X is not good; and if S thinks truly that X is good, then X's being good is neither identical with nor dependent on S's thinking it good. In fact, while theory (A) deserves the most serious consideration, and it is excessively hard to be sure whether one is right in rejecting it or may not have been guilty of some logical confusion, theory (B) may be rejected out of hand. Professor Perry, as one might expect, repudiates it with vigour.

I turn to a reconsideration of theory (A) in the light of Professor Perry's discussion. He divides all possible theories of value into four types, according to the view they take of the relation of value to interest, interest being identified 'with the motive-affective life; that is to say, with instinct, desire, feeling; these, and all their family of states, acts, and attitudes'.[1] 'There are four possible relations of value to interest. In the first place, value may be, in its essential nature, quite irrelevant to interest. . . . In the second place, value may be held to be the character of an object which qualifies it to be an end; in other words, that which implies, evokes or regulates interest. . . In the third place, value may be assigned to the objects of certain duly qualified interests, such as the final, harmonious, absolute, or imperative interest. Finally, there is the simpler and more comprehensive view, that value in the generic sense attaches promiscuously to all objects of all interest.'[2]
I am not specially concerned with the two intermediate views, and agree with many of Professor Perry's criticisms of them. I am mainly interested in the first, which I believe to be true,[3] and in the fourth, which he believes to be true. He takes as a typical expression of the first view Professor Moore's

[1] *A General Theory of Value*, 27.   [2] Ib.
[3] I think, of course, that a thing may arouse interest, and will arouse it in a well-constituted mind, *because of* its goodness. What I wish to deny is that its goodness either is or depends on its arousing interest.

remark 'my point is that "good" is a simple notion, just as
"yellow" is a simple notion; that, just as you cannot, by any
manner of means, explain to any one who does not already
know it, what yellow is, so you cannot explain what good is';
and he treats this view as being best 'understood as an extension
of that pan-objectivism which, having concluded that the so-
called "secondary qualities", such as colour, have as good a
title to extra-mental existence as the so-called primary qualities,
such as figure, sees no reason why the so-called "tertiary"
qualities, such as good, should not be assigned the same
status'.[1]

There may be in some minds a connexion between a realistic
view of the secondary qualities and an objective view of goodness, but it should be pointed out that there is no necessary
connexion between the two views. For my own part, reflection
on the facts of perception and of its illusions forces me to think
that there is no such thing as objective colour, for example;
I am driven to suppose that colour-sensation is a mental state
which is not perception of colour. But colour-sensation[2] is an
indubitable fact, and I can with a certain modification accept
Professor Moore's comparison. I can say that goodness is a
quality which can no more be defined in terms of anything
other than itself, than can the quality of the sensation which we
describe as being one of 'seeing yellow'. Whatever we may
think about the objectivity of colour, there can, I imagine, be
no doubt of the indefinability of the character of our sensation.
Thus the adoption of this comparison is in no way bound up
with an objective view of secondary qualities. Nor, again, do
I think of goodness as 'extra-mental'; for while I do not think
it is essentially for minds, I think it is essentially a quality of
states of mind.

Professor Perry's first criticism of the objective view of good
is that 'one who upholds this view of good must be prepared
to point to a distinct *quale* which appears in that region which
our value terms roughly indicate, and which is different from

---

[1] *A General Theory of Value*, 29.
[2] i. e. the experience which we habitually, whether rightly or (as I suggest) wrongly,
describe as that of seeing colour.

the object's shape and size, from the inter-relation of its parts, from its relation to other objects, or to a subject; and from all the other factors which belong to the same context, but are designated by words other than "good". The present writer, for one, finds no such residuum.'[1] The existence of such a residuum is just the point at issue. So far we have only the word of those who agree with Professor Moore that they do discern in certain things a unique quality which can only be expressed by the term 'goodness' or some synonym of 'goodness', and the word of those who agree with Professor Perry that they do not; and so long as the question is considered on these lines, all that we can do is to invite others to contemplate, for instance, conscientious action, and try for themselves whether they do or do not discern such a quality in it. But Professor Perry is, of course, not content with his *ipse dixit*. He argues that if goodness were an indefinable quality like yellowness its presence, when it is present, should be equally self-evident; and he points to the hesitancy of Professor Moore's report as to what things are good, as showing that the presence of goodness is *not* equally self-evident with that of yellowness. Here he seems to be stressing too much the analogy which Professor Moore has alleged to exist between goodness and yellowness. The analogy exists only in respect of the indefinability of both. It is not argued that in other respects the two qualities are on all fours. In particular, the one is apprehended (if apprehended at all)[2] by sense-perception, the other by intelligence; and there is no reason to anticipate that what is discerned by the intelligence should be as easily discerned as what is discerned by sense-perception. But Professor Perry exaggerates the difference between the ease of discernment in the two cases. There is, he says, 'no serious difference of opinion as to the distribution of terms connoting empirical qualities. "Things wear them in public, and any passer-by may note them." '[3] But does not yellow merge into green, and into orange, and are there not

---

[1] *A General Theory of Value*, 30.
[2] This caution seems necessary in view of the doubt I have expressed on p. 86 as to whether colour is something apprehended at all. The sentence in the text *without* the parenthesis would state the defence which I believe Professor Moore would make of his view.   [3] *A General Theory of Value*, 30.

border-line cases in which it is extremely difficult to say whether what we have before us is yellow or green, or whether it is yellow or orange? And if there are things about whose goodness there is room for difference of opinion, are there not other things, such as conscientious action, whose goodness is matter of general agreement?

But I should not like to rest the case for the indefinability of goodness merely on this *argumentum ad hominem*. It seems to me more important to point out that the question whether the presence of a given quality in some particular thing is easily discerned has nothing to do with the question whether the quality is indefinable. If two people differ, for instance, as to whether a particular action is good, their differing implies, no less than their agreeing would have done, that they mean by 'goodness' a definite quality; and their mere differing does not imply that that quality is *not* indefinable any more than their agreement would imply that it *is*. The questions of its definability and of its discernibility are different and not logically connected.

But if I attempt to vindicate Professor Moore's comparison of goodness with yellowness as being like it an indefinable quality, I do not wish (any more than I imagine he would) to be thought to suppose that it is a quality in other respects like yellowness. The most salient difference is that it is a quality which anything that has it can have only in virtue of having some other characteristic; as e. g. a conscientious act is good in virtue of being conscientious. This I express later by describing it as a consequential and not a fundamental quality.[1]

Professor Perry turns next to mention Professor Laird's presentment of the objective view. Professor Laird, he says, 'appeals to the fact that there is an immediate objectivity in the appreciation of beauty, or in the admiration of conduct. These are not mere subjective states *caused* by an object; they *present* the object, clothed in its quality of charm or moral worth.'[2] Professor Perry points out that there are many adjectives which we apply to objects, and which therefore *prima facie* might appear to stand for qualities of objects apart from any relation

[1] Cf. pp. 121-2.   [2] *A General Theory of Value*, 31.

to persons, but which on examination turn out to refer simply to the existence of some such relation,—adjectives like 'coveted', 'boresome', 'tiresome', 'hopeful'; and that on the other hand adjectives like 'red' resist all attempts to localize them in the subject and insist on being localized in the object. But it is surely unfair to argue from words like 'coveted', 'boresome', 'tiresome', 'hopeful', which by their very formation point to a relation between a subject and an object, and the word 'good', which equally clearly points to nothing of the kind but to a quality resident in the object itself, independent of any subject's reaction to the object. As regards 'beautiful' I am, as I shall point out later,[1] inclined to agree that the fact that lies at the back of our predications of it *is* simply the power something has of producing a certain kind of emotion in us; and the frequent use of such words as 'charming', 'delightful', almost as synonyms of 'beautiful' may be held to lend this view some support. But it is surely a strange reversal of the natural order of thought to say that our admiring an action either is, or is what necessitates, its being good. We think of its goodness as what we admire in it, and as something it would have even if no one admired it, something that it has in itself. We could suppose, for instance, an action of self-denial which neither the doer nor any one else had ever admired. If now some one were to become aware of it and admire it, he would surely pronounce that it had been good even when no one had been admiring it.

Professor Perry makes the further objection that the 'objective' theory derives all its plausibility from its exponents' being preoccupied with 'the aesthetic and contemplative values', and that it precludes them from giving a comprehensive account of all values. 'The most serious defect of this type of theory is its failure to provide any systematic principle whatsoever. There are as many indefinable values as there are feeling attitudes, and since these are to be regarded as objective qualities rather than as modes of feeling, there is nothing to unite them, not even the principle of feeling. If "good" is a unique quality, then so are "pleasant", "bad", and "ought". There is no way of subsuming pleasant under good, or of defining the opposi-

---

[1] pp. 127–30.

tion of good and bad, or of subsuming both good and ought
under a more general category such as value. If, on the other
hand, value is defined in terms of interest, then the variability
of interest seems to account for both the unity and the diversity
of values.'[1] His assumption, then, is that there must be some
single sense of 'valuable' in which the word is always used,
and his contention is that a subjective theory alone will serve
to assign such a single meaning and to show the relations
between the various specific kinds of value. And under the
heading of 'valuable' he includes both things which would not
naturally be described as being valuable at all, and things which
we can surely recognize to have value only in fundamentally
different senses. Does any one really think that obligatoriness
is a special form of being valuable?[2] Is it not a hasty assumption to assume that it is an instance of the same kind of thing
of which moral goodness or beauty is another instance? And
is it not clear that what we call economic values[3] are merely
instrumental values, different in kind from the goodness of
virtue or of pleasure? The assumption that there must be 'a
general theory of value' applicable to value in all the senses of
that word seems to me to be unjustified.

At the same time, I am inclined to agree with Professor Perry
in one of his contentions, though not in what he (if I understand
him aright) seeks to deduce from it. He is seeking to find a
single thread of identity which unites all our *applications* of the
word good, and to infer from this that the word 'good' has the
single *meaning* which he assigns to it. Now when I consider
the variety of meanings of 'good' indicated in the preceding
chapter—the predicative and the attributive use, the meanings 'successful in his endeavour' and 'useful', the instrumental
and the intrinsic sense—though I cannot agree that what we
mean in all or any of these cases by '*X* is good' is '*X* is an object
of interest to some one', I am inclined to think that the only
thread that connects our *application* of the word in all these
senses—i. e. the only common fact that is present whenever we
use the term 'good'—is that in each case the *judger* has some
feeling of approval or interest towards what he calls good. But

---

[1] *A General Theory of Value.* 34.   [2] Ib.   [3] Ib.

this in no way proves that we are always using 'good' in the same *sense*. The *senses* 'intrinsically good' and 'useful' appear to me entirely different, though whether we use the word good in one or the other we have in both cases a feeling of approval or interest towards what we call good. What common thread there is, is one that connects not the various meanings of good, but our use of it in these various meanings. The attempt to find a common thread in our *application* of the term is not what I am chiefly interested in. What I am interested in, and what I cannot but think to be the more important question for philosophy, is whether there is not a sense of good in which it can be applied to things not as meaning that they are successful or useful members of a class, and not as meaning that they are instrumental to a good beyond themselves, but as meaning that they are good in themselves. And it is surely plain that when we state, for instance, that courage is good, this is what we mean— even if some one may maintain that we are mistaken in making this statement. I have tried to do some justice, briefly, to the other senses, in the preceding chapter, and from that point onwards I have been interested solely in this other and more fundamental sense of 'good'. And of this I feel pretty clear, that though our applications of it are always accompanied by an interest in what we thus call good, the existence of that interest is not what we assert when we so describe things.

Professor Perry turns next to consider in detail Professor Moore's argument for the indefinability of 'good'. He quotes the remark 'it would be absolutely meaningless to say that oranges were yellow, unless yellow did in the end mean just "yellow" and nothing else whatever—unless it were absolutely indefinable.' [1] And to this, taken alone, his objection is well founded. 'It is *not* meaningless', he points out, 'to say that "the conception of substance is pre-historic", or that "the painting is post-impressionistic", or that "the argument is circular"; and yet in these cases the assigned predicates are definable.' [2] The statement 'oranges are yellow' certainly is meaningless unless 'yellow' has in this statement a single self-identical meaning. In a sense 'yellow' must mean yellow and nothing

[1] G. E. Moore, *Principia Ethica*, 14.   [2] *A General Theory of Value*, 35.

else whatever. But this does not show it to be indefinable. For if we could correctly define 'yellow' as, say, '*x* which is *y*', we should not be saying that 'yellow' means anything other than 'yellow', for '*x* which is *y*' would be just what yellow is. But, it might be said in support of the view that 'good' is obviously indefinable, there is a great difference between 'good' and such attributes as 'pre-historic', 'post-impressionistic', 'circular'. If a term is definable, i. e. stands for a certain complex,[1] we can use the term intelligently and intelligibly only if we have the definition to some extent before our minds; and we have in fact at least rough definitions of such terms in our minds when we use them. On the other hand, the fact that we use the term 'good' intelligently and intelligibly without having any definition of it in our minds shows that it is indefinable.

Professor Moore uses an argument of somewhat the same type when he argues, against any attempt to define 'good', that given any set of concepts not containing good, it is always possible to inquire whether a thing answering to this set of concepts is good.[2] Suppose some one claims that 'being-desired-by-anybody is being good', this claim is met by the fact that even if we know that war is desired by some people, we may still doubt whether it is good.

Both of these arguments amount, I think, to saying that if 'good' stood for any complex (as on any relational theory it does), we ought, if we use the word intelligently, to have in our minds the notion of a definite relation between definite things. It seems to me clear that we have no such notion in our minds when we use the word in ordinary discourse.

But I cannot be sure that this entirely settles the question. For there seem to be cases in which we seek for the definition of a term and finally accept one as correct. The fact that we accept some definition as correct shows that the term did somehow stand for a complex of elements; yet the fact that we are

---

[1] I should explain that I mean by a complex here a complex of elements co-ordinate in respect of universality, in distinction from another class of terms which *might* be called complex, and which are indefinable, viz. those that involve elements *not* co-ordinate in respect of universality, as 'red' involves both colour and redness. Cf. Cook Wilson, *Statement and Inference*, ii. 502–4.

[2] *Principia Ethica*, 15.

for some time in doubt whether the term is analysable, and if so, what the correct analysis is, shows that this complex of elements was not distinctly present to our mind before, or during, the search for a definition. It appears as if we cannot avoid recognizing that there is such a thing as using a term which implicitly refers to a certain complex, while yet the complex is not explicitly present to our minds. And in principle this might, it seems, be true of 'good'. The absence of an explicit reference to a complex in our ordinary use of the term should therefore not be taken as necessarily implying that the term is indefinable, nor, in particular, as excluding the possibility of its standing for a relation. The method should, I think, rather be that of attending to any proposed definition that seems at all plausible. If it is the correct definition, what should happen is that after a certain amount of attention to it we should be able to say, 'yes, that is what I meant by "good" all along, though I was not clearly conscious till now that it was what I meant'. If on the other hand the result is that we feel clear that 'that was not what I meant by good', the proposed definition must be rejected. If, after we have examined all the definitions that possess any initial plausibility, we have found this negative result in every case, we may feel fairly confident that 'good' is indefinable. And there is no initial presumption that it is definable. For it seems clear that there could be no complex entities unless there were some simple ones; and, in a universe so various as the universe is, there is no reason to suppose that the simple entities are few in number.

In the process of criticizing proposed definitions of a term, there are two moments. Perhaps the most obvious ground for rejection of a definition is that we are able to point to things of which the term is predicable but the definition not, or *vice versa*. And any one will be able without difficulty to think of definitions of 'good' that have been proposed, which come to grief on one or other of these two objections. But even when the denotations of the term and of the definition coincide (or when we cannot be sure that they do not), we can often see that a proposed definition does not express what we *mean* by the term to be defined. It would be on this ground, for example, that we should reject a definition of 'equilateral triangle' as 'triangle with all its angles equal'. And it is on this ground that most of the proposed definitions of 'good' can be rejected —many of the metaphysical definitions, such as those which identify goodness with comprehensiveness or with reality; and many of the psychological definitions, such as those which identify it with being productive of pleasure or with being an object of desire. The point is not that the proposed definition is not seen at first sight to be true, or that it needs inquiry, but that it does not survive inquiry.

Professor Perry's own criticism of Professor Moore takes the following form. Suppose that 'good' be defined as 'desired by some one'. This definition is disproved, says Professor Moore, by the fact that even if war is desired by some one, it is still possible to inquire whether war is good. Professor Perry seems to admit this as fatal to the proposed definition, for he proposes to substitute for it what he evidently thinks of as a different definition, 'good in some sense = desired by some one'. And he endeavours to turn the edge of Professor Moore's objection by saying that the correctness of *this* definition is quite compatible with our still being able to inquire (as we evidently can) whether war, if it is good in this sense, is also good in some other sense, e. g. desired by all men, or obligatory, or beautiful.[1]

This seems to me strangely to miss the point. No one would, I suppose, dream of objecting to the equating of 'good in some sense' with 'desired by some one' on the ground that war though desired by some persons is not desired by every one, or not beautiful, or not obligatory. The objections are (1) that, even though desired by some persons, war is not in any sense good (though there may be elements in it that are good), and (2) that, even if it were in some sense good, what would be *meant* by calling it good is most certainly not that it is desired by some one.

Professor Perry further tries to base an argument for the relativity of good to the interests of individuals, on the fact 'that the question may be submitted once again to each indi-

[1] *A General Theory of Value*, 36–7.

vidual judge'. 'If when a given object *a* is already acknowledged to be good the question of its goodness is nevertheless put to a subject *M*, the question is assumed to refer to the special sense of good which is relative to *M*.'[1] This would surely be a nonsensical procedure. If the goodness of *a* is already 'acknowledged', i. e. admitted by both the persons involved, there is *no* sense in the one asking the other whether the object is good; and anything that the other may say such as 'I desire it' or 'I don't desire it' has *no* relevance to the question whether it is good, which has already *ex hypothesi* been settled in the affirmative.

The advocates of the view he is criticizing are, Professor Perry points out, anxious to secure for 'good' a meaning which shall 'provide judgments of value with a common object which will determine their truth or falsity'. And for this purpose, he insists, 'an interest is as good an object as any other. The fact that *M* takes an interest in *a*, consists in a relation of *a* to *M*; but this fact itself is not relative to *M*'s judgment about it, or to the judgment of any other subject.'[2] There is, in fact, a great difference between a view which makes the goodness of an object depend on a subject's judgement that it is good, and one which makes it depend on his interest in it. The former view is one that will not stand a moment's examination; the latter is one that does provide judgements of value with some reality to judge about, and that therefore requires serious consideration. But while it provides for our judgements of value an object independent of our judgements, it fails to do justice to what is also implied in our judgements of value, that when one person says an object is good and another says it is not, they are contradicting one another. For if *M* only meant 'I take an interest in *a*' and *N* only meant 'I do not', they would *not* be contradicting each other.

Professor Perry sometimes, for brevity, uses as equivalent to 'good' 'enjoyed by a subject', and sometimes 'desired by a subject'. Neither of these phrases does full justice to his theory. His theory is that to be good is to be an object of *interest*, and interest is thought of as covering both desire and enjoyment;

[1] Ib. 37.　　　　　　　　　　[2] Ib. 38.

i. e. the goodness of some things consists in their being enjoyed, that of others in their being desired, and that of others, perhaps, in their being both enjoyed and desired (though this, as we shall see, is impossible). Now so long as we say (as he is apt to say) that 'the goodness of the primrose consists in its being desired',[1] the theory seems at first sight attractive enough. But obviously it is only a rough and ready description of my desire to say I desire a primrose. What I desire is to be seeing it or smelling it or possessing it. As soon as we describe definitely what it is that we desire, we see that it is something which does not yet exist. There are no doubt cases in which we desire to go on doing what we are doing, or being in the same sort of state that we are in. But even if I desire, for instance, to go on looking at a primrose, what I desire is not the looking which is taking place at present, but the looking which I wish to take place in the immediate future. The object of desire is always something non-existent. If it be said that it exists as a possibility, we must reply that that is an inexact way of saying that the possibility of it exists, which means that though it does not exist, the nature of some or all of the things that do exist is not incompatible with its coming into existence.

It is plain that in so far as goodness were either identical with or dependent upon being desired, nothing could both exist and be good. Now I suppose that we are all convinced both that some things that exist now are good, and that things of certain kinds, which may come into existence in the future, will be good if and when they exist; and I suppose that apart from these convictions we should have little or no interest in the topic of 'good', and ethics in particular would go by the board. Yet in so far as the theory identifies the good with the desired, it denies both these convictions. But it might be replied that the goodness of existent things consists in their being enjoyed, and the goodness of non-existent things in their being desired. I must take leave, however, to doubt whether we can say of a non-existent thing that it *is* good. However much one were convinced that conscientiousness, for example, is good, and that *A* might *become* conscientious, no one would say '*A*'s

---

[1] Cf. *A General Theory of Value*, 133.

conscientiousness is good' if he were convinced that A is not in fact conscientious. But, our opponent might reply, we can say of *kinds* of thing that they are good even if we are not convinced that any instances of these kinds exist. We might say 'perfectly conscientious action is good', even if (as Kant suggests) we are not convinced that there has ever been such an action. But that is only a short-hand way of saying that without being sure that such an action ever has existed, we can be sure that *if* any existed it would be good. Hypothetical goodness presupposes hypothetical existence just as actual goodness presupposes actual existence. And if so, being good can never be identical with being desired, or even compatible with it.

The relation in which the primrose stands to desire is not that of being desired but that of exciting desire. This is a relation in which existing things *can* stand to desire, and the theory might be transmuted into the form, 'the good is that which excites desire'. But the excitants of desire fall into two classes. There are things our experience of which is such as to make us desire to remain in our existing relation to them, or to get into some closer relation to them, and to others like them; and there are things our experience of which is such as to make us desire to get away from them. Things of the second class are just as decidedly excitants of some desires as things of the first class are of others. And obviously one main sub-class (if not the whole) of the second class consists of things that cause pain. Thus if 'good' meant 'excitant of desire' we should be led to the conclusion that things that cause pain are, as such, an important class of goods. This conclusion would evidently not be accepted, and therefore the theory would have to be modified into the form 'the good is that which excites the desire to maintain our relations with it, or to get into closer relations with it, and with others of its kind'—what we may, for short, call 'positive desire'.

Now, on the face of it, some of the things that excite positive desire[1] do so because they are judged to be good. *Prima facie* one would say that if the consciousness of a good disposition

---

[1] Desire, of course, not for them to exist but for us to be in some new relation to them or to continue to be in the same relation to them.

in oneself or the contemplation of it in another leads me to wish to maintain and develop that sort of disposition, it is not because I feel it to be pleasant but because I judge it to be good. But this alternative is not open to Professor Perry, for, in basing our taking an interest in the thing on our thinking it good, it would involve the giving up of his main thesis, that a thing's being good either is or is based upon our taking an interest in it. All that is left for him therefore is to identify what is good with that which by virtue of the pleasure it causes excites desire for a closer relation with it and with other things like it. What is good, then, for him is that which excites pleasure and thereby excites such a desire. And though he includes both these elements in his formula, the fact of exciting pleasure is evidently the root fact of which the other is a mere consequence.

Not only, however, is pleasantness the fundamental and tendency to excite desire only a consequential element in goodness, according to the theory in the form in which it seems necessary to restate it, but it is far more plausible to put forward pleasantness, than to put forward this tendency, as the essence of goodness. If we say 'that which produces so-and-so is, as doing so, good', we are evidently implying that what is produced is intrinsically good, and what produces it instrumentally good. And it is plausible enough to say 'pleasure is intrinsically good, and what produces it instrumentally good'; there is a pretty general agreement that pleasure, whether it is the good or not, is at least good. But there is no general agreement that desire, or even positive desire, is good. If we take the moral standpoint we must say that some desires are good and others bad, and that when desires are good they are good not because they are desires but because they are the sort of desires they are. And if we take the hedonistic standpoint, we must say that desires are good or bad (which will mean 'pleasant or unpleasant') not in virtue of being desires but mainly (I suppose) in virtue of their being supposed to be likely or unlikely to be fulfilled. Desire (even positive desire) thus not being a thing necessarily good in itself, there is no reason why, in general, things that excite desire (or positive desire) should be good. So long as we thought of things as objects of desire, it was perhaps not unplausible to say that objects of desire are good even when the desire is not; but if we recast the theory in the form in which we have found it necessary to recast it, and say the good is that which excites positive desire, i. e. which is to it as cause to effect, there is no reason (obvious or alleged) why, positive desires not being always good, their excitants should nevertheless always be so.

The most favourable way, then, of presenting the theory we are examining is to exclude from it the reference to desire and to reduce it to the form 'what is good is that which produces pleasure'.[1] But no one would in fact say that everything which produces pleasure is good unless he thought pleasure itself good;[2] and the theory emerges in the final form 'pleasure, and pleasure alone, is good by its own nature; and what produces pleasure, and only what produces pleasure, is good because it produces something good.' The heart of the theory, then, in spite of all it has said by way of attack on ordinary notions of intrinsic good, is that there is one thing, and one thing only, that is intrinsically good, viz. pleasure. The theory when reduced to its simple terms seems to be our old friend, hedonism. After all the able refutations of hedonism that have been published in recent years, it seems to me unnecessary to tread once more on this rather hackneyed ground, and I suppose that Professor Perry would agree that hedonism is untenable, and claim that his own theory is tenable only in virtue of elements that distinguish it from hedonism. But these elements are, if I am not mistaken, among the least tenable elements in his theory.

There is, however, one more point of view from which the theory may be examined. Professor Perry describes 'the most popular' objection to it as being that 'the fact of desire is not accepted as final in most judgments of value. Objects of desire

---

[1] This is ambiguous, since it may mean ' "good" means "productive of pleasure" ', or 'what is good is good because it produces pleasure'; i.e. the ambiguity involved in the theory from the start (cf. pp. 80–1) still remains.

[2] And inferred from this that what produces it is good. But it is surely plain that it does *not* follow from a thing's being good that what produces it is good, in the same sense of 'good'. It must be admitted that we often call 'good' things that are merely useful, but then 'good' is being used improperly. Where I use the phrase 'instrumentally good', I use it to indicate this common but loose sense of 'good'.

are held to be bad in spite of their being desired, and desires themselves are held to be bad whether or no they are satisfied'.[1] I need not consider (*a*) one form of this objection with which I have no sympathy—the view of Schopenhauer and others that *all* desire is bad; that is an extravagance of quietism for which there is little to be said. (*b*) The first real difficulty to which the theory is exposed is that named next by Professor Perry, viz. the fact that 'the same object may be liked or desired by one man, and disliked or avoided by another'.[2] This fact, taken with the identification of 'good' with 'object of interest', leads to the conclusion that the same thing may be both good and bad. On the face of it, this result is paradoxical, and all but self-contradictory; but he claims that 'a relational definition, such as that here proposed, is the only means of *avoiding* contradiction'.[3] The claim is an odd one: by identifying good with object of interest we get into the paradox of calling the same thing good and bad (a paradox which an absolute theory at least escapes, whatever be its other merits or demerits); and then we triumphantly get out of the difficulty by saying, 'Oh, but good only means good for one person, and bad only means bad for another person, so that there is no paradox.'

Is it not clear that when we assert the goodness of anything we do assert something which we believe to be incompatible with the same thing's being bad? We may describe a thing as 'both good and bad', but such language is not strict. (i) We may mean that the thing contains some elements that are good and some that are bad, but then *that* is the right way of putting the matter, and 'the thing is both good and bad' is only a loose way of putting it. It is implied in our thought on the subject both that if we push our analysis far enough we shall find some elements that are simply good and others that are simply bad, *and* that the whole is not both good and bad but is either on the whole good or on the whole bad. (ii) It may be suggested that, without thinking of a thing as consisting of good and bad elements, we may judge it to be good from one point of view and bad from another—that a state of mind, say, may be morally good and intellectually bad. But this turns out to be reducible

---

[1] *A General Theory of Value*, 134.   [2] Ib. 135.   [3] Ib. 136.

to the former case, in which analysis reveals a good and a bad element. If we take a temporal section of the history of a mind, however short be the section there will be elements in it of knowledge and opinion which have a certain value, and actions or dispositions to act which have a certain value (positive or negative). The whole state of mind, then, cannot be judged from the moral point of view, nor from the intellectual, but some elements in it from the one and some from the other. And each such element will have a goodness that is incompatible with its being bad, or a badness that is incompatible with its being good; and the whole state of mind will have a degree of goodness or *else* a degree of badness, which can be assessed only from a point of view in which we transcend both the moral and the intellectual point of view.

(*c*) 'The case which has most deeply affected popular habits of thought, and which is mainly responsible for the prejudice against the present theory of value', says Professor Perry, 'is the case in which an interest or its object is morally condemned.'[1] It is certainly an obvious objection to the theory that all objects of interest are good, that in point of fact we do judge to be bad many things in which nevertheless some one or other takes or has taken an interest. Professor Perry's answer to this objection is to urge that in such a case we are performing a *moral* judgement, and that 'moral judgments are not concerned with value in the generic sense, but with a specific and complex *aspect* of it. . . . They do not deal with interests *per se*, but with the relation of interests to the complex purposes in which they are incorporated.'[2]

In answer to this it is important to point out that the term 'moral judgement' contains a serious ambiguity. There are three types of judgement which have by various writers been termed moral judgements. These are (i) the judgements in which an act is pronounced to be right or wrong; (ii) the judgements in which an action or disposition is judged to be morally good, or bad, or indifferent, i. e. to have (or fail to have) the kind of goodness or badness that only dispositions and actions can have; (iii) the judgements in which something is said to be

[1] Ib. 136.   [2] Ib. 136-7.

good or bad or indifferent *sans phrase.* The first two may be said to be departmental judgements, in the sense that each of them is applicable only to one class of objects, the first to acts considered apart from their motives, the second to dispositions and actions considered in respect of their motives. Judgements of the third class are not in any way departmental; they may be made about anything in the whole world. It can be said of some things—I suggest, as at any rate an adumbration of the things of which it can be said, virtue, knowledge and well-grounded opinion, and pleasure¹—that they are good; of others—vice, badly grounded opinion, and pain—that they are bad; and of other things that they are indifferent, i. e. considered in themselves, though many of them may be instrumental to good or to evil. In making such judgements we are not adopting a *narrowly* ethical standpoint; we are saying for instance that wisdom and pleasure are good, though they are not morally good. We are taking the most commanding point of view that can be taken with regard to the value of the things in the universe. Yet this is a point of view which a moral philosopher should, in part of his inquiry, adopt, since ethics is the study of that which we ought to do, and of what is involved in its being what we ought to do, and since what we ought to do depends to a large extent (though, as I have urged, not entirely) on the goodness or the badness of the things we can in our acts bring into being.

It would, however, be a mistake to spend time in arguing the question whether the theory of good in general belongs to ethics or to metaphysics. The other two types of judgement belong exclusively to ethics. Goodness in general runs out beyond the strict scope of ethics, if ethics be the philosophical study of good conduct; for some of the things that are good are neither conduct nor dispositions to conduct. But the study of the meaning of good in general, and of the types of thing that are good, is either a part of ethics, or a part of metaphysics to which the study of purely ethical problems inevitably leads us: which it is, depends on how we define ethics and meta-

¹ To avoid making my statement too complicated, I omit a further kind of good which will be mentioned later, cf. p. 138.

physics. Neither ethics nor metaphysics is a study to which definite limits have hitherto been set, or one, probably, to which they can profitably be set. The only way, perhaps, in which we could prescribe a quite rigid programme for metaphysics would be by saying that it is the study of the characteristics possessed in common by everything that is; and from this point of view the theory of goodness would have to be pronounced not to be part of metaphysics. But whether we widen our notion of metaphysics to make it include the theory of all very widely distributed characteristics (among which goodness and badness are included), or treat the study of value as a part of ethics, or recognize an intermediate science of axiology (or theory of value) less wide than metaphysics and wider than ethics, is a question the discussion of which does not lead us any distance at all towards understanding the facts.

We must return, however, to the objection Professor Perry is at the moment considering, and to his answer to it. The objection is that many of the things in which people find pleasure and which they desire are nevertheless bad. His answer is that they are not bad in general but only bad from the ethical standpoint. And our answer to that is that while there is what may be called a narrowly ethical standpoint from which we judge such and such an action to be vicious or morally bad, there is also a more commanding standpoint from which we view the agent's total state of mind at the time and judge that in spite of any elements of pleasure-value it may contain it is on the whole a bad thing, a thing for whose occurrence the world is the worse. This is not the narrowly ethical standpoint, for it is the same standpoint from which we judge that the occurrence of a pain is, considered apart from its accompaniments, a bad thing, though a pain is not morally bad. Now if from this, which is the most commanding standpoint, we say that many states of mind in which their owners have taken interest and found pleasure are nevertheless bad, 'good' cannot be identical with 'object of interest'.

My general conclusion is that Professor Perry's arguments have not succeeded either in refuting the view that goodness is an intrinsic quality of certain things, or in defending from attack the view that it is identical with being an object of interest to some mind.[1]

But the view that goodness is an intrinsic quality is exposed to attack from another quarter. Professor Urban, whose work on the question of values entitles him to the most serious consideration, attacks this view and puts forward another.[2] He considers that there is a certain ambiguity in speaking of value as a quality of objects. 'On the one hand, by value is often understood such qualities as the good and the bad, the beautiful and the ugly, the pleasant and unpleasant, etc. They are qualities like yellow, hard, loud, etc. On the other hand, the value *quale* is characterized, often by the same authors (Russell, Meinong), as that which "ought to be on its own account" or "as worthiness to be, or to be of interest".'[3] The expression *value*, he says, is not necessarily used 'merely as a general term for these qualities; it may also refer to the proposition that the object ought to be, to *something judged because of these qualities*'.[4]

Professor Urban admits then that goodness is a quality, and a quality like yellowness. But he thinks that besides the value judgement 'so-and-so is good', there is another type of value judgement, 'so-and-so ought to be because it is good'; and it is the latter type of judgement that leads him to reject a quality theory of value. Here he seems to me both to admit too much and to make a claim that cannot be sustained. (1) On the one hand he admits that 'good', 'beautiful', 'pleasant' are qualities like 'yellow', 'hard', 'loud'. This seems to me to overlook two important distinctions. (*a*) Even if 'good' and 'beautiful' are qualities, they are not qualities like 'yellow' and 'hard'. There is the vital difference—to be dwelt on later [5]—that while the latter are constitutive qualities, the former are resultant quali-

---

[1] I may refer here to the weighty final chapter of Meinong's last treatment of the problem of value, in his *Zur Grundlegung der allgemeinen Werttheorie*. It is remarkable that though he approaches the problem from the side of the subjective act of valuation, and of the analysis of this, he concludes that there are 'unpersonal goods', in the sense that there are goods which are not essentially for a subject at all, though they are in a subject (cf. p. 147 of his work). This is exactly the position I wish to establish.

[2] *Journal of Philosophy*, &c., 1916, 455–65.

[3] Ib. 456.   [4] Ib.   [5] Cf. pp. 121–2.

ties, depending on constitutive qualities. And (*b*) there is a vital difference between 'good' on the one hand and 'pleasant' or 'beautiful' on the other; for while it can be intelligently asked whether the pleasant or beautiful has value, it cannot be intelligently asked whether the good has value, since to be good is just to be valuable. 'Good' is a more general term than 'beautiful' and 'pleasant', and if we sometimes use 'good' with a narrower reference to moral good, it is with the knowledge that 'good' has a wider scope than this.

(2) But while he is content to regard not only 'pleasant' and 'beautiful' but 'good' as mere qualities, Professor Urban thinks there is something further that may be asserted of things that have these qualities, because they have them, viz. that they ought to be on their own account, or that they are worthy to be or to be of interest; and it is this that he identifies with value proper, and asserts not to be a quality. This seems to me, with all respect, to be a mistake. 'Ought' properly asserts an obligation, and it would be absurd to assert of, say, a state of pleasure or a beautiful object that it is under an obligation to be, or of a state of pain or an ugly object that it is under an obligation not to be. It is true that we sometimes *say* of such things that they ought or ought not to be, but it is always, if we use language with any approach to strictness, with the underlying thought that it is or was or will be some one's duty to bring them into being, or to prevent them from being. It may further be pointed out that it does not even *follow* from a thing's being good that it ought to be, even in this loose sense, for if a thing, though good, would add less to the sum of good in the universe than some other good thing that can be produced by an alternative act, it is (when no special obligations exist) our duty not to bring it into being; and again there are special obligations which over-ride the obligation to bring a particular good into being.

'This is worthy to be' or 'this is worthy to be an object of interest' seems either (*a*) to be a metaphorical ascription of moral merit, i. e. of a *deserving* to be brought into being or to be made an object of interest, to things many of which (e. g. states of pleasure or beautiful objects) obviously have no moral merit; or else (*b*) to be a mere synonym for the phrase we have already criticized—'this ought to be' or 'this ought to be of interest'—and open to the same objection as these. These two mistakes, as I venture to think them ((1) and (2)) are logically connected. It is because Professor Urban degrades 'good', the universal adjective of value, to the level of 'pleasant' and 'beautiful', which are departmental adjectives of value, and degrades all of these alike to the level of constitutive qualities like 'yellow', 'hard', 'loud', that he feels a necessity to seek value in something beyond goodness, and to express it in the loose and metaphorical phrases he uses for it.

Further, he does not seem to be clear about the relation between goodness, pleasantness, or beauty, and 'ought-to-beness'. For on one page [1] he describes the proposition that an object ought to be as 'something judged because of these qualities', and on the next he says that from the presence of these qualities 'the positive value of the object itself does not follow'. Why then should one judge that it ought to be, 'because of these qualities'?

Professor Urban is seeking to show that value, like existence, is not a quality, and states this in the following way. 'As an object may have its full quota of qualities and the question of its existence or non-existence still be left open, so an object may have its full quota of qualities, including its so-called value qualities, and we may still have to ask whether it ought to be or not.'[2] Here he seems to be on the track of a true distinction, which, however, I should prefer to state in another way. There are a number of characteristics which evoke some sort of approval or preference and in virtue of which anything that has them has some intrinsic goodness. Yet to say of a thing that it has one of these is not to say that it is intrinsically good. Treating beauty as a form of instrumental goodness (i.e. not as a form of goodness in the strict sense but as a way of being productive of something good),[3] I do not reckon it among these characteristics. The three which seem to me to cover the ground (though I may easily be mistaken) are the characteristics of being virtuous, of being an instance of knowing, of

[1] *Journal of Philosophy,* &c., 456.　　　　[2] Ib. 457.
[3] Cf. pp. 127-31.

being an instance of being pleased.[1] If therefore a state of mind possessed one of these valuable characteristics and did not possess any of the opposite characteristics, we should necessarily judge it to be good. But concrete states of mind, perhaps always and certainly sometimes, occupy positions on all three scales—that of virtue-vice, that of intelligence-unintelligence, that of pleasure-pain; and it therefore does not follow, because a state of mind has one, or two, of the characteristics which in themselves are good, that it is good on the whole. Thus to judge of a state of mind (or of a state of society) that it is on the whole virtuous, or intelligent, or pleasant, is not necessarily to judge that it is good on the whole. The judgement that a state of mind is good on the whole is what I should put in place of Professor Urban's judgement that a thing ought to be, as distinguished from the judgement that it is virtuous or pleasant or beautiful. And if I am right in holding that 'this is good' is the true expression of this ultimate valuation, rather than 'this ought to be', the argument for the view that goodness is not a quality, and for the assertion that its affinities are rather with existence, falls to the ground. I would distinguish as Professor Urban does between the possession of moral goodness or of intellectual goodness or of feeling-goodness by a thing (i. e. by a state of mind) and its possession of goodness on the whole. But I see no ground for his view that while these departmental values are qualities, value 'is not a "what" at all, either quality or relation: it is a "that" '. Is it not clear that value must fall within the same category as its own varieties?

Professor Urban admits this as a *possible* view, i. e. that ultimate value may be a quality, though different from the 'valuable qualities'.[2] But he holds that this view has been refuted by Croce. Croce's argument,[3] as summarized by Professor Urban, is this: 'Take . . . the value-judgement in its usual form, A is as it should be, or negatively, A is as it should not be. The first, he holds, is tautology, the second a logical absurdity. If A exists, it is already as it should be, for it can not be other than it is.'[4] The conclusion Croce draws is that

[1] This last requires some modification; cf. pp. 135–8.   [2] *Journal of Philosophy*, &c., 459.   [3] *Saggio sullo Hegel*, 409.   [4] *Journal of Philosophy*, &c., 459.

the so-called value judgement is not a judgement at all but a mere expression of feeling. Professor Urban draws a different conclusion—that value is not a quality. But let us see if either of these conclusions really follows. It is necessary to distinguish between two types of subject of which it might conceivably be asserted that it is (or is not) as it should be. (1) It might conceivably be said 'pleasure is as it should be', 'pain is not as it should be'. And against any such judgement Croce's criticism is justified. To say for instance that pleasure is as it should be implies that pleasure, while remaining pleasure, might have different natures, that it is better that it should have one of them than any other, and that it has that which it is best that it should have. And so with any similar judgement. Of all such judgements we may say, not with Croce that some are tautological and others are absurd, but that all are absurd. For in naming the subjects of our judgements as we have named them, we have ascribed to them a certain nature and excluded the possibility of their having a different nature, and also (since the value of things depends on their nature) the possibility of their having a different value, from that which they have. This is just what distinguishes intrinsic from instrumental value; for if a thing is only instrumentally good or bad, then even when its nature remains the same it might have a different instrumental value if the causal laws of the universe, or the other things in the universe, were different.

But it is to be observed that, so far, Croce is fighting a man of straw. No one can judge that 'pleasure is as it should be' unless he has adopted (as Croce does) the artificial view that 'A is as it should be' is the correct form of the value judgement. If we adopt instead the natural form, 'pleasure is good', 'pain is bad', his argument leaves us quite untouched. For to point out that pleasure or pain could not be other than it is, has not the slightest tendency to show that the judgement 'pleasure is good' is tautological or the judgement 'pain is bad' absurd.

(2) There is another and quite different type of judgement, in which we can and do assert of something that it is or is not as it should be. We may say 'the state of so-and-so's mind is not as it should be', or 'the state of England is not as it should be'.

Here we do not in naming our subject already describe its nature and exclude the possibility of its having a different nature, and a different value, from that which it has. We mean that the existing state of things is bad, with the further implication that it is the duty of some person or persons to substitute for it a different state which would be good. And this again is left entirely untouched by Croce's argument.

The supposed conclusiveness, then, of Croce's argument against value being a quality arises partly from the use of the phrase '*A* is as it should be' as the true expression of the value judgement, and partly from a confusion between a kind of judgement of this form which is absurd but which no one actually makes, and another type of judgement of this form which we do make but which is not tautological nor absurd.

It is possible to exhibit in yet another way the falsity of Professor Urban's view that the affinity of value is with existence and not with qualities. 'Qualities inhere in objects,' he says, 'since it is the quality that makes the object precisely what it is; the judgement of quality presupposes that the thing is not other than it is. But the object may have its full quota of qualities without being judged valuable any more than existent.' [1] He is thinking, no doubt, of Kant's famous criticism of the ontological argument on the ground that it treats existence as a quality among others. An imaginary thaler may have (or rather be imagined to have) exactly the same qualities as an actual thaler in my pocket; existence is not one of the qualities constitutive of a thing's nature, nor something that follows from them. But surely the analogy entirely breaks down. For whereas from the fact that an imaginary thaler is imagined to have exactly the same qualities as a real thaler has, it does not follow that since the one exists the other exists, from two things' having exactly the same qualities other than goodness, it most decidedly does follow that if the one is good the other is good. While existence is not a quality, goodness is a quality consequent on the other qualities of that which has it.

Value is, Professor Urban maintains, 'not an adjectival predicate, but an attributive predicate. . . . It is a predicate only in the sense that existence and truth are predicates';[1] i. e. he considers that there is a class of judgements of which '*A* exists', '*A* is good', '*A* is true' are instances, in which no quality or relation is ascribed to a subject. And though, as I have tried to show, there is a quite essential difference between our predications of existence and our predications of value, to which his view does not do justice, it is perhaps worth while also to attack the view that there is a class of non-qualitative, non-relational predicates, of which 'existent' is merely one. The judgement '*A* is true' is plainly a judgement in which another judgement is asserted to possess a certain quality, which in turn depends on a certain relation between the judgement that is judged about and an existing fact. It is *not* of the same type as the existential judgement, and there is no argument from analogy for supposing that the judgment '*A* is good' is so.

In contrast with the views that value is a relation, or a quality, Professor Urban inclines to the view that value is 'an objective, or specific form of objectivity',[2] and he selects three points as sufficient to characterize this view. '(1) Value is ultimately indefinable in the terms or categories of matter of fact—as object, or quality, or relation; (2) the judgment of intrinsic value, that an object ought to be, or to be so-and-so, on its own account apprehends an ultimate and irreducible aspect of objects; (3) this value is itself, not a *quale* of some objects, but is a form of objectivity, in contrast with being and existence.'[3] I may be allowed to sum up my own attitude towards the theory as follows. (1) If 'object' here means, as I suppose it must, 'substance', value is certainly not that. And I have tried to give reasons for holding that it is not a relation. But the arguments against the *prima facie* view that it is a quality seem to have completely broken down. (2) I agree that the judgement of intrinsic value apprehends an ultimate and irreducible aspect of objects, and think that this is the sole element of truth —and a very important element of truth—in the view. (3) I reject the view that the true form of the value judgement is not '*A* is good' but '*A* ought to be' or '*A* is as it ought to be', which if accepted might lend some colour to the theory that the value judgement is akin to the existential judgement '*A* is' rather than to the predicative judgement '*A* is *B*'.

Under the third head, Professor Urban recognizes two types of the theory, one which holds that value is what ought to be, another which holds that it is what ought to be acknowledged.[1] The second form is no more acceptable than the first; for the only conceivable ground for holding that a thing ought to be acknowledged, i. e. acknowledged to exist, is that it exists, so that the fact that it ought to be acknowledged is not the fundamental fact about it but only a consequential one.

Professor Urban adds two points which he considers to tell in favour of his view. (1) The first consists in emphasizing the verbal form of the value judgement. 'In the value judgment', he insists *passim*,[2] 'we apprehend a "that", not a "what".' And the ground here given is that what we judge is not an object but an objective, i. e. something which can only be expressed by a that-construction. Now we may if we please call anything of which the proper expression is a that-clause an objective; I will accept this language for the moment. And if so we must agree that what is judged in a value judgement is an objective. But how does this prove that value is an objective? For it is equally true of *any* judgement that what is judged in it is an objective. But the fact that 'that *A* is red' is an objective does not show red to be an objective and not a quality; how then does the fact that 'that *A* is good' is an objective show good to be an objective and not a quality? In this respect the two judgements are precisely parallel.

But while value appears not to be an objective, I am inclined to think that it is only objectives that in the long run have value, or that have ultimate value. This fact, if it be a fact (the question seems to me a very difficult one), is obscured by certain perfectly natural and not really misleading but nevertheless not strictly accurate ways of speaking. We say for instance of a *man* that he is good. But if we ask ourselves what is really good in or about him, we find that it is not all that he is or all that he does, but those actions, dispositions, or states of him which have a certain character; his acting, say, on certain occasions

[1] *Journal of Philosophy*, &c., 461.   [2] e. g. ib. 462.

from love of duty. Now that which is valued, like that which is desired, is not so *obviously* an objective as that which is judged. For the latter we have only one proper form of expression. No one ever says 'I judge his goodness'; we have to say 'I judge that he is good'. For the object of valuation, and for the object of desire, we have other forms of expression. We can say 'his acting from such and such a motive is good', or 'his insight into a comprehensive law of the universe is good', or 'his being pleased is good'; and we can say 'he desires the happiness of his children'. But in both cases we can quite naturally substitute the that-form. We can say 'that he is acting from a sense of duty is good', or 'that he has insight, &c., is good', or 'that he is experiencing pleasure is good'; and in the case of desire we can say 'he desires that his children shall be happy'. Thus the that-construction seems to be a comprehensive form applicable to what we value and to what we desire, as much as to what we judge, though in the former two cases language has provided us with alternative expressions which mean the same as the 'that' clause.

This, if true, is important; for it enables us, without denying goodness to be a quality, to recognize a great difference between it and most qualities. Most of our adjectives, I suppose, refer to qualities that belong to substances; 'good' is the name of a quality which attaches, quite directly, only to 'objectives', and since an objective is an entity more complex than a substance, standing as it does for a substance's having a certain quality or being in a certain relation, 'good' may be called a quality of a different type from those that attach to substances. To this it might be objected that I judge that so-and-so's acting conscientiously, or knowing an important law of the universe, or being pleased, is good, simply because I judge that virtue, knowledge, or pleasure is good. But it is surely clear that 'virtue', 'knowledge', and 'pleasure' are just short-hand ways of referring to the fact that some mind or other is in a certain condition, i. e. to entities that are complex as contrasted with mere substances, or mere qualities, or mere relations; in other words, to objectives.

But if I use the word 'objective' as a convenient way of

referring to the things that can be expressed by the 'class-construction', by 'that'-clauses, I am far from thinking that these taken together form a class of real entities. If I think 'that *A* is *B*', this does not imply that there is a real entity 'that *A* is *B*'—an independently real proposition with which my mind is in a certain relation. If I say 'I think that *A* is *B*', it is my state of mind and not any independently existing entity that I am describing. The reasons which have led some logicians to recognize propositions as entities distinct both from objective facts and from the activity of thinking appear to be false; as the subject is foreign to our inquiry, I am content to refer to Mr. McTaggart's refutation of them.[1] And similarly, if I desire 'that *A* shall be *B*', this does not imply that 'that *A* shall be *B*' is a real entity. In saying 'I desire that *A* shall be *B*' I am describing the state of my mind and nothing else; there is no entity 'that *A* shall be *B*' with which my mind enters into relation. Thus the whole variety of things that are expressed by 'that'-clauses do not form a class of entities. But *some* of the things so expressed are real entities. If I *know* 'that *A* is *B*', it is implied that 'that *A* is *B*' is a real element in the nature of the universe. And if 'that mind *A* is in state *B*' is good, then again it is implied that 'that mind *A* is in state *B*' is a real element in the nature of the universe. But the proper name for what is expressed in *such* 'that'-clauses, which are real elements in the nature of the universe, is not 'objectives' (which suggests an affinity that does not really exist between these and what is expressed in the other 'that'-clauses mentioned above), but 'facts'. It is better therefore to say that the things that have ultimate value are facts. And since these are entities of a higher order of complexity than substances, we get an important distinction between value judgements and the judgements in which we judge about substances.

(2) Professor Urban argues that 'in order to know that an object ought to be or is as it ought to be, it is not necessary to know whether the object is or is not'.[2] This statement, in the second of its alternative forms, is plainly not acceptable. It is clearly impossible to know that anything 'is as it ought to be'

---

[1] *The Nature of Existence*, i. 9–32.   [2] *Journal of Philosophy*, &c., 463.

without knowing whether it is at all. The other form, 'such and such an object ought to be', contains no such obvious pre-supposition of the object's existence. But we have already given reasons for rejecting this as a correct expression of the value judgement. The true expression of that judgement is '*A* is good'. Does *this* presuppose *A*'s existence? Professor Urban maintains that it does not, and this is, I think, involved in his view that value is 'a form of objectivity, in contrast with being and existence',[1] 'lying between being and non-being, but itself not a form of being'.[2] He maintains that such a thing as perfect happiness can be judged to be good, without being known to be possible, let alone existent. But it seems clear that if we do not judge perfect happiness to exist, the proper form of ex-pression is not 'perfect happiness is good' but 'perfect happiness would be good', i. e. if it existed—where its being good pre-supposes its existence; just as it is the case that, if we do not judge that *A* is happy, we cannot say '*A*'s happiness is good' but only '*A*'s happiness would be good'. The judgement that a thing is good presupposes the judgement that it exists; and the judgement that it would be good presupposes the sup-position of its existence. We can, of course, make the judgement that it would be good if it existed, without knowing or even judging that it exists, or even that it is possible. But that in no way tends to show that value is independent of existence. Actual value presupposes actual existence, and conditional value supposed existence.

I conclude, then, that the arguments in favour of thinking of value as an objective are no more successful than those in favour of treating it as a relation, and that the arguments against its being a quality put forward by those who hold the 'objec-tive'-theory are no more valid than those put forward by the advocates of the 'relation'-theory. The natural view that value is a quality therefore holds its ground, and we may proceed to consider whether we can say anything about the sort of quality it is, and its relation to other qualities. In considering this I have been much helped by Professor Moore's study of the

[1] *Journal of Philosophy*, &c., 461.   [2] Ib. 464.

conception of intrinsic value,[1] the main points of which I will briefly summarize. 'To say that a kind of value is intrinsic is to say that the question how far a thing possesses it depends entirely on the intrinsic nature of the thing, i. e. (1) that it is impossible for a self-same thing to possess the value at one time and not at another, or to possess it more at one time and less at another; (2) that if a thing possesses any kind of intrinsic value in a certain degree, anything exactly like it must in all circumstances possess it in the same degree. Or to put it otherwise, if of two things not having a different intrinsic nature one has a certain value, the other must also have it.

'Intrinsic difference is not qualitative difference (though *most* intrinsic difference is qualitative difference). For things that possess the same quality in different degrees are intrinsically different, e. g. a loud sound and a soft one, or two things of different sizes; and so are a yellow circle with a red centre and a yellow circle with a blue centre, although not these wholes but only single elements of each are qualitatively different.

'What is meant by "impossible" when we say "a kind of value is intrinsic if and only if it is impossible that X and Y should have different values of this kind unless they differ in intrinsic nature"? (i) It is sometimes said that "it is impossible for that which has attribute F to have attribute G" means simply that things that possess F never in fact possess G. But more is meant than this.[2]

'(ii) There are *causal laws* in virtue of knowing which we seem able to say that if a thing had a property F it would have a property G. But when we say that if a thing has a value in a certain degree, anything exactly like it would have the value in the same degree, we mean that this is so independently of any causal laws.

'It is clear that there is such a sense of necessity. If you take a particular patch of colour, it is certain that any patch exactly like it must in any universe be yellow. It is in a similar sense that we assert that two things exactly alike must have the same value.

---

[1] *Philosophical Studies*, 253–75.
[2] I omit Professor Moore's reasons for this assertion, which is (I think) obviously true.

'(iii) The necessity we are examining is, finally, not identical with logical necessity, such as that which we assert when we say that whatever is a right-angled triangle must be a triangle. "I do not see how it can be deduced from any logical law that, if a given patch of colour be yellow, then any patch which were exactly like the first were yellow too." So too it cannot be deduced from any logical law that if A is beautiful anything exactly like A would have the same degree of beauty.

'But while both yellowness and beauty depend only on the intrinsic nature of what possesses them, yellowness is and beauty is not an intrinsic predicate. No predicate of value is an intrinsic predicate in the sense in which yellowness, or being a state of pleasure, is intrinsic. Apparently certain predicates of value are the only attributes that share with intrinsic properties the characteristic of depending solely on the intrinsic nature of what possesses them. The fact that many people have thought that values were subjective, points to some great difference between them and such attributes as yellow. What is the difference, if values are *not* subjective? It may be vaguely expressed by saying that intrinsic properties *describe* the nature of what possesses them in a way in which values do not. If you could enumerate all its intrinsic properties you would have given a complete description of the object. It is true both of intrinsic properties and of values that if one thing possess them and another do not, the intrinsic nature of the two things must be different. Is the necessity of a different kind in the two cases? If it is, we have two senses of "must", both unconditional, and both different from the logical "must".'

This analysis seems to me a valuable one. I agree both with Professor Moore's account of what is implied in a value's being intrinsic, and with what I take to be his view, that goodness, in its most fundamental meaning, the meaning to which I have tried to call attention by eliminating the 'good of its kind' and the 'instrumentally good', is intrinsic. But I wish to express a difference of opinion with regard to rightness and beauty, the two attributes which he describes as the main value-attributes other than goodness; to examine further the way in which the goodness of a thing depends on its intrinsic nature; and to

comment on some points of detail. I begin with the latter.
(1) The first concerns the distinction which Professor Moore
draws between difference in intrinsic nature and difference in
quality. He holds that there are things that differ in intrinsic
nature without differing in quality, and he gives two types of
instance of this. (*a*) 'Nobody would say that a very loud sound
was exactly like a very soft one, even if they were exactly like
in quality; and yet it is plain there is a sense in which their
intrinsic nature is different.'[1] Similarly no one would hold
that a particular patch of colour was 'exactly like' another patch
of identical quality but a million times larger or smaller, or that
if the one were beautiful the other must have exactly the same
degree of beauty. On this I would observe that if loudness and
size are not qualities (a question on which I offer no opinion),
the point will be met by saying that the intrinsic nature of a
thing includes besides its quality whatever quantity (intensive
or extensive) it may have.

(*b*) The second illustration of difference in intrinsic nature
as distinct from difference in quality is 'the difference between
two patches consisting in the fact that the one is a yellow circle
with a red spot in the middle, and the other a yellow circle with
a blue spot in the middle'.[2] This, which is obviously a difference in the intrinsic nature of the two patches, is described
by Professor Moore as only loosely to be called a difference
of quality. But surely he holds that two things not different in
quality are identical in quality, and surely no one would ascribe
identity in quality to two such patches. The expression 'difference in quality' seems quite sufficient to cover such a case as
this, if only we recognize that 'different in quality' means
'having *any* difference in quality', not necessarily 'different
throughout in quality'.

It would seem then as if we might say that the intrinsic nature
of a thing includes its quality and its quantity. But the question
may naturally be asked, should not relations also be brought
into our account of the intrinsic nature of a thing? Obviously
the relations of a thing to things other than it and other than
its elements should not. For the very view that a thing has an

[1] *Philosophical Studies*, 264.   [2] Ib.

intrinsic nature is the view that it has a nature which does not include any relations of it to other things.[1] There remain, however, (a) the relations of the thing to its own parts or elements, and (b) the relations between its elements. Must these be included in its intrinsic nature as separate factors, over and above its quality and its quantity? It will be agreed that two patches of colour have not the same nature if one consists of three bands of red, white, and blue, in that order, and the other of red, blue, and white, in *that* order; and that if one was beautiful it would not follow that the other was. And this difference of intrinsic nature rests on a difference not between the quality or quantity, but between the relations, of the elements of the two wholes. Nevertheless it seems clear that it is part of the *quality* of the one *whole* to consist of the three bands in one order, and part of the quality of the other *whole* to consist of the three bands in a different order. And if this be so, the relations of the parts need not be included in the intrinsic nature of the whole, *over and above* the quality of the whole. And for a similar reason the relations of the whole to the parts need not be included as a separate factor. For if one patch contained a yellow part which was half the size of the whole, and another a yellow patch which was a third of the size of the whole, these facts would be part of the quality of the wholes. It would appear, then, as if intrinsic nature included simply quality and quantity.

(2) Another point which invites comment is the nature of the necessity or necessities by which (a) if one patch of colour is yellow, another having the same intrinsic nature must be yellow, and (b) if one patch is beautiful, another having the same intrinsic nature must be beautiful. I agree with Professor Moore in thinking that in neither case does the necessity mean (i) that in fact no two patches of colour of identical nature are respectively yellow and not yellow, or respectively beautiful and not beautiful. This will be true, of course, but we mean more than this. Nor does it mean (ii) that in this universe there is a causal law which ensures that no two patches of colour

---

[1] Cf. Cook Wilson's analysis of the meaning of 'what a thing is in itself', *Statement and Inference*, i. 152–3.

intrinsically alike are respectively yellow and not yellow, or respectively beautiful and not beautiful. I think that we can see that this must be so in any universe, and cannot depend on the causal laws of this universe. When he asserts (iii) that the necessity is not logical necessity, the question becomes more difficult. He describes logical necessity as 'the kind of necessity, which we assert to hold, for instance, when we say that whatever is a right-angled triangle *must* be a triangle, or that whatever is yellow *must* be either yellow or blue'.[1] I agree that from the single proposition 'these two patches of colour are intrinsically alike' it does not follow that if one is yellow the other must be yellow, or that if one is beautiful the other must be beautiful. But elsewhere he gives, and is, I think, evidently right in giving, as a further instance of logical necessity, the fact that 'from the proposition with regard to any term that it is red it *follows* that it is coloured'.[2] Here I suppose the conclusion follows strictly not from the one proposition 'this is red' but from this plus the self-evident proposition that red is a colour. I suggest that the necessity by which if two patches of colour are intrinsically alike it follows that if one is yellow the other is yellow, is of the same nature; i. e. this follows not from the bare proposition 'these two patches of colour are intrinsically alike', but from this plus the self-evident propositions that yellow is a quality (which is of the same type as 'that red is a colour' above), and that intrinsic likeness involves identity in quality. The necessity is what Professor Moore calls a logical necessity; I should prefer to say that it is an instance of implication and not of causality.

What are we to say of the necessity by which if two things are exactly alike it follows that if one is beautiful the other is beautiful? This question is perhaps better left till we examine the difference which Professor Moore now points out to exist between beauty and such attributes as yellowness. 'The difference I mean is one which I am inclined to express by saying that though both yellowness and beauty are predicates which *depend* only on the intrinsic nature of what possesses them, yet while yellowness is itself an *intrinsic* predicate, *beauty* is not.'

<hr>

[1] *Philosophical Studies*, 271.   [2] Ib. 284-5.

He suggests that intrinsic kinds of value, if any exist, are unique in respect of the fact that, though not intrinsic properties, they 'share with intrinsic properties this characteristic of depending only on the intrinsic nature of what possesses them'.[1] He confesses himself unable to define further the difference between value and intrinsic properties except 'by saying that intrinsic properties seem to *describe* the intrinsic character of what possesses them in a sense in which predicates of value never do. If you could enumerate *all* the intrinsic properties a given thing possessed, you would have given a complete description of it, and would not need to mention any predicate of value it possessed; whereas no description of a given thing would be *complete* which omitted any intrinsic property'.[2]

Here the use of the terms 'depend' and 'complete description' seems to me open to criticism. To say that both intrinsic properties and value depend on the nature of their possessors is to suggest that it has an intrinsic nature apart from both and on which both are based. But Professor Moore's conception, and the true conception, of intrinsic properties is that they are just the things that make up the intrinsic nature of their possessors. What are the minimum conditions that must be fulfilled if two patches of colour are to have the same intrinsic nature? Let us say that they are that the two patches must be (1) of the same colour-tone, (2) of the same brightness, (3) of the same size, (4) of the same shape. Any of these may vary independently of any and all of the others. The essential difference between them and beauty is that beauty, and the degree of beauty, cannot vary independently of them taken together. Two patches of colour exactly alike in these other respects must be alike in beauty. In other words, while these others are constitutive characteristics, beauty is, in some way (which we must later [3] try to describe more precisely), a dependent or consequential characteristic. The necessity that if the intrinsic nature of the two patches is the same their colour (or brightness, or size, or shape) must be the same is analytic; the necessity that their degree of beauty must be the same is synthetic.

Again, I cannot agree that a description of a patch of colour

---

[1] *Philosophical Studies*, 272.   [2] Ib. 274.   [3] Cf. pp. 121-3.

would be *complete* without the statement that it is beautiful (if
it is so); for its beauty might be for some purposes the most
important fact about it. But it would be, in a certain respect
(i. e. for a certain purpose), *sufficient*; in that respect in which a
description of a triangle as being an equilateral triangle with
sides a foot long would be sufficient. Any such triangle would
have many more attributes; it would be equiangular, its angles
would be angles of sixty degrees, it would have a certain area,
&c.; but a description that omitted such attributes but mentioned its equilaterality and the length of its sides (or of one
side) would be sufficient in the sense that two triangles alike in
these respects must be alike in all respects, and that it would
state the attributes from which all the other geometrical attributes of such a triangle necessarily follow. But it would not be
sufficient in respect of telling us all that the triangle is; and no
more would be the description of a patch of colour which
omitted to say whether it is beautiful or not.

In fact, as a first approximation at any rate, we may say that
the difference between goodness or value and such attributes as
yellowness is that whereas the latter are *differentiae* (i. e. fundamental or constitutive attributes) of their possessors, the former
is a *property* (i. e. a consequential attribute) of them. And in
this respect goodness may be compared to the properties that
geometry proves to hold good of various types of figure. But
if we recognize the affinity, we must also recognize the marked
difference between the two cases. (1) In the first place, it is
quite arbitrary which of the attributes equilaterality and
equiangularity is selected as the differentia of the kind of
triangle which in fact possesses both; it is just as proper to
say that the relative size of the angles determines the relative
length of the sides, as *vice versa*. Value, on the other hand,
seems quite definitely to be based on certain other qualities of
its possessors, and not the other qualities on the value. In fact
the distinction between differentia and property as fundamental
and consequential attributes respectively is far more appropriate in this case than in most of those to which it is applied,
since this is one of the comparatively few cases in which one of
the attributes is objectively fundamental and the other objec-

tively consequential. We might call value a genuine as opposed to an arbitrarily chosen resultant (or property).

(2) Another respect in which value differs from mathematical properties, as well as from certain other resultant properties, is that while mathematical (i. e. spatial, temporal, and numerical) properties follow from part of the intrinsic nature of their possessors, value follows from the *whole* intrinsic nature of its possessors. If a patch of colour is in shape an equilateral triangle, it will be an equiangular triangle, whatever be its size or colour; if it is of a certain colour, it will match certain other patches, whatever be its shape or size; if it is of a certain size, it will be equal in size to certain other patches, whatever be its colour or shape. These attributes which are based on some single element in the nature of their possessors may be called parti-resultant properties. In contrast with these, value is a toti-resultant property, based on the whole nature of its possessors. And this is true not only of 'good', the adjective which expresses intrinsic value, but also of 'right' and 'beautiful', which are often classed with it; though 'right' does not stand for a form of value at all,[1] and 'beautiful' does not stand for an intrinsic form of value.

(a) Take first the attribute 'good' in the sense we are examining, i. e. that in which it means 'intrinsically good'. If I may be allowed to anticipate positions which I shall try to commend independently of the present argument, good is a characteristic belonging primarily only to states of mind, and belonging to them in virtue of three characteristics—the moral virtue included in them, the intelligence included in them, and the pleasure included in them.[2] The precise degree of goodness belonging to any state of mind will belong to it not in virtue of any one or two of these elements but in respect of all of them, or of all which it possesses. Two states of mind alike in respect of virtue and intelligence are not equally good if they differ in their degree of pleasantness; nor two states alike in virtue and pleasantness equally good if they differ in their degree of intelligence; nor two states alike in intelligence

---

[1] What has value is the doing of the right act because it is right.
[2] Cf. n. 1 on p. 107.

and pleasantness equally good if they differ in their degree of virtuousness.

(*b*) An act that is right is right in virtue of its whole intrinsic nature[1] and not of any part of it. In respect of certain elements in its nature it may be *prima facie* right, and in respect of others *prima facie* wrong; whether it is actually right or wrong, and if it is wrong the degree of its wrongness, are determined only by its whole nature. This point has been, I hope, sufficiently dealt with in our second chapter.

(*c*) It is, I suppose, still more clear that it is only in virtue of its whole intrinsic nature that any beautiful thing has the precise degree of beauty that it possesses. Take a simple case. A patch of colour might have been more, or less, beautiful than it is if either its shade of colour or its degree of brightness or its size or its shape had been different. Or, to take a more complicated case, the alteration of a poem in any syllable may, in principle, make it more, or less, beautiful.

If we are agreed that goodness, rightness, and beauty depend on nothing less than the whole intrinsic nature of their possessors, we must consider whether they depend on anything *more* than this. Only if they do not, only if we can say 'if *A* is good, right, or beautiful, anything exactly like *A* will be equally good, right, or beautiful', will goodness, rightness, and beauty be intrinsic properties. An apparent objection naturally arises in the case of beauty. There might be two patches of colour *A*, *A'* exactly alike. Yet if one lay beside a patch of colour *B* which harmonized with it, and the other beside a patch *C* which clashed with it, it would seem natural to say that the one might be beautiful and the other ugly. The objection is, however, illusory. For strictly it is not the two like patches *A*, *A'* that would be respectively beautiful and ugly, but the wholes *A B*, *A' C*. On reflection we should admit that though *A B* is beautiful and *A' C* ugly, still if *A* is beautiful, *A'* if exactly like it must be beautiful too; though to apprehend its beauty we should have to do what it may be difficult to do, viz. contemplate it in abstraction from *C*.

---

[1] i. e. in virtue of being the origination of all that it is the origination of. But cf. the qualification in n. 2, p. 33.

It is, I think, clear that the only types of theory which deny that beauty is intrinsic to beautiful objects are those which make it consist in or depend on the fact that some mind or minds do or undergo something in face of them. And such theories, as we have seen,[1] fall into two main kinds, according as beauty is held to depend on the occurrence of (*A*) a feeling or (*B*) a judgement. We have seen, too, that such theories may connect beauty with the occurrence of some feeling or judgement (1) in at least one person, no matter in whom, (2) in the person who judges the object beautiful, (3) in a majority of persons of some class or other—say aesthetically cultivated people, or people belonging to a particular stage in the history of civilization, (4) in a majority of mankind, or (5) in all mankind. The most appropriate names for the feeling in question are, I suppose, 'aesthetic enjoyment' or 'aesthetic thrill', and for the opposite feeling 'aesthetic repulsion'. Into the precise nature of these feelings it is not necessary for our argument to inquire. It is perhaps enough to say that we all know these feelings by experience, and have a general idea of what they are like.

Corresponding theories, we have seen,[2] may be held with regard to 'right' and with regard to 'good'. Professor Moore rejects theory (*A* 1) with regard to 'right' on the ground (*a*) that 'a man may doubt whether an action is right, even when he does *not* doubt that *some man or other* has the required feeling towards it'.[3] The argument seems to me conclusive in the case of 'right'; but a corresponding argument is not equally conclusive in the case of 'beautiful'. For it must surely be admitted that the nature of aesthetic enjoyment and of aesthetic repulsion is more obscure, and more liable to be confused with something different, than is that of moral approval or disapproval. A man who thinks that he himself gets aesthetic enjoyment from a certain object may well doubt whether any one has ever experienced genuine aesthetic repulsion to it. He may hold that what the other feels is a non-aesthetic repulsion to it arising from, e. g., moral or religious or patriotic motives, or from the shock of novelty, though the other may wrongly think and say that his repulsion is aesthetic. And similarly a man who

[1] p. 80.   [2] pp. 11, 80.   [3] *Ethics*, 111.

thinks that he himself experiences aesthetic repulsion to an object may well think that no one has ever experienced genuine aesthetic enjoyment from it, and that those who thought they did were mistaking a pleasant feeling of some other kind (moral approval, or religious enthusiasm, or the like) for the genuine aesthetic thrill. Is not this, in fact, the account we are most likely to give when we find ourselves differing from other people about the beauty or ugliness of an object? It is not, therefore, clear that 'a man may doubt whether an object is beautiful (or ugly), even when he does not doubt that some one or other has experienced aesthetic enjoyment of (or repulsion to) it'. And if this is not clear, this argument falls to the ground.

(b) We may, however, fall back on Professor Moore's second argument against this theory. If what I mean when I call an object beautiful is that some one or other gets aesthetic enjoyment from it, and if what any other person means when he calls it ugly is that some one or other feels aesthetic repulsion to it, we are not at variance, because both propositions might be true. Yet if anything is clear, it is that we do suppose ourselves to be making incompatible statements about the object.

(c) And finally, it might have been enough to ask quite simply whether any one finds it plausible to suppose that what I mean when I call a thing beautiful is that some one or other, quite irrespective of who it may be, has felt aesthetic enjoyment of it. Until some such person is found, the theory may simply be ignored; and I have dealt with it only for the sake of logical completeness.

(2) The second theory, that what I mean is that *I* experience aesthetic enjoyment from the object, is, however, often held. The objection which Professor Moore makes to the corresponding theory about rightness is equally fatal to this theory about beauty. If all I mean when I say that an object is beautiful is that I experience aesthetic enjoyment from it, and all you mean when you say it is ugly is that you experience aesthetic repulsion to it, we are not at variance, for we may both be right. Yet if anything is clear, it is that we suppose ourselves to be making incompatible statements.

At the same time it is worth noting that, owing to the obscurity of the nature of aesthetic enjoyment in comparison with that of moral approval, each of two people who call a thing respectively beautiful and ugly would be more inclined to deny that the other is experiencing genuine aesthetic repulsion or enjoyment than he would be to take the corresponding line in an analogous moral dispute. And in many, if not in all, cases this denial would pretty clearly be correct.

(3) The third theory is that in calling an object beautiful I mean that a majority of some class of people experience aesthetic enjoyment from it. To save needless repetition, I may simply refer to the previous refutation of the corresponding theory about goodness.[1] I may add that all the historical instances of artistic revolt against tradition, all the claims to have discovered some new form of beauty, are clear evidence of the falsity of the theory. Nay, any one who acclaims the beauty of a newly discovered mountain or flower, or of a neglected gem of poetry, is evidently not claiming to express the feelings of any majority.

Finally, theories (4) and (5), and theory (*B*) in all its five possible forms, may be refuted by the same arguments as the corresponding theories about rightness or about goodness.

We have now seen the falsity of all purely subjective theories of beauty, i. e. of all theories which identify the beauty of an object with its arousing of either a feeling or an opinion in any man or class of men. But a doubt remains whether beauty can be purely objective, whether it must not in some more complicated way have necessary reference to a mind. The difficulty arises partly from the fact that so much of beauty—the whole of it, I suppose, strictly speaking—is sensuous. Very much of it is inseparably bound up with colours and sounds, and unless we give a completely objective account of these we cannot give a completely objective account of beauty. Now the view which holds that colours and sounds, exactly as they are (or seem to be) perceived, are characteristic of physical bodies, is pretty generally given up. Those who believe in their objectivity are now more inclined to describe them as forming a separate class of objects to which the name of *sensa* is given. And again most

[1] Cf. pp. 83-4.

of the sensum-theories regard sensa as owing their nature not solely to the nature of the physical object but partly to the nature of the perceiver's body, or of his mind, or of both. The only form of sensum-theory which gives a purely objective account of colours and sounds, the only one therefore that is compatible with a purely objective account of beauty, is one which regards them as pure products of the physical object, and the mind's function with regard to them as being purely that of perceiving a selection of them. This is obviously not the place to embark upon a discussion of the 'object of perception' (particularly as beauty is not one of our main subjects but is being examined only in order to bring out by contrast the nature of goodness). But we may perhaps be allowed to assume that the purely selective theory is highly improbable. Personally I would go further and say that to me any form of sensum-theory seems less probable than a purely causal theory of perception; one, that is to say, which regards all our sensuous experience as not being apprehension at all but simply a set of mental events produced by the operation of external bodies on our bodies and through them on our minds. But the commending of this view would need a book to itself, and in anything I say which presupposes this view I can only hope to win the assent of those to whom such a view of perception already commends itself.

If we are right in holding that beauty is bound up with what is sensuous and that what is sensuous is at any rate partly dependent on a mind, can any account of beauty be given which will do justice to this fact and at the same time avoid the fatal objections which we have seen to arise against a purely subjective account of beauty, i. e. one which identifies 'this is beautiful' with 'this arouses some particular feeling or opinion in some mind or minds'? The view to which I find myself driven, in the attempt to avoid the difficulties that beset both a purely objective and a purely subjective view, is one which identifies beauty with the *power* of producing a certain sort of experience in minds, the sort of experience which we are familiar with under such names as aesthetic enjoyment or aesthetic thrill. Does such a theory really escape the objections to a purely subjective theory? We shall see the position of affairs if we suppose first two people maintaining respectively that a certain object is beautiful and that it is not beautiful; and secondly two people maintaining respectively that an object is beautiful and that it is ugly. (1) When a man thinks an object to be beautiful, either he is holding an independent personal opinion, or he is judging the object to be beautiful out of deference to the opinion of some other person or persons. For brevity's sake I will omit the latter or conventional type of opinion, which raises no special difficulty, and concentrate on the former. Every independent opinion that an object is beautiful has for antecedent, it will be agreed, a feeling of enjoyment which either is, or is taken to be, aesthetic; there is no other basis for thinking an object beautiful than such an experience. Yet what the judger is judging is not that he has this experience. For (*a*) the judgement is a judgement about the object, not about the judger's state of mind. And (*b*) though we cannot judge an object to be beautiful till we think we have been aesthetically thrilled by it, we judge that it was beautiful before we were thrilled by it, and will be beautiful when we have ceased to be thrilled by it. The judgement, while it is not a judgement about the judger's state of mind, is one in which, on the strength of his knowledge of (or opinion about) his state of mind, he ascribes an attribute to an object. And if we ask ourselves what is the common attribute belonging to all beautiful objects, we can, I believe, find none other than the power of producing the kind of enjoyment known as aesthetic.[1]

Now observe the difference between this view and that which identifies 'this is beautiful' with 'this produces a certain feeling in me'. The latter view is open to the fatal objection that it leaves no real point at issue between the man who says 'this is beautiful' and the man who says 'no, it is not'; for it may

---

[1] I think, however, that it must be admitted (and this is, for what it is worth, an objection to the view suggested) that we do not *mean* by 'beautiful' an attribute having even this sort of reference to a mind, but something entirely resident in the object, apart from relation to a mind. What I am suggesting is that we are deceived in thinking that beautiful things have any such common attribute over and above the power of producing aesthetic enjoyment.

well be true *both* that the object produces aesthetic enjoyment
in one man *and* that it does not produce it in the other. But if
one is in effect saying 'the object has it in it to produce aesthetic
enjoyment in any one sufficiently capable of feeling such', there
is a question really at issue between him and one who says 'no,
it has not'.

That this is no unnatural account of the question at issue
between them may be seen by considering separately the two
cases in which the person who asserts the object to be beautiful
is right, and is wrong, respectively. (*a*) When he is right, he is
actually having or has had genuine aesthetic enjoyment of the
object; the other has had no such enjoyment and is inferring
from this that the object has no power of producing such enjoyment in any one. But the actual occurrence of the enjoyment
depends on conditions in the experient as well as on conditions in the object. While his own lack of susceptibility
or of aesthetic education is at fault, he is supposing that the
conditions in the *object* are not those required for aesthetic
enjoyment.

(*b*) When the man who pronounces the object beautiful is
wrong, what is happening is that he is receiving *some* kind of
pleasurable thrill from the object, confusing this with aesthetic
enjoyment, and on the strength of this mistake wrongly at-
tributing to the object the power of producing the aesthetic
thrill.

(2) When one person pronounces an object beautiful and
another pronounces it *ugly*, there are, I think it must be admitted, four possibilities. The first person alone may be right,
or the second alone be right, while the other is mistaking some
other emotion for aesthetic repulsion or enjoyment, or making
a conventional judgement based on his opinion that some one
else thinks the object ugly or beautiful. Thirdly, both may be
wrong, both making the sort of mistake that in the first two
cases one of them has made. But fourthly, it appears that both
may conceivably be right. For when we consider how beauty
is bound up with sense-perception, and how dependent sense-
perception is on our equipment of sense-organs, it seems not
improbable that owing to differences in the sense-organs of

different individuals, or of different races, the same object may produce (or minister to) genuine aesthetic enjoyment in one individual or race and genuine aesthetic repulsion in another. And if so, the same object will be both beautiful and ugly; whether we think this probable or not, it seems clear that it cannot be ruled out as impossible. And to this extent our ordinary ideas about beauty and ugliness require revision; for we certainly in general mean by 'beautiful' and 'ugly' attributes which cannot belong to the same thing (i. e. to the same thing taken as a whole; we well know that some *elements* in a thing may be beautiful and others ugly).

In a sense, then, beauty is perfectly objective. An object may be beautiful though no one has ever felt or will ever feel its beauty, provided that there is some mind which if confronted with it would get aesthetic enjoyment from it, or could be so educated as to get such enjoyment. The further question may be asked, whether there could be beauty in a world in which there were no minds at all. If it is possible for a mind to *come into being* in such a world (a question on which I offer no opinion), there too there might be beauty; for an object in a mindless universe might be such as to produce aesthetic enjoyment in some mind which might come into existence. So far the theory is purely objective; but in so far as it holds beauty to be indefinable except by reference to a possible effect on a mind, and to involve a certain relation between the nature of the object and that of mind (or of some mind), our theory might be called subjective. And its objectivity in the one sense seems to be quite compatible with its subjectivity in the other.

Finally we may ask whether beauty is an intrinsic value. Apparently we must say that it is not. For even if it be held that beauty might exist in a mindless universe, there is no reason for regarding the beautiful things in such a universe as having any value in themselves. Their value would be solely instrumental to the production of aesthetic enjoyment in such minds as might later come into being. Aesthetic enjoyment is good in itself, and beauty is valuable simply as productive of it; in any assignment of intrinsic value to a mindless universe or to anything in it there is a surreptitious introduction of a subjective factor, namely of oneself imagined as contemplating such a universe or the things in it.

We may turn now from beauty to goodness. We have already seen the failure of all purely subjective theories of goodness. Are we, then, to adopt a purely objective theory, or an intermediate theory such as I have suggested about beauty? Such a theory would hold that goodness is a power in certain things to produce a certain sort of feeling in minds—or, it might be, to produce in minds the opinion that these things are good. These two sub-types of theory must be considered separately. (*A*) There seems to be a great difference between our predications of beauty and of goodness. All predications of beauty seem to rest on the opinion that the judger, or some one else, has derived aesthetic enjoyment from the object. If for brevity we eliminate the derivative or conventional predications of beauty in which we rely on some one else's supposed enjoyment of the object, and if we concentrate on independent predications of beauty, we find that it is quite impossible to make such a predication unless we have ourselves first derived aesthetic enjoyment from the object. The feeling is the primary thing and the judgement is based upon it. In my attitude towards the things I call good, on the other hand, my opinion that they are good seems to be the primary thing, and my feeling to be consequent upon this. It seems even evident that I may judge something to be very good or very bad, when owing to preoccupation I have no strong feeling about it at all; while (apart from conventional judgements) no one can judge an object to be very beautiful or very ugly except on the strength of a vivid feeling towards it. This is a matter of psychological analysis, and it is difficult to be certain about it. But after a good deal of reflection I feel pretty clear that if I delight in contemplating a virtuous action, for instance, it is because I think the action to be good, and not *vice versa*.[*] If we think that feeling is here the primary thing, I suppose the most natural name for it would be 'approval'; but if we ask ourselves what approval is we find that the basic element in it is not feeling at all but the judgement that an object is good.

Further, the chaotic condition of aesthetic theory seems to show that it is extremely difficult, if not impossible, to specify the characteristic or characteristics of beautiful things (apart from the way in which they can affect minds) on which beauty depends. But we can give an account of what the goodness of good things depends upon without introducing any reference to the feelings they produce in a spectator. The goodness of an action depends on its springing from one or other of certain nameable motives; the goodness of an intellectual activity, on its being an instance of knowledge, or of well-grounded opinion; the goodness of a state of feeling, on its being pleasant.

(B) If goodness is not a power of producing a certain feeling, is it a power of producing a certain opinion—the opinion that the object is good? This suggestion can be refuted much more decisively. For opinions have the characteristic, which feelings have not, of being necessarily either true or false. No one will say that an object is good because it is capable of so affecting him, or any one, as to produce the opinion that it is good, irrespective of whether the opinion is true or false. If the opinion is false, the object is not good; and if the opinion is true, the truth of the opinion that the object is good rests on the *fact* that the object is good, and not *vice versa*.

It seems then that an intermediate view of goodness is no more satisfactory than a purely subjective view, and that goodness is entirely objective and intrinsic to the things that are good.

What are we to say of rightness? We must, I think, say that it is intrinsic, but that in so far as a right act has value its value is not intrinsic. The rightness of an act, if the contention of our second chapter is correct, is intrinsic to the act, depending solely on its nature. But if we contemplate a right act alone, it is seen to have no intrinsic *value*. Suppose for instance that it is right for a man to pay a certain debt, and he pays it. This is in itself no addition to the sum of values in the universe. If he does it from a good motive, *that* adds to the sum of values in the universe; if from a morally indifferent motive, *that* leaves the sum of values unchanged; if from a bad motive, *that* detracts from the balance of values in the universe. Whatever intrinsic value, positive or negative, the action may have, it owes to the nature of its motive and not to the act's being right or wrong; and whatever value it has independently of its motive is instrumental value, i. e. not goodness at all, but the property of producing something that is good.

Our arguments seem to show, then, that rightness no more than beauty is an intrinsic value, and that the only correct way of expressing intrinsic value is the word 'good'.

V

WHAT THINGS ARE GOOD?

OUR next step is to inquire what kinds of thing are intrinsically good. (1) The first thing for which I would claim
that it is intrinsically good is virtuous disposition and action,
i. e. action, or disposition to act, from any one of certain motives,
of which at all events the most notable are the desire to do one's
duty, the desire to bring into being something that is good,
and the desire to give pleasure or save pain to others. It seems
clear that we regard all such actions and dispositions as having
value in themselves apart from any consequence. And if any one
is inclined to doubt this and to think that, say, pleasure alone is
intrinsically good, it seems to me enough to ask the question
whether, of two states of the universe holding equal amounts of
pleasure, we should really think no better of one in which the
actions and dispositions of all the persons in it were thoroughly
virtuous than of one in which they were highly vicious. To
this there can be only one answer. Most hedonists would shrink
from giving the plainly false answer which their theory requires,
and would take refuge in saying that the question rests on a
false abstraction. Since virtue, as they conceive it, is a disposition to do just the acts which will produce most pleasure,
a universe full of virtuous persons would be bound, they might
say, to contain more pleasure than a universe full of vicious
persons. To this two answers may be made. (a) Much pleasure,
and much pain, do not spring from virtuous or vicious actions
at all but from the operation of natural laws. Thus even if a
universe filled with virtuous persons were bound to contain
more of the pleasure and less of the pain that springs from
human action than a universe filled with vicious persons would,
that inequality of pleasantness might easily be supposed to be
precisely counteracted by, for instance, a much greater inci-
dence of disease. The two states of affairs would then, on
balance, be equally pleasant; would they be equally good?
And (b) even if we could not imagine any circumstances in
which two states of the universe equal in pleasantness but

unequal in virtue could exist, the supposition is a legitimate one, since it is only intended to bring before us in a vivid way what is really self-evident, that virtue is good apart from its consequences.

(2) It seems at first sight equally clear that pleasure is good in itself. * Some will perhaps be helped to realize this if they make the corresponding supposition to that we have just made; if they suppose two states of the universe including equal amounts of virtue but the one including also widespread and intense pleasure and the other widespread and intense pain. Here too it might be objected that the supposition is an impossible one, since virtue always tends to promote general pleasure, and vice to promote general misery. But this objection may be answered just as we have answered the corresponding objection above.

Apart from this, however, there are two ways in which even the most austere moralists and the most anti-hedonistic philosophers are apt to betray the conviction that pleasure is good in itself. (a) One is the attitude which they, like all other normal human beings, take towards kindness and towards cruelty. If the desire to give pleasure to others is approved, and the desire to inflict pain on others condemned, this seems to imply the conviction that pleasure is good and pain bad. Some may think, no doubt, that the mere thought that a certain state of affairs would be *painful* for another person is enough to account for our conviction that the desire to produce it is bad. But I am inclined to think that there is involved the further thought that a state of affairs in virtue of being painful is *prima facie* (i.e. where other considerations do not enter into the case) one that a rational spectator would not approve, i.e. is *bad*; and that similarly our attitude towards kindness involves the thought that pleasure is good. (b) The other is the insistence, which we find in the most austere moralists as in other people, on the conception of merit. If virtue deserves to be rewarded by happiness (whether or not vice also deserves to be rewarded by unhappiness), this seems at first sight to imply that happiness and unhappiness are not in themselves things indifferent, but are good and bad respectively.

Kant's view on this question is not as clear as might be wished. He points out that the Latin *bonum* covers two notions, distinguished in German as *das Gute* (the good) and *das Wohl* (well-being, i. e. pleasure or happiness); and he speaks of 'good' as being properly applied only to actions,[1] i. e. he treats 'good' as equivalent to 'morally good', and by implication denies that pleasure (even deserved pleasure) is good. It might seem then that when he speaks of the union of virtue with the happiness it deserves as the *bonum consummatum* he is not thinking of deserved happiness as good but only as *das Wohl*, a source of satisfaction to the person who has it. But if this exhausted his meaning, he would have no right to speak of virtue, as he repeatedly does, as *das oberste Gut*; he should call it simply *das Gute*, and happiness *das Wohl*. Further, he describes the union of virtue with happiness not merely as 'the object of the desires of rational finite beings', but adds that it approves itself 'even in the judgement of an impartial reason' as 'the whole and perfect good', rather than virtue alone. And he adds that 'happiness, while it is pleasant to the possessor of it, is not of itself absolutely and in all respects good, but always presupposes morally right behaviour as its condition'; which implies that *when* that condition is fulfilled, happiness *is* good.[2] All this seems to point to the conclusion that in the end he had to recognize that while virtue alone is morally good, deserved happiness also is not merely a source of satisfaction to its possessor, but objectively good.

But reflection on the conception of merit does not support the view that pleasure is always good in itself and pain always bad in itself. For while this conception implies the conviction that pleasure when deserved is good, and pain when undeserved bad, it also suggests strongly that pleasure when undeserved is bad and pain when deserved good.

There is also another set of facts which casts doubt on the view that pleasure is always good and pain always bad. We have a decided conviction that there are bad pleasures and

---

[1] *Kritik der pr. Vernunft*, 59–60 (Akad. Ausgabe, vol. v), 150–1 (Abbott's Trans., ed. 6).

[2] Ib. 110–11 (Akad. Ausgabe), 206–7 (Abbott).

(though this is less obvious) that there are good pains. We think that the pleasure taken either by the agent or by a spectator in, for instance, a lustful or cruel action is bad; and we think it a good thing that people should be pained rather than pleased by contemplating vice or misery.

Thus the view that pleasure is always good and pain always bad, while it seems to be strongly supported by some of our convictions, seems to be equally strongly opposed by others. The difficulty can, I think, be removed by ceasing to speak simply of pleasure and pain as good or bad, and by asking more carefully what it is that we mean. Consideration of the question is aided if we adopt the view (tentatively adopted already)[1] that what is good or bad is always something properly expressed by a that-clause, i. e. an objective, or as I should prefer to call it, a *fact*. If we look at the matter thus, I think we can agree that the fact that a sentient being is in a state of pleasure is always in itself good, and the fact that a sentient being is in a state of pain always in itself bad, when this fact is not an element in a more complex fact having some other characteristic relevant to goodness or badness. And where considerations of desert or of moral good or evil do not enter, i. e. in the case of animals, the fact that a sentient being is feeling pleasure or pain is the whole fact (or the fact sufficiently described to enable us to judge of its goodness or badness), and we need not hesitate to say that the pleasure of animals is always good, and the pain of animals always bad, in itself and apart from its consequences. But when a moral being is feeling a pleasure or pain that is deserved or undeserved, or a pleasure or pain that implies a good or a bad disposition, the total fact is quite inadequately described if we say 'a sentient being is feeling pleasure, or pain'. The total fact may be that 'a sentient and moral being is feeling a pleasure that is undeserved, or that is the realization of a vicious disposition', and though the fact included in this, that 'a sentient being is feeling pleasure' would be good if it stood alone, that creates only a presumption that the total fact is good, and a presumption that is outweighed by the other element in the total fact.

[1] pp. 111–13.

Pleasure seems, indeed, to have a property analogous to that which we have previously recognized under the name of conditional or *prima facie* rightness. An act of promise-keeping has the property, not necessarily of being right but of being something that is right if the act has no other morally significant characteristic (such as that of causing much pain to another person). And similarly a state of pleasure has the property, not necessarily of being good, but of being something that is good if the state has no other characteristic that prevents it from being good. The two characteristics that may interfere with its being good are (*a*) that of being contrary to desert, and (*b*) that of being a state which is the realization of a bad disposition. Thus the pleasures of which we can say without doubt that they are good are (i) the pleasures of non-moral beings (animals), (ii) the pleasures of moral beings that are deserved and are either realizations of good moral dispositions or realizations of neutral capacities (such as the pleasures of the senses).

In so far as the goodness or badness of a particular pleasure depends on its being the realization of a virtuous or vicious disposition, this has been allowed for by our recognition of virtue as a thing good in itself. But the mere recognition of virtue as a thing good in itself, and of pleasure as a thing *prima facie* good in itself, does not do justice to the conception of merit. If we compare two imaginary states of the universe, alike in the total amounts of virtue and vice and of pleasure and pain present in the two, but in one of which the virtuous were all happy and the vicious miserable, while in the other the virtuous were miserable and the vicious happy, very few people would hesitate to say that the first was a much better state of the universe than the second. It would seem then that, besides virtue and pleasure, we must recognize (3), as a third independent good, the apportionment of pleasure and pain to the virtuous and the vicious respectively. And it is on the recognition of this as a separate good that the recognition of the duty of justice, in distinction from fidelity to promises on the one hand and from beneficence on the other, rests.

(4) It seems clear that knowledge, and in a less degree what

we may for the present call 'right opinion', are states of mind
good in themselves. Here too we may, if we please, help ourselves to realize the fact by supposing two states of the universe
equal in respect of virtue and of pleasure and of the allocation
of pleasure to the virtuous, but such that the persons in the one
had a far greater understanding of the nature and laws of the
universe than those in the other. Can any one doubt that the
first would be a better state of the universe?

From one point of view it seems doubtful whether knowledge
and right opinion, no matter what it is of or about, should be
considered good. Knowledge of mere matters of fact (say of
the number of stories in a building), without knowledge of
their relation to other facts, might seem to be worthless; it
certainly seems to be worth much less than the knowledge of
general principles, or of facts as depending on general principles
—what we might call insight or understanding as opposed to
mere knowledge. But on reflection it seems clear that even
about matters of fact right opinion is in itself a better state of
mind to be in than wrong, and knowledge than right opinion.

There is another objection which may naturally be made to
the view that knowledge is as such good. There are many pieces
of knowledge which we in fact think it well for people *not* to
have; e. g. we may think it a bad thing for a sick man to know
how ill he is, or for a vicious man to know how he may most
conveniently indulge his vicious tendencies. But it seems that
in such cases it is not the knowledge but the consequences in
the way of pain or of vicious action that we think bad.

It might perhaps be objected that knowledge is not a better
state than right opinion, but merely a source of greater satisfaction to its possessor. It no doubt is a source of greater
satisfaction. Curiosity is the desire to *know*, and is never really
satisfied by mere opinion. Yet there are two facts which seem
to show that this is not the whole truth. (*a*) While opinion
recognized to be such is never thoroughly satisfactory to its
possessor, there is another state of mind which is not knowledge
—which may even be mistaken—yet which through lack of
reflection is not distinguished from knowledge by its possessor,
the state of mind which Professor Cook Wilson has called

'that of being under the impression that so-and-so is the case'.[1] Such a state of mind may be as great a source of satisfaction to its possessor as knowledge, yet we should all think it to be an inferior state of mind to knowledge. This surely points to a recognition by us that knowledge has a worth other than that of being a source of satisfaction to its possessor. (b) Wrong opinion, so long as its wrongness is not discovered, may be as great a source of satisfaction as right. Yet we should agree that it is an inferior state of mind, because it is to a less extent founded on knowledge and is itself a less close approximation to knowledge; which again seems to point to our recognizing knowledge as something good in itself.

Four things, then, seem to be intrinsically good—virtue, pleasure, the allocation of pleasure to the virtuous, and knowledge (and in a less degree right opinion). And I am unable to discover anything that is intrinsically good, which is not either one of these or a combination of two or more of them. And while this list of goods has been arrived at on its own merits, by reflection on what we really think to be good, it perhaps derives some support from the fact that it harmonizes with a widely accepted classification of the elements in the life of the soul. It is usual to enumerate these as cognition, feeling, and conation. Now knowledge is the ideal state of the mind, and right opinion an approximation to the ideal, on the cognitive or intellectual side; pleasure is its ideal state on the side of feeling; and virtue is its ideal state on the side of conation; while the allocation of happiness to virtue is a good which we recognize when we reflect on the ideal relation between the conative side and the side of feeling. It might of course be objected that there are or may be intrinsic goods that are not states of mind or relations between states of mind at all, but in this suggestion I can find no plausibility. Contemplate any imaginary universe from which you suppose mind entirely absent, and you will fail to find anything in it that you can call good in itself. That is not to say, of course, that the existence of a material universe may not be a necessary condition for the existence of many things that are good in themselves. Our

---

[1] *Statement and Inference*, i. 113.

knowledge and our true opinions are to a large extent about the material world, and to that extent could not exist unless it existed. Our pleasures are to a large extent derived from material objects. Virtue owes many of its opportunities to the existence of material conditions of good and material hindrances to good. But the value of material things appears to be purely instrumental, not intrinsic.

Of the three elements virtue, knowledge, and pleasure are compounded all the complex states of mind that we think good in themselves. Aesthetic enjoyment, for example, seems to be a blend of pleasure with insight into the nature of the object that inspires it. Mutual love seems to be a blend of virtuous disposition of two minds towards each other, with the knowledge which each has of the character and disposition of the other, and with the pleasure which arises from such disposition and knowledge. And a similar analysis may probably be applied to all other complex goods.

VI

DEGREES OF GOODNESS

THE next question which seems to face us is the question whether goods are commensurable. As a preliminary to this, we may ask the narrower question whether pleasures are commensurable. And as a preliminary to that again, we may ask whether pleasures are comparable; whether we can properly say that one pleasure is greater or more pleasant than another. That this is so there seems to be no doubt. Any denial of it usually proceeds by asking us to say which of two extremely disparate pleasures is the greater. It is true that often we cannot do this. But one who maintains the comparability of pleasures is not bound to maintain that he can say of any two pleasures which is the greater. He may not, for instance, have recently enjoyed the two; and undoubtedly memory of the intensity of pleasures is treacherous when it has to cover any long span of time. Or again one or both of the pleasures may be very complex, and the introspection necessary for the assessment of their pleasantness may be difficult. But this much is clear, that if we compare two comparatively simple and comparatively similar pleasures recently experienced, we may have no difficulty in seeing one to have been more pleasant than the other; and this is enough to show that pleasures have different intensities. If we proceed from these to others that are more complex or less similar or were experienced less recently, it is plain that there is no point at which we can stop and say, some pleasures are in their nature comparable and others are not. The truth is that pleasures have the only characteristic on their side that is necessary to comparability, viz. difference of intensity; but that some of the conditions on our side which would enable us to compare them are often lacking.[1]

If this is clear, we may next argue that pleasures are com-

[1] It is hardly necessary to say that I am not ascribing to pleasures an existence independent of a mind to feel them; I am thinking of them as existing independently of our activity in *comparing* them.

mensurable, i. e. that one pleasure may not only be more intense than another, but may be, say, just twice as intense. This surely follows from our previous conclusion. For if one pleasure is more intense than another, it must have a definite amount of extra intensity. True (as is often pointed out), the difference between two pleasures is not a pleasure, as the difference between two lengths is a length. That is part of what we mean by distinguishing intensity from extension. But the difference between the intensity of two pleasures is an amount of intensity, and of course a definite amount. And this may be exactly equal to the intensity of the less pleasure; and if so, the greater pleasure is just twice as great as the less.

On their side, then, pleasures have the characteristic requisite for commensurability. And on our side too the conditions necessary for rough commensuration are sometimes fulfilled. For there seems to be no doubt that in comparing two comparatively simple and similar pleasures, recently experienced, we can sometimes say with the greatest confidence that one was, say, at least twice as intense as the other. We cannot be more precise than this and say that one was just twice, or three times, as intense as the other. That points to the absence of some of the conditions needed for exact commensuration on our side and not to the lack of the conditions needed for commensurability on theirs. Or perhaps this statement should be modified. The pleasures have precise intensities, which in principle makes them commensurable. But they have not the characteristics that make material objects comparatively easy to measure, the characteristics of being fairly permanent and of being easily compared with standards of measurement which may be applied to each in turn.

At the same time it is worth while to point out that the difference between physical and mental objects in respect of commensurability is not so complete as it might appear. We can never say that one material object is precisely twice as long, say, as another, but only at most that it either is this or fails to be this by an amount which our senses do not enable us to detect. And similarly we can, under favourable circumstances, say that one pleasure either is just twice as intense as another, or differs from this by an amount which introspection does not enable us to detect.

If pleasures are commensurable, it does not necessarily follow that all goods are; that, say, pleasure can be measured in respect of goodness against virtue or knowledge. But the arguments that have been urged against the commensurability of goods are to a large extent the same that have been urged against the commensurability of pleasures. The case against the commensurability of goods gets much of its plausibility by confronting us with two goods, highly complex or highly dissimilar or not recently experienced, or perhaps never experienced at all by the person who is asked to give judgement, or a good which ranks high in a low order with one which ranks low in a higher order.[1] The proper reply is to point to other goods *not* so characterized which we have little difficulty in comparing and even in measuring roughly against one another. Few people, except those who are committed to hedonism, would hesitate to say that an action of sublime heroism is many times as good a thing as some faint and passing shade of pleasure. If we can ever commeasure two goods, that is much stronger evidence that goods are in principle commensurable, than the fact that we sometimes cannot commeasure two goods is for goods *not* being in principle commensurable.[2] Yet the conclusion to which this preliminary consideration points is faced with great difficulties when we try to commeasure good things of very different types.

When we turn to the attempt actually to measure goods against each other, it will be prudent to begin with goods of the same order, i. e. with the balancing of one pleasure against another, of one state of knowledge against another, of one virtuous action or disposition against another. (1) Much has been written about the calculus of pleasures, and I shall be forgiven, and perhaps thanked, for not saying much more. Bentham has enumerated the 'dimensions' on which depend the calculus of pleasures, but it is evident that two of them—

[1] Cf. pp. 149–54.
[2] I note with satisfaction that Mr. McTaggart argues in favour of the commensurability of pleasures, and of goods (*The Nature of Existence*, ii. 242–3, 447–8).

fecundity and purity—refer not to the intrinsic value of pleasures but to their tendency to produce other pleasures, or pains; that certainty and propinquity, again, do not belong to pleasures in themselves; and that extension refers not to the intrinsic value of a particular pleasure but to the number of people for whom pleasure will be produced by a particular act. We are left with intensity and duration as the characteristics on which depend the value of a pleasure *qua* pleasure; and to these there is nothing to add. Mill argued that pleasures have 'quality' as well, and that this affects their hedonistic value. The first of these contentions is true, and the second false. It is obviously true that a pleasure, i. e. a pleasant state of mind, always has a quality over and above its intensity and duration. If we compare, for instance, the pleasure of reading good literature and that of a country walk (even supposing that in some case their intensity and duration were the same), we do not find a pleasant feeling identical in the two plus cognitive and conational elements different in the two. Pleasant feeling is coloured through and through by what we are taking pleasure *in*. But Mill should have gone on to say that however interesting a fact this may be, it is from the point of view of the hedonistic calculus quite irrelevant. For a hedonist holds that pleasantness is the only characteristic of states of mind that makes them good, and one state of mind can have more pleasantness than another only by being more intensely pleasant or by being pleasant for a longer time. Mill's introduction of quality of pleasures into the hedonistic calculus is, as has been widely recognized, an unconscious departure from hedonism and a half-hearted admission that there are other qualities than pleasantness in virtue of which states of mind are good.

(2) The commensuration of different states of knowledge against each other, and of states of knowledge against states of right opinion, has been much less discussed. It is clear that we all do in practice treat some forms of knowledge as more valuable than others, but we do not as a rule stop to distinguish whether we are valuing them for their own nature or for their results. Our concern here is solely with their intrinsic value.

The problem is complicated by the fact that while we assign

value, and a kindred (though not equal) value, both to knowledge and to right opinion, these are not species of a single
genus. Knowledge is apprehension of fact, and right opinion
is ñot that, but is simply a state of mind in which things are
believed (*not* apprehended) to be related as they are in fact
related; and there seems to be no single genus of which these
are species. We cannot say that knowledge and right opinion
are species of a single genus (say, 'cognition'), differing in degree
of certainty; for knowledge alone has certainty, and opinion
has merely varying degrees of approach to certainty. What
we can say, by way of bringing knowledge and opinion into
relation with one another, is (*a*) that knowledge is the ideal we
always have in mind in the forming of opinions, and opinions
are the results of more or less unsuccessful attempts at reaching
knowledge, and (*b*) that opinion always rests in part on knowledge. These two characteristics are closely bound up together,
for while opinions are the result of a variety of psychological
causes (largely irrational), it is just in so far as they rest on
knowledge that they approximate to being knowledge.

It seems natural to say that the value of a state of knowledge
or opinion rests partly on the nature of the state of mind, and
partly on the nature of the fact it is in relation to. We must not
say 'of the fact apprehended', for in opinion the fact is not
apprehended. If we want to substitute something more definite
for the phrase 'the fact it is in relation to', we can only say 'the
fact apprehended, or believed to exist'.

Now (*a*) in respect of the nature of the state of mind, there
appear to be two characteristics which mark knowledge off
from opinion, and on which the superiority of knowledge
seems to rest. (i) The first is that knowledge is either the direct
non-inferential apprehension of fact, or the inferential apprehension of one fact as necessitated by other facts, while opinion
is never either completely non-inferential or completely inferential, but is always the holding of a view which is partly
grounded on apprehension of fact and partly the product of
other psychical events such as wishes, hopes, fears, or the
mere association of ideas. In this respect all knowledge is
of equal value, and opinion is of value as it approximates to

being completely grounded on apprehension of fact, i. e. to being knowledge. (ii) The other respect in which knowledge differs from and is superior to opinion is that of certainty or complete absence of doubt. But we cannot say that opinion approximates in value to knowledge in proportion as it approaches to certainty. It rises in value not by being held with more conviction, but by being held with a degree of conviction which answers more closely to the degree to which the opinion is grounded on knowledge. It might seem as if it were a worse intellectual fault to hold an opinion with more, than to hold it with less, conviction than it deserves. It is certainly a fault to which we are more liable, and it is probably more dangerous in its consequences; but it does not seem to be either a greater or a less fault. To mis-estimate the probability of our opinions is equally bad, whether we over-estimate it or under-estimate it.

Thus in what renders a state of opinion good there are two elements, (i) its degree of groundedness, and (ii) the extent to which the degree of conviction corresponds to the degree of groundedness.

It may be added that knowledge can only be possessed with the degree of conviction it deserves, i. e. complete conviction. An opinion on the other hand can rarely, if ever, be held with the precisely appropriate degree of conviction; to make sure of that we should have to know factors in the situation which *ex hypothesi* we do not know. Thus in respect (ii) as well as in respect (i) opinion is in principle inferior to knowledge, and can only by accident fail to be so.

But (*b*) our states of knowledge and opinion seem to derive some of their value from the nature of the fact apprehended, or believed to exist. The only rule I have to suggest here is that which has been stated impressively by Mr. Bradley,[1] that knowledge of general principles is intellectually more valuable than knowledge of isolated matters of fact, and that the more general the principle—the more facts it is capable of explaining—the better the knowledge. Our ideal in the pursuit of knowledge is system, and system involves the tracing of consequents to their ultimate grounds. Our aim is to know

---

[1] *Principles of Logic*, ed. 2, ii. 685–8.

not only the 'that' but the 'why' also, when the 'that' has a 'why'. I venture, however, to think that it is a mistake to rest the value of knowledge on its being inferential. Inferential knowledge, and its value, are entirely inseparable from non-inferential knowledge, first of the ultimate premisses from which inference must start, and secondly of the fact that the premisses warrant the conclusions. It is better to know why a thing is so than merely that it is so, not because your knowledge is inferential, but because you are knowing more, and knowing what is more general. Any attempt to elevate either inferential knowledge above non-inferential, or non-inferential above inferential, is fundamentally mistaken.

There are no doubt particular matters of fact which it is more important for our welfare that we should know, than many general principles. It is very likely more important for our happiness to know the characters of the people we live among (if we can be said ever to know them) than to know highly general mathematical principles. But this is an instrumental value. From the purely intellectual point of view, with which alone we are concerned in speaking of the *intrinsic* value of knowledge, generality (I venture to think) is the only valuable element in knowledge or opinion arising from the nature of the fact apprehended or believed in.

The intrinsic value of a state of knowledge or opinion seems, then, to depend on three elements, (i) the degree of its groundedness on fact, (ii) the degree to which the strength of conviction with which it is held corresponds to its groundedness, (iii) the generality of the fact known, or believed to exist. How these factors are to be balanced against one another in estimating the value of any knowledge or opinion I do not profess to know. The question is practically less important than it might seem to be. In choosing a subject of study, we may choose either one (like metaphysics) in which we are unlikely to obtain much knowledge or even fairly grounded opinion, but in which the knowledge or opinion if obtained would be more general, or one (such as chemistry) in which we are more likely to gain knowledge or fairly grounded opinion, but about something less general. But what we do in such a case is not to try to estimate the value of what we are likely to gain, but to follow our strongest interests; and in this we are justified, for interest is the most important condition of our gaining anything valuable at all.

(3) As regards the balancing of virtuous actions and dispositions against one another, I would refer to my next chapter, which contains all I have to say on the subject.

The 'greatest wave' now awaits us—the question whether virtue, knowledge, and pleasure can be compared with one another in value, and whether they can be measured against one another. I do not pretend that the views I shall express are certainly true, still less that I can prove them to be so. I will only say that they are the result of a good deal of reflection about the comparative value of these things, and that they agree, so far as I can judge, with the views of many others who have reflected on it. I think, then, that pleasure is definitely inferior in value to virtue and knowledge. There are certain facts which support this view. (1) Most people are convinced that human life is in itself something more valuable than animal life, though it seems highly probable that the lives of many animals contain a greater balance of pleasure over pain than the lives of many human beings. Most people would accept Mill's dictum that 'it is better to be a human being dissatisfied than a pig satisfied',[1] though they may think such a view inconsistent with Mill's own principles. The very fact that he felt bound to make an admission so fatal to his cherished hedonism is some testimony to the truth of the admission. (2) Many people whose opinion deserves the greatest respect have undoubtedly thought that the promotion of the general happiness was the highest possible ideal. But the happy state of the human race which they aimed at producing was such a state as the progress of civilization naturally leads us to look forward to, a state much of whose pleasantness would spring from such things as the practice of virtue, the knowledge of truth, and the appreciation of beauty. The ideal has owed its attractiveness in a large degree not to its being a state of maximum happiness, but to its being a state whose happiness would spring from such sources; and if they

[1] *Util.*, 14 (copyright editions).

thought that the state of maximum happiness would be one whose happiness sprang from such things as the indulgence of cruelty, the light-hearted adoption of ill-grounded opinions, and enjoyment of the ugly, they would immediately reject such an ideal. They would no doubt argue that such a state as I have just described could not in fact be one of maximum happiness. But that, if true, is simply a consequence of the laws of the world we live in, and does not absolve them from facing the problem, what if the laws of nature *were* such as to make such a life the most pleasant possible? Would they then prefer it to a state less pleasant but more virtuous and intelligent? They have, in fact, in pronouncing pleasure to be the sole good, not had in mind mere pleasant consciousness, such as we suppose animals to enjoy, but to a very large extent what I have called[1] good (i. e. morally good) pleasures, those which are themselves actualizations of morally good dispositions (such as love for other men and love of truth and beauty) and which owe their goodness much more to this than to their pleasantness.

This argument, if it is sound, only proves that a certain amount of virtue and knowledge would more than outweigh a certain amount of pleasure, and it might still be held that a certain larger amount of pleasure would more than outweigh the given amount of virtue and intelligence. But if we take this view we are faced by the question, *what* amount of pleasure is precisely equal in value to a given amount of virtue or of knowledge? And to this question, so long as we think that *some* amount is equal, I see no possibility of an answer or of an approach to one. With regard to pleasure and virtue, it seems to me much more likely to be the truth that *no* amount of pleasure is equal to any amount of virtue, that in fact virtue belongs to a higher order of value, beginning at a point higher on the scale of value than that which pleasure ever reaches; in other words, that while pleasure is comparable in value with virtue (i. e. can be said to be less valuable than virtue) it is not commensurable with it, as a finite duration is not commensurable with infinite duration.* Pleasure will then be an object worthy

[1] Cf. p. 166.

of production, but only when this does not interfere with the production of virtue.

(3) The question seems to become clearer when one turns from considering virtue and pleasure in the abstract to consider which of them seems the most worth while to get for ourselves. It seems clear that, viewed in this way, pleasure reveals itself as a cheap and ignoble object in comparison with virtue. This manifests itself clearly in the fact that the acquisition of pleasure for oneself rarely, if ever, presents itself as a duty, and usually only as something permissible when it does not interfere with duty, while the attainment of moral goodness habitually presents itself as a duty. This surely points to an infinite superiority of virtue over pleasure, a superiority such that no gain in pleasure can make up for a loss in virtue.

But if virtue is better worth aiming at for ourselves than pleasure, it is better worth trying to promote for man in general. For that which is good owes its goodness not to being possessed by one person or by another, but to its nature.

(4) A further argument in favour of this view seems to arise from the consideration of pleasures which are realizations of a bad disposition, such as the pleasure of cruelty. It seems clear that when we consider such a pleasure we are able to say at once that it is bad, that it would have been better that it should not have existed. If the goodness of pleasure were commensurable with the goodness or badness of moral disposition, it would be possible that such a pleasure if sufficiently intense should be good on the whole. But in fact its intensity is a measure of its badness, because it is a measure of the viciousness of the disposition realized.

(5) It is, on the face of it, much less obvious that knowledge completely transcends pleasure in value than that virtue does so. In fact it would be paradoxical to say that the slightest possible increase in knowledge would outweigh the greatest possible loss of pleasure; I do not think that this can reasonably be maintained about knowledge considered simply as a condition of the intellect. But in fact most (if not all) states of knowledge are themselves to some extent the actualization of a desire for knowledge. And the desire or disposition expressed and

manifested in them has *moral* worth, is of the nature of virtue, and has thus a value completely transcending that of pleasure (i. e. pleasure that is the actualization not of a good disposition but of a neutral capacity, as sensuous pleasure is). It is to be noted, however, that this desire is expressed just as much in the search for knowledge as in the attainment of it. While in its own nature knowledge seems to be a better state than inquiry, the moral virtue of desire for knowledge may be much more fully present in many an unsuccessful search for difficult knowledge than in the successful attainment of knowledge that is easy to get.

The view that virtue and knowledge are much better things than pleasure does not in practice work out in so ascetic a way as might appear, and that for two reasons. (1) It is quite certain that by promoting virtue and knowledge in ourselves and in others we shall inevitably produce much pleasant consciousness. These are, by general agreement, among the surest sources of happiness for their possessors. And still more are they among the surest sources of general happiness, for a variety of reasons which will readily suggest themselves. And (2) it is pretty clear that our pursuit of the greater goods is made all the more effective by intervals in which we give ourselves up to enjoying ourselves and helping others to enjoy themselves. The desire for pleasure is so strong in every one that any one who tries to ignore or suppress it entirely will find himself defeated by the laws of human nature; *naturam expellas furca, tamen usque recurret*. There is a place for asceticism in the best life, but it cannot safely be made the general rule of the best life.

When we turn to consider the relative value of moral goodness and knowledge as ends, here again I am inclined to think that moral goodness is infinitely better than knowledge. Here too the question seems to become clearer when one considers these two goods not in the abstract but as objects to be striven after for ourselves as individuals. When I ask myself whether any increase of knowledge, however great, is worth having at the cost of a wilful failure to do my duty or of a deterioration of character, I can only answer in the negative. The infinite superiority of moral goodness to anything else is clearest in the case of the highest form of moral goodness, the desire to do one's duty. But even of the lesser virtues the same appears to be true. And if virtue is always the thing best worth aiming at for oneself, it is the thing best worth trying to promote in others.

This doctrine will no doubt appear to many unduly moralistic; and two remarks may be made which may perhaps do something to diminish their repugnance to it. (1) I do not wish to introduce moralistic considerations into other spheres than that of morals. Scientific questions must be dealt with on scientific grounds, and aesthetic questions on aesthetic grounds. That a belief would conduce to the promotion of morality does not tend to show that it is true; and that the contemplation of a work of art would conduce to immorality does not show that it is not beautiful. But science and aesthetic enjoyment fall within human life as a whole, and I do maintain that in human life there is a greater good than either.

(2) The doctrine that morality is entirely social, that all duty consists in promoting the good of others, seems to me a profound mistake. Intellectual integrity, the love of truth for its own sake, is among the most salient elements in a good moral character. It is a thing which, with the other virtues, we should try to cultivate in ourselves and to promote in others; and it will perhaps not seem paradoxical to say that it is a better thing to love truth than it would be to have it (if we could do so) without loving it. That which (I am suggesting) is less good than virtue is not the intellectual life in its concreteness, which is the manifestation of a high and a precious excellence of character, but the bare being in possession of knowledge irrespective of the character from which this springs.

The superiority of virtue to all other goods is illustrated once more if we compare it with the more complex good we have recognized, consisting of the proportionment of pleasure to virtue. For suppose that some one's life as a whole contained just that amount of pleasure which was appropriate to the degree of virtue that characterized him, but that some of his pleasures were the expressions of a bad disposition (e. g. pleasures of cruelty), we should, I think, certainly judge that the state of affairs would have been better if he had been without both these pleasures and the defect of character they presuppose; although the state of affairs thus produced would have been one of much less perfect proportionment of pleasure to virtue, since he would both have been *more* virtuous and have enjoyed *less* pleasure.

The suggestion that there are two orders or classes of good things such that those in one class are not commensurable, though they are comparable, with those in the other, is obviously not free from difficulties. But it is the conclusion to which we are led if it be admitted that on the one hand virtue and, say, pleasure are both of them good, and that on the other we are totally unable to see how any amount of one of these could be equal in goodness to any amount of the other. The problem seems to me not to have been faced by those who repudiate both the Kantian view that only virtue is good in itself and the hedonistic view that only pleasure is good in itself; and I am satisfied to have called attention to the importance and difficulty of the problem. Its theoretical importance is evident; but it is also practically important, for pretty evidently one of our chief duties is that of producing as much good as we can, and clear views as to the comparative goodness of different kinds of good things are an essential preliminary to this.

MORAL GOODNESS

GOODNESS is always a consequential attribute; that which is good is good by virtue of something else in its nature, by being of a certain kind. I think that I can best explain what I understand by '*morally* good' by saying that it means 'good either by being a certain sort of character or by being related in one of certain definite ways to a certain sort of character'. It seems necessary to put the matter in this alternative way, because a variety of kinds of thing can be said to be morally good. We may say that such and such a *man* is morally good or that a certain *action* or a certain sort of *feeling* (e.g. sympathy with misfortune) is morally good. But it seems clear that a man is morally good by virtue of having a character of a certain kind, and that an action or a feeling is morally good by virtue of proceeding from a character of a certain kind. This account of the meaning of 'morally good' seems to be confirmed by studying the usage of the phrase. Suppose it were said, for instance, that while conscientious action, knowledge, and pleasure are all good, conscientious action is the only one of the three that is morally good, what we should mean is that while conscientious action is good in virtue of proceeding from a certain sort of character, knowledge and pleasure are good not in virtue of this but in virtue of being, respectively, know- ledge and pleasure.

If this account of what we mean by 'morally good' is correct, the general answer to our next question, what kinds of thing are morally good, is clear. Only what is a certain sort of charac- ter or is related to a certain sort of character in one of certain ways, can be good in virtue of being a certain sort of character or of being so related to it. Of the things that are morally good, I will take for consideration morally good actions, and ask what can be said about the nature of these. If we could agree about this, we are not likely to disagree about what sort of men or what sort of feelings are morally good; they will be the men that have, and the feelings that spring from, the same sort of character that morally good actions spring from. Now when we ask what is the general nature of morally good actions, it seems quite clear that it is in virtue of the motives that they proceed from that actions are morally good. Moral goodness is quite distinct from and independent of rightness,* which (as we have seen)[1] belongs to acts *not* in virtue of the motives they proceed from, but in virtue of the nature of what is done. Thus a morally good action need not be the doing of a right act, and the doing of a right act need not be a morally good action. The ethical theories that stress the thing done and those that stress the motive from which it is done both have some justification, for both 'the right act' and 'the morally good action' are notions of the first importance in ethics; but the two types of theory have been at cross-purposes, because they have failed to notice that they are talking about different things. Thus Kant has tried to deduce from his conception of the nature of a morally good action rules as to what types of act are right; and others have held a view which amounts to saying that so long as our motive is good it does not matter what we do. And, on the other side, the tendency of acts to produce good or bad results has sometimes been treated as if it made them morally good or bad. The drawing of a rigid distinction between the right and the morally good frees us from such confusion.

We can perhaps now substitute something more definite for our preliminary statement that moral goodness is that goodness which is connected with a certain type or types of character. If we ask in particular what the moral goodness of morally good actions arises from, the answer seems (as we have seen) to be 'from a certain kind of motivation'. When we ask what the moral goodness of morally good *feelings* arises from, we cannot answer 'from motivation', for the term 'motive' is inappropriate here, being appropriate only when action is in question. But cannot we say that the moral goodness both of actions and of feelings arises from their proceeding from a certain kind of desire? We think that sorrow at the misfortune of others is morally good because we think that it springs from an interest in their happiness, or, to put the matter more plainly, from a

[1] pp. 4–6.

desire that they shall be happy. As regards actions, the only
objection that might be made to saying their goodness is due
to their proceeding from a certain sort of desire would be the
objection that conscientious action does not spring from desire,
but from something quite different.

Kant, whose greatest service to ethics is the vindication of
the distinct character and the supreme worth of conscientious
action, against the open or covert egoism of most of the eigh-
teenth-century theories, insists that what is operative in it is
something distinct from desire of any kind. It is for him something so mysterious that he is driven to assign it not to man's
phenomenal nature, which he believes to be moved solely by
desire, but to his real or noumenal nature, and to hold (as his
theory of freedom implies) that it is not operative in time at all.
Against this it must be maintained that while a general sense
of duty (i. e. an apprehension that there are things we ought to
do) is present, active or latent, in us throughout our adult lives,
it is no more true to say that than to say that a desire for food,
for instance, is present in us, active or latent, throughout our
lives; and that the thought of a particular act as being our duty,
which is what operates when we act from the sense of duty,
arises in us at a particular time just as does the particular desire to
eat, which is what operates when we, in fact, proceed to eat. The
familiar conflict between the sense of duty and other motives
could not take place unless both were operating in the same field,
and that the field of ordinary 'phenomenal' consciousness.

Regarding the sense of duty as an operation of reason distinct from any form of desire, and accepting the *general* truth
of Aristotle's dictum that thought alone sets nothing going,[1]
Kant found one of his greatest puzzles to lie in the fact that pure
reason can become practical, that the mere thought of an act as
one's duty can by itself induce us to do the act. In comparison
with this, actions from desire seemed to him easily intelligible.
But it may be maintained that there is no more mystery in the
fact that the thought of an act as one's duty should arouse an
impulse to do it, than in the fact that the thought of an act as
pleasant, or as leading to pleasure, should arouse an impulse to

[1] *Nic. Eth.* 1139ᵃ 35.

do it. Human nature being what it is, the latter thought arouses an impulse to action much more constantly than the former; but it is only if we have already assumed (on quite insufficient grounds) that pleasure is the only object of desire, that we shall find it difficult to suppose that the thought of an act as right can arouse a desire to do it. Kant himself, of course, allows that the thought of duty arouses *emotion*—the emotion which he calls *Achtung*, respect or reverence; and this seems to be part of the truth. But to hold this is not incompatible with holding that the thought of duty also arouses desire. Now people often describe themselves as 'wanting' to do their duty. It seems to be often a perfectly straightforward description of their state of mind, and when we examine ourselves we find something of which this appears to be a correct description. All that Kant has said of the uniqueness and the moral supremacy of action arising from the awareness of duty is justified; but it owes its uniqueness and supremacy not to not proceeding from desire, but to proceeding from a desire which is specifically distinct because it is a desire for a specifically distinct object, not for the attainment of pleasure nor even for the conferring of it on others, but just for the doing of our duty. It is in virtue of the specific quality of the attribute 'obligatory', and not of arousing something other than desire, that the thought of duty has the humbling and at the same time uplifting effect that Kant ascribes to it.

When it is denied that we desire to do our duty, that in us which leads us to do our duty tends to be thought of as being in necessary conflict with desire. The sense of duty tends to be described as the sense that one should do certain acts, though on other grounds (e. g. on the ground of their painfulness) one wants not to do them. But 'the sense of duty' really means the sense that we ought to do certain acts, *whether or not* on other grounds we desire to do them, and no matter with what intensity we may desire, on other grounds, not to do them. One of the effects of the forming of a habit of dutiful action is that any natural repugnance one may have to dutiful acts on other grounds tends to diminish. If we form a habit of early rising, for example, it becomes easier, and less unpleasant, to rise early.

But when the doing of a dutiful action is thought of as necessarily involving a resistance to desire, the paradoxical consequence follows that the forming of a good habit, since it leads to less and less resistance to desire being necessary, has to be held to involve that we act less and less from a sense of duty as the habit grows stronger, so that (if, as Kant holds, sense of duty is the only good motive, or even if it is the best motive) to form a good habit is to become a person who acts less well, and therefore a less good person.

If habitual action could become so automatic that it ceased to be done from the thought that it is right, there would certainly be less moral worth in the doing of it. But so long as the act is still done because it is right, it will have no less moral worth because it has become easy. The agent's devotion to duty has not been impaired, but its whole intensity is not needed, as it was at the beginning, to enable him to do the right act. Some of it has now become surplus. The view that there may be a reserve or surplus of good motive, more than is needed to produce the right act,[1] enables us to avoid the paradoxical consequence that to form good habits is to become less good. Goodness is measured not by the intensity of the conflict but by the strength of the devotion to duty. The stronger the motives that oppose the doing of the right act, the more *sure* we can be that when the right act has been done the sense of duty must have been strong; but it may well *be* equally strong when resisting motives are feeble or non-existent.

Tending, as he does, to think of obligation as thwarting desire, and holding that a perfect character must have no desires adverse to the doing of what is right, Kant finds himself obliged to say that a perfect character or 'holy will' would act not under a sense of obligation but only under a sense of the goodness or rightness of certain acts. But, as we have seen, an act, as distinct from the doing of it from a certain motive, is never *good*; and to think of an act as *right* is to think of it either as being obligatory or as being one of certain alternatives, the doing of one or other of which is obligatory;[2] so that the distinction which Kant draws between the right and the obligatory does not answer to the real difference. When we realize that obligation is not necessarily in conflict with desire, but merely independent of desire, we need not hesitate to say that a holy will would act under a sense of obligation; only it would be an obligation that would not necessarily be irksome, because there need not be actually present any desire adverse to it. In fact, the better a man is, the more intensely will he feel himself bound to act in certain ways and not in others, though it will also be true that he will have less desire to act in these other ways. It would, however, be a mistake to say that *all* internal conflict is incompatible with a perfect character. A perfect character would, *ex hypothesi*, have no bad desires; it would not, for instance, desire the pleasure of contemplating another's pain. But its perfection would not exclude the desire for innocent sensuous pleasures, such as those of food or rest, and these desires might incidentally be in conflict with the desire to do what was right. The possibility of such conflict as this seems inseparable from human nature, and at the same time quite compatible with a perfect character.

It would seem, then, that conscientious action springs from a certain desire (the desire to do one's duty), and owes its goodness to the specific nature of this desire. And if this be granted, we have removed the only objection that seems likely to be made to the contention that all morally good actions (and feelings) owe their goodness to the kind of desire they spring from.

If 'morally good' means what I have taken it to mean, it seems that besides (1) conscientious action two other kinds of action are morally good; and these too owe their goodness to the nature of the desire they spring from. These are (2) action springing from the desire to bring into being something good, and (3) action springing from the desire to produce some pleasure, or prevent some pain, for another being.

Under (2) I would include actions in which we are aiming at improving our own character or that of another, without thinking of this as a duty. And believing as I do that a certain state of our intellectual nature also is good, I would include actions in which we are aiming at improving our own intellectual condition or that of others. Some writers would maintain that such action, and that in which we aim at producing pleasure for others, is not morally good, but virtuous. But if I am right in the account I have given of what we mean by moral goodness, viz. that it is goodness due to the character, or (more definitely) to the desire, involved, it seems clear that such actions are morally good. And it would seem contrary to the natural usage of the word 'virtuous' to deny that conscientious action is virtuous. In fact 'morally good' and 'virtuous' appear to mean the same thing, and to be applicable to actions from any one of these three desires.

It may seem at first sight doubtful whether the second and third of these desires are really different. Some might be inclined to hold, and I have sometimes myself believed, that to think of something as being a pleasant state of consciousness for another being necessarily involves thinking of it as good, or *is* thinking of it as good in a particular way, just as thinking of an action as virtuous is thinking of it as good in another particular way. There is no doubt that the two thoughts are often closely associated. Many people undoubtedly do think that pleasure is good, and in aiming at the production of pleasure for another are aiming at the production of something thought of as good. Nevertheless it appears to me that the thought of something as pleasant for another being is both different and separable from the thought of it as good.[1] For (*a*) there are many states of consciousness of other people that we think to be pleasant and also bad (e. g. states of enjoying the contemplation of some one else's pain). It can only be by overlooking such cases that any one can come to hold that to think of something as pleasant for another being either is or necessarily involves thinking of it as good. And (*b*) quite apart from such vicious pleasures, it seems clear that (i) the thought of a state of consciousness as pleasant for another cannot be the thought of it as good in a particular way; for if it were, the thought of a state of consciousness as pleasant for oneself would equally be the thought of it as good in a particular way (since being pleasant is, on this view, just being good in a particular way);

---

[1] On this question, as on some others, I wish to retract the view put forward by me in *Proceedings of the Aristotelian Society*, 1928–9, 251–74.

and then the desire to get such an experience for oneself would be the desire to bring into being something thought of as good, and would itself have to be deemed morally good; whereas we are convinced that the desire of an innocent sensuous pleasure (such as that of rest after work) is morally indifferent. And (ii) it seems clear that the thought of a state of mind as pleasant either for oneself or for another does not necessarily *involve* the thought of it as good, since we should then on reflection always be able to detect the distinct presence of the second thought whenever the first is present; which we certainly are not.

It seems, therefore, that we must distinguish the desire to bring something pleasant for another person into being, from the desire to bring something good into being (of which an instance would be the desire to help a friend to improve his character).[1] And both are evidently different from the desire to do what is right. Yet there is this amount of connexion between the thought of an act as right on the one hand and the thought of a good, or pleasure for another, to be brought into being, on the other hand, that when we think of an act as right we think that either something good or some pleasure for another will be brought into being. When we consider ourselves bound, for instance, to fulfil a promise, we think of the fulfilment of the promise as the bringing into existence of some source of pleasure or satisfaction for the person to whom we have made the promise. And when we consider the other main types of duty—the duties of reparation, of gratitude, of justice, of beneficence, of self-improvement—we find that in the thought of any of these there is involved the thought that what the dutiful act is the origination of is either an objective good or a pleasure (or source of pleasure) for some one else. The conscientious attitude is one which *involves* the thought either of good or of pleasure for some one else, but it is a more reflective attitude than that in which we aim directly at the production of some good or some pleasure for another, since in it the mere thought of some particular good, or of a particular

---

[1] This may be held whether or not we consider that all pleasures, or that some pleasures, are in fact good. The desire to bring them into being *qua* pleasant for another will in either case be different from the desire to bring them into being *qua* good.

pleasure for another, does not immediately incite us to action, but we stop to think whether in all the circumstances the bringing of that good or pleasure into existence is what is really incumbent upon us; the difference is well illustrated by that between discriminate and indiscriminate charity.

If there be these three types of virtuous action, it seems that in principle there might be three corresponding types of vicious action, (1) the desire to do what is wrong, (2) the desire to bring into being some particular evil, (3) the desire to inflict some pain on another. It seems clear that all of these, if they exist, are vicious, and that they are different from one another as are the three corresponding forms of good action. But it is not quite obvious that any one of them ever really occurs. (1) Men seem to be attracted to the doing of wrong acts by the thought of the pleasantness of the particular acts or of their consequences, or it may be by the thought of the pleasure of flouting authority and convention; it seems very doubtful whether they are ever attracted by the mere thought of the wrongness of an act. 'Evil, be thou my good', which is (I suppose) meant to indicate this attitude, is the maxim not of a man but of a devil. (2) Again, when some one sets himself to bring something evil into existence, e. g. to corrupt some one's character, it may be doubted whether it is the badness of what he is bringing into being that attracts him, or the pleasant sense of power or some other pleasure that will attend the action. The corrupting of the character of another, for the sake of corrupting it, is again the traditional role of the devil; but I am inclined to think it not impossible for a man. (3) The existence of disinterested malevolence seems at first sight doubtful; it may be argued that what incites any one to do a malevolent act is not the thought of the pain of his victim, but the thought of the pleasure he will himself derive from watching or thinking of the other's pain. But the true view seems to be that the very thought that that experience will be pleasant to oneself presupposes the existence of an independent desire for the pain of the victim. And a vindictive death-bed will is pretty good evidence of disinterested malevolence, as one of the opposite kind is of disinterested benevolence.

Between the three types of good desire (and of consequent good action), and similarly between the three conceivable types of bad desire and action, it seems possible to establish a scale of goodness, or of badness. For, firstly, it seems clear that the desire to do one's duty is the morally best motive. Many will question this, and think that acts springing from love, from an interest in the well-being of a particular person or persons, are better than those dictated by the 'cold', 'hard', and 'rigid' sense of duty. But let us reflect. Suppose that some one is drawn towards doing act *A* by a sense of duty, and towards doing another, incompatible, act *B* by love for a particular person. *Ex hypothesi*, he thinks he will not be doing his duty in doing *B*. Can we possibly say that he will be acting better if he does what he thinks not his duty than if he does what he thinks *is* his duty? Evidently not. What those who hold this view mean by 'acting from the sense of duty' is obeying a traditional, conventional code rather than following the warm impulses of the heart. But what is properly meant by the sense of duty is the thought that one *ought* to act in a certain way, not the thought that one has been brought up to or is expected to act in a certain way. And it seems clear that when a genuine sense of duty is in conflict with any other motive we must recognize its precedence. If you seriously think you ought to do *A*, you are bound to think you will be acting morally worse in doing anything else instead. *

Suppose, now, that love and sense of duty incline us to the *same* act. Will our action be morally better if we act from the first motive or from the second? It seems clear that since the sense of duty is recognized as the better motive when the two are in conflict, it is still the better when they are in agreement. We may like better the man who acts more instinctively, from love, but we are bound to think the man who acts from sense of duty the better man. And this is not merely because instinctive affection is a more wayward, capricious motive than sense of duty, more apt to lead to wrong acts. It is because the sense of duty is different in kind from, and superior in kind to, any other motive.

We have considered (*a*) the case in which sense of duty and another motive, present in the same person, point to different acts, (*b*) that in which they point to the same act. But there is a third comparison to be considered. Many people would say that a man who helps his neighbour from sympathy, without thinking whether this or any other action is his duty, does a better action than another man who helps his neighbour from a sense of duty; though thay might admit that *when* the sense of duty arises in a man, it is better that he should act from it than from any other motive; and this is at first sight an attractive view. Nevertheless, it appears that action from the sense of duty, which we have seen to be better than action from any motive which conflicts or conspires with it, is also better than action not preceded by the thought of duty. The attractiveness of the opposite view seems to arise from the following fact: The sense of duty is more obviously present when it has to fight against opposing inclinations; i. e. is more obviously present in an imperfect character than in one all of whose inclinations urge it in the direction which duty also indicates.[1] We are therefore apt to associate it with an imperfect character, and to prefer the characters of those whose inclinations are good and who act on them without thought of duty. But in truth the thought that an act is my duty is not the thought that an act is my duty though I want to do something else, but the thought that an act is my duty whether or not I want to do something else; though *if* I do not want to do things incompatible with duty the act done from sense of duty is done immediately, without the necessity of a moral conflict and without the thought of duty having to be held for any length of time before the mind. The man who acts from a sense of duty without fuss or conflict appears to be a better character than the man who acts from inclination without any thought of duty; though, as I suggest later, the man who acts from both sense of duty and virtuous inclination is in a still better state.

Next, it seems plain that the desire to bring into being some-

---

[1] Cf. Kant, *Grundlegung* (Akad. Ausg. iv. 397–9. Abbott's *Kant's Theory of Ethics*, 13–15). One fact which makes the presence of the sense of duty more obvious in the former case is that in this case there is present not only the thought that I ought to do so-and-so, but also the consequential thought that I ought to resist the inclination which would prevent me from doing so-and-so.

thing good is a better desire than the desire to bring into being a pleasure for another. This is plainly seen in the fact that we should think concern for the character of one's children or friends a better moral state than concern for their pleasure.

Similarly it seems clear that the desire to bring something bad into being is worse than the desire to produce pain for another; just as concern for the character of another is better than concern for his pleasure, the desire to corrupt some one's character would seem to be more villainous than the desire to inflict pain on him. On the other hand, it is less bad than is or would be (for its existence seems improbable) the completely anti-moral attitude of desiring to do what was wrong, simply because it was wrong.

There seem then to be three types of good desire (and consequent action) of diminishing goodness, and three conceivable types of bad desire (and action) of increasing badness. But it is clear that most bad actions do not belong to any of these types, but are selfish actions, in which the desire involved is none of the bad desires but desire for one's own pleasure. One is at first sight tempted to say that this desire is in itself morally indifferent. But it seems that a distinction must be drawn between good pleasures, bad pleasures, and indifferent pleasures. By a good pleasure I mean one which springs from the satisfaction of a good desire, as e. g. the pleasures of a good conscience spring from the satisfaction of the desire to do right, or the pleasure of doing a kind action springs from the satisfaction of the desire to produce pleasure for another. By a bad pleasure I mean one which springs from the satisfaction of a bad desire, as e. g. the pleasure of making another suffer springs from the satisfaction of the desire to make him suffer. By an indifferent pleasure I mean one which does not spring from either of these sources; and it is plain that most selfish actions are dictated by desire for such pleasures, as a rule for the pleasures of the senses. It seems clear that the desire of an indifferent pleasure is in itself indifferent; that the desire of a good pleasure is either indifferent (as I am inclined to think) or less good than any of the three good desires previously named; and that the desire of a bad pleasure is bad, but less bad than any of the three bad desires previously named.

The general character of selfish action, in distinction from the three forms of bad action first mentioned, is that it proceeds not from a bad, but from an indifferent desire. When one asks on what its badness depends, one is at first sight tempted to say that there is some badness in feeling any desire more strongly than one feels another desire higher in the scale. But this clearly will not do. Take, for instance, a soldier whose duty it is to rest before the battle of the following day. He may be so tired that the desire for the morally indifferent pleasure of resting is much stronger in him than the desire to do his duty; and no one would think him selfish or think any the worse of him for that. It is, therefore, not the mere feeling of a lower desire with greater intensity than a higher that constitutes selfishness and is morally bad. It is only when the action aimed at securing pleasure for oneself excludes and makes impossible the doing of one's duty or the bringing into being of something that is good, or some pleasure for another, that the action in question is deemed to be morally bad.   Such action seems to be of two types, or rather (since these probably shade off into one another) to range between two extremes. At one extreme, it is the choosing of one's own pleasure in deliberate preference to the doing of duty or to the bringing into being of a good, or of a pleasure for another. At the other, it is the doing of an act which in fact excludes the doing of duty or the bringing of some good or some pleasure for another into being, though the thought of a duty that should be done, or of a good, or of a pleasure for another, that might be brought into being, is not present to the agent's mind. The two types might be called deliberate and impulsive selfishness respectively; of the two, deliberate selfishness is the worse. But even what might be called impulsive selfishness usually includes the vague awareness that if one stopped to think one would see that, in doing what one does, one is omitting an opportunity of doing one's duty, or of bringing some good, or some pleasure for another, into being.

There are these two main kinds of bad actions—a simpler and

worse kind which consists in acting on a bad desire, and a more complicated and less bad kind which consists in acting on an indifferent desire to the exclusion of an action to which a good desire prompts us, or would prompt us if we stopped to think.

One thing which I have taken for granted may at first sight appear somewhat paradoxical, viz. that while the desire to bring something good into being is good whether the good thing is to be a state of oneself or of another (e. g. an improvement in one's own character or in that of a friend), the desire to bring a pleasure into being for another is good, but the desire to get a pleasure for oneself is indifferent when the pleasure is indifferent (perhaps we should add 'or when it is good'), and bad when the pleasure is bad. A complication must be introduced here which I have omitted from my main statement in order that its general outline might be clearer: viz. this. The distinction between good, bad, and indifferent pleasures may be applied to the pleasures we desire to produce for others as well as to those we desire to get for ourselves; and when we apply it we see that the desire to secure a bad pleasure for another (e.g. the pleasure of watching some one suffer) is itself bad. Still, the main contrast is clear, that the desire to produce an indifferent pleasure for another is good, and the desire to produce it for oneself indifferent. That this is what we really think seems perfectly clear. And it is not really paradoxical. For though the pleasure will be similar whether it is enjoyed by the agent or by another, the desire for pleasure for oneself is quite a different thing from the desire to produce it for another, since one's relation to oneself is entirely different from one's relation to any other person.

So far I have spoken as if each action sprang from one and only one motive; we have next to consider actions (if there are any) done from mixed motives. Is it possible to do an act partly from sense of duty, partly from love, and, if so, is such an action morally better or worse than one done from pure sense of duty? Again, is it possible to do an act partly from a good, partly from an indifferent or bad motive, and, if so, what are we to say of the moral value of such an action?

It is clear that a mother, for instance, may want her child to be happy or good, and may also think it her duty to produce for it the conditions of happiness or of goodness. But can she really act from both motives together; must not one be operative and the other ineffective? The metaphor of 'mixture of motives' seems a questionable one, but we must at least recognize the co-operation of motives, or perhaps we should rather say 'the co-operation of elements to form a single motive'. We are familiar, I think, with cases in which conscience alone or self-interest alone would not have induced some one to do some difficult act, but the two together have induced him to do it. The activities of most statesmen are probably correctly attributed to the co-operation of ambition, party feeling, and patriotism, in varying proportions; and it does not seem as if we can always say, 'This act was due to ambition and that to party feeling and that to patriotism'; in many of their acts it seems that two, or perhaps all three, of these motives are at work. Again, if we want to induce a man to undertake a certain task, we probably put various arguments before him representing the points in its favour, and we do so not merely in the faith that if one point does not appeal to him another will, but in the belief that the various points, or some of them, may have a cumulative influence on him; and this seems, in fact, often to be the case.

Can we go further, and say that all motives that are present at all in a man's mind at a particular moment are *bound* to co-operate in producing his action, the mind being subject to a law of composition of forces of its own? This is clearly not the case. If motive A inclines us towards a certain act and motive B towards a different act, our doing of the first act is not necessarily altered (though the state of feeling with which we do it is) by our desire to do the second, nor do we necessarily do an act intermediate in character between the two. The doing of such an act (e. g. when there are two safe ways across a street, and we take an unsafe way between them) is a mark of distraction and loss of self-control. When we act with self-control we do the one act resolutely, irrespective of a lingering wish to do the other. We must, how-

ever, consider separately the case in which two motives point
to the *same* act. We *may* act from both motives together;
must we do so? We have seen that a motive adverse to the
doing of a particular act may be so disregarded that the act is
done just as it would have been done had the motive been
absent; it seems reasonable to suppose that a motive favourable to the doing of the act may equally be disregarded; e. g.
that when both sense of duty and ambition would incline a
man to do an act, he may, though he is sensible of both motives,
do the act wholly from the one or wholly from the other;
and attention to one's own experience seems to support this
view.

Where, however, a higher and a lower motive do co-operate
in inducing us to act, what degree of moral worth has the action
—more, or less, than if it had been done from the higher motive
only? Kant assumes that its worth will be less, since it will no
longer be 'pure'. The question can be looked at in either of
two entirely different ways. It will suffice if we take account
of two morally good motives, one higher than the other, of
one morally indifferent motive, and of one bad motive; and
must suppose that each of these motives has a definite
amount of effectiveness in inducing the agent to act. We are
far from being in a position to assign correctly definite numerical amounts either to the value or to the strength of motives;
but it will help us to attack the problem if we assign (admittedly
arbitrarily) such amounts. Let us suppose, then, that in the
scale of values sense of duty is represented by 10, love by 8,
desire of an innocent sensuous pleasure by 0, malice by -8:
and let us suppose an act in which two of these motives co-
operate with equal strength in producing an act. To assign
other values to the motives, or unequal strengths to them,
would not affect the argument. Kant, in insisting that the worth
of an action is degraded by the presence in it of any motive
lower than the sense of duty, is really assuming that its value
must then be the value half-way between that which it would
have had if done wholly from sense of duty, and that which it
would have had if done wholly from the lower motive; e. g. an
act done from sense of duty + desire of an innocent sensuous

pleasure will have the value $\dfrac{10+0}{2}$. An action done from

sense of duty + malice[1] will have the value $\dfrac{10-8}{2}$. And since

Kant assigns no value, positive or negative, to 'pathological'
love, an action done from sense of duty + love will have the

value $\dfrac{10+0}{2}$. If we amend his view, as we have seen reason to

do,[2] by assigning a positive value (say 8) to love, an action done

from sense of duty + love will have the value $\dfrac{10+8}{2}$.

It is, however, possible to take quite a different view; to hold
that, for instance, sense of duty may be present with undimi-
nished strength when another motive co-operates with it, and
that when it is, the addition of a morally indifferent motive does
not lessen the value of the action, and the addition of a good,
though less good, motive increases it. The action done from
sense of duty + desire of an innocent sensuous pleasure may be
estimated at 10+0; that done from sense of duty + malice at
10 − 8; that done from sense of duty + love at 10 + 8. If we call
sense of duty A, love B, desire of innocent sensuous pleasure
C, malice D, the value of the actions we have been considering
will be estimated thus:

	Kant.	Kant modified.	The alternative view.
Action from A	10	10	10
„ „ $A+B$	5	9	18
„ „ $A+C$	5	5	10
„ „ $A+D$	1	1	2

It is now, perhaps, easier to see the principles on which the
two modes of estimation are based. In insisting (as in principle
he does) that when two motives are equally effective, their
total (or net) value must be divided by two in order to assess
the value of the action, Kant is really assuming that all similar
actions have an equal total intensity of motivation, so that by

[1] This combination may sound paradoxical; but a little reflection will show that it
is not impossible, nor, indeed, at all uncommon.
[2] Cf. pp. 160–1.

the extent to which any other motive is effective, the sense of duty must be less effective than it would have been if acting alone. We, on the other hand, are suggesting that the sense of duty may be present with equal intensity and effectiveness whether another motive is or is not effective. Or, to put it otherwise, he is assuming that the motivation is always exactly enough to produce the doing of the given act, while we are suggesting that there may be some to spare, so that in a man who does an act, e. g., from sense of duty+love, the sense of duty may yet be strong enough to have secured the doing of the act from it alone; i. e., while we agree with Kant that there are cases in which, say, sense of duty+a morally indifferent motive are just strong enough to produce a certain act, and that then the value of the act, if both motives are equally effective, is only half what it would have been if done from pure sense of duty, we suggest that there are other actions in which, while a morally indifferent motive is present, the sense of duty is strong enough to have secured by itself the doing of the act, and that in that case the action is as good as if it had been done from sense of duty alone. And while we hold that there are actions in which sense of duty+an inferior good motive are just enough to secure the doing of the act, and that in that case the value of the action is reduced, we suggest that there are other cases in which, though an inferior good motive is present, the sense of duty is strong enough to have secured by itself the doing of the act, and that in such a case the value of the action is greater than if it had been done from duty alone. On the question whether such a reserve or surplus of motivation exists, there seems to be no appeal except to introspection, and it seems clear on introspection that there are many cases in which, while a variety of motives inclines us to do an act, one of them or some of them would have been enough to induce us to do it. Thus we can, while agreeing with Kant that the sense of duty is the best motive, justify the generally entertained preference for actions in which some more instinctive generous impulse is present as well. And experience suggests that the presence and effectiveness of instinctive generous emotions are by no means adverse to the operation of the sense of duty. It is *not* the case that men in whom the sense of duty is strong are usually less affected by the generous emotions than those in whom it is weak. And it is possible, as we have tried to show, to value highly the presence and operation of warm personal feeling, without disparaging, as it has so often been thought necessary to do, the supreme moral value of the sense of duty.

EDITOR'S NOTES

5   *that 'I ought' implies 'I can'*: Although Ross does not state it here, he thinks that rightness is not constrained by ability in this way. For example, he maintains that 'we can still call grief the right or fitting emotion in certain situations . . . even if we do not suppose the person we are thinking about has it in his power to feel grief in those circumstances' (*The Foundations of Ethics* (Clarendon Press: Oxford, 1939), 55). Ross does, however, go on to say that 'it must be granted that when we use 'right' of acts, as opposed to emotions, we usually think of them as being in the agent's power' (*The Foundations of Ethics*, 55). But the implication here seems to be merely conversational rather than the strict entailment he thinks holds between 'I ought' and 'I can'.

7   *the thing done*: In *The Foundations of Ethics* Ross changed his mind about this. He there thinks that what we should do is not certain acts, but 'set ourselves' to do certain acts. Following H. A. Prichard ('Duty and Ignorance of Fact', in Prichard, *Moral Obligation*, ed. W. D. Ross (Clarendon Press: Oxford, 1949)), he wrote: 'contrary to the implication of ordinary language and of moral rules in particular, an obligation must be an obligation, not to *do* something, but to perform an activity of a totally different kind, that of setting or exerting ourselves to do something, i.e. to bring something about'. On his later view, therefore, success in doing what one sets oneself to do is irrelevant to whether one has succeeded in doing what one should. This contradicts what he says later in *The Right and the Good* about success (42–7).

7   *from which it is done*: In *The Foundations of Ethics* Ross modified his view slightly. He maintained that the moral goodness of an action is determined not only by the agent's actual motives, but also by the motives he would have if he were responsive to all of the morally relevant considerations in the right proportion (*Foundations*, 306–10). See note to p. 156.

7   *our moral thought*: In *The Foundations of Ethics* Ross makes it clear that he does not suppose that acts are independent of motives in the sense that the former could exist without the latter. All he is keen to maintain here is that the rightness of acts is independent of the motives from which they are done, and so should be considered in abstraction from their motives (*Foundations*, 127–8).

20   whole *nature*: Although Ross does not tell us here why he chose the misleading term '*prima facie* duty', he does in *The Foundations of Ethics*. First, this term picks out the fact that when we consider what we should do in particular situations it is the fitness or unfitness of an imagined act *in certain respects* that first catches our attention. '. . . it is only by recognizing these different features one by one that we can approach the forming of a judgement on the totality of its nature; our first look reveals these features in isolation, one by one; they are what appears *prima facie*' (*Foundations*, 84). Secondly, it picks out the deontic nature of these features—the fact that they make certain actions in some respect right or wrong, or better, fitting or unfitting to different aspects of the situation (ibid.).

20   *a claim on oneself*: Although Ross rejected Prichard's suggestion of the term 'claim', he later accepts Carritt's suggestion of the term 'responsibility' (*The Foundations of Ethics*, 85). He also seems happy to use the term 'fitting' or 'suitable' as a good substitute for '*prima facie* duty' (ibid. 51–5 and 79– 82, especially pp. 53 and 84). His view is, then, that to be *prima facie* right is to be fitting to some aspect of the situation—that is, to some responsibility we have. To say that an act is our duty proper is to say that it is the one which is most fitting to all of the relevant features of the situation, that it is the one that fulfils as many of our responsibilities as is possible. A right act which is nonetheless *prima facie* wrong is one that fulfils as many of our responsibilities as is possible, and is thus the act that is most fitting to the situation, though it fails to fulfil some responsibility, and is thus unfit to an aspect of the situation.

26   *in this way*: In *The Foundations of Ethics* Ross abandoned the view that we have a *prima facie* duty to promote our own innocent pleasures (pp. 272–4). In fact he goes so far as to say: 'That we are conscious of no duty to maximize pleasure for ourselves seems to be so clear as not to need argument' (p. 273). He makes no reference here to his earlier view in *The Right and the Good*.

30   *need no proof*: In a paper published three years before *The Right and the Good* Ross maintains that self-evident principles *require* no proof, but rejects the view that they *cannot* be proved. He writes, 'the fact that something can be inferred does not prove that it cannot be seen intuitively' ('The Basis of Objective Judgements in Ethics', *International Journal of Ethics*, 37 (1927), 121). If he thinks that some proposition can be inferred from (justified by) other propositions

and be self-evident, he clearly thinks that its being self-evident does not rule out the possibility of a proof.

32 *morally good action*: In *The Foundations of Ethics* Ross completely changed his mind on this topic. There he argues that what we should do is not determined by the objective facts—certain relations in which we stand to others—but by certain subjective facts, namely, what we believe is right or morally suitable in the circumstances as we take them to be (*Foundations*, 161–4).

131 *not* vice versa: In *The Foundations of Ethics* (pp. 254–5) Ross adds that evaluative judgements *express* our favourable attitude towards the object, but notes that this does not imply that what we are asserting of the object is that it is the object of such a favourable attitude.

135 *is good in itself*: In *The Foundations of Ethics* Ross abandoned the view that pleasure is intrinsically good (*Foundations*, 283). He still maintained that it is good, but argued that it is good in a relational sense—that is, in the sense that it is a worthy object of sympathetic satisfaction (*Foundations*, 275–6).

150 *with infinite duration*: In *The Foundations of Ethics* Ross realized that the view he expressed here must be wrong. He notes that 'if virtue were really on the same scale of goodness as pleasure, then pleasure of a certain intensity, if enjoyed by a sufficiently large number of persons or for a sufficient time, would counterbalance virtue possessed or manifested only by a small number or only for a short time' (*Foundations*, 275). Since he could not accept that pleasure is ever better than virtue, he rejected the view that they are on the same evaluative scale, and maintained that pleasure is good in a different sense from that in which virtue is good (ibid.). See note to p. 135.

156 *independent of rightness*: In *The Foundations of Ethics* Ross weakened his claim about the independence of moral rightness and goodness.

> . . . an action will be completely good only if it manifests the whole range of motivations by which an ideally good man would be affected in the circumstances, a sensitiveness to every result for good or for evil that the act is foreseen as likely to have, as well as to any special *prima facie* obligations or disobligations that may be involved; and only if it manifests sensitiveness to all these considerations in their right proportions. But if the agent is responsive to all the morally relevant considerations in their right proportions, he will in fact do the *right* act. Thus no

action will have the utmost moral excellence which an action in the circumstances can have, unless it is also the right action. (*Foundations*, 308–9)

164 *anything else instead*: Ross never abandoned the view that the sense of duty is the best motive (*The Foundations of Ethics*, 303–5). But because he came to believe that the moral worth of an action depends not only on one's actual motive, but also on motives one would have if one were appropriately responsive to all the moral considerations in the situation (see note to p. 156), he came to believe that an action done from a sense of duty could be morally bad.

The nepotist may act from the thought that he *ought* to bestow the job on B; and so far there is an element of goodness in his action. But in so far as he is failing to be influenced by the thought that he ought to do justice to C, D, and the rest, his action is a bad one; and it is easy to imagine a case in which the *prima facie* obligations he is failing to be influenced by are much more weighty than those he is being influenced by; and in such a case his action will be on the whole positively bad. (*Foundations*, 307–8)

INDEX